AAT
INTERACTIVE TEXT

Technician Unit 10

Managing Accounting Systems

May 2000 edition

- Layout designed to be easy on the eye – and easy to use

- Icons to guide you through a 'fast track' approach if you wish

- Thorough reliable updating of mateial to 1 May 2000 takinginto account changes to auditing standards and guidance

FOR 2000 AND 2001 DEVOLVED ASSESSMENTS

BPP Publishing
May 2000

Second edition May 1998
Third edition May 2000

ISBN 0 7517 6217 2 (previous edition 0 7517 6163 X)

British Library Cataloguing-in-Publication Data
A catalogue record for this book
is available from the British Library

Published by

BPP Publishing Limited
Aldine House, Aldine Place
London W12 8AW

www.bpp.com

We are grateful to the Auditing Practices Board for permission to reproduce the glossary of auditing terms.

We are also grateful to the Lead Body for Accounting for permission to reproduce extracts from the Standards of Competence for Accounting and to the AAT for permission to reproduce extracts from the mapping and guidance notes.

Page

INTRODUCTION   (v)

How to use this Interactive Text – Technician Qualification Structure – Unit 10
Standards of Competence – Assessment Strategy

PART A: CO-ORDINATING WORK ACTIVITIES

PART B: IDENTIFYING OPPORTUNITIES TO IMPROVE THE EFFECTIVENESS OF AN ACCOUNTING SYSTEM

PART C: PREVENTING FRAUD

ORDER FORM

REVIEW FORM & FREE PRIZE DRAW

BPP PUBLISHING

HOW TO USE THIS INTERACTIVE TEXT

Aims of this Interactive Text

To provide the knowledge and practice to help you succeed in the devolved assessment for Technician Unit 10 *Managing Accounting Systems.*

To pass the devolved assessment you need a thorough understanding in all areas covered by the standards of competence.

To tie in with the other components of the BPP Effective Study Package to ensure you have the best possible chance of success.

Interactive Text

This covers all you need to know for the devolved assessment for Unit 10 *Managing Accounting Systems*. Icons clearly mark key areas of the text. Numerous activities throughout the text help you practise what you have just learnt.

Devolved Assessment Kit

When you have understood and practised the material in the Interactive Text, you will have the knowledge and experience to tackle the Devolved Assessment Kit for Unit 10 *Managing Accounting Systems*. This aims to get you through the devolved assessment, whether in the form of the AAT simulation or in the workplace.

Recommended approach to this Interactive Text

(a) To achieve competence in Unit 10 (and all the other units), you need to be able to do **everything** specified by the standards. Study the Interactive Text carefully and do not skip any of it.

(b) Learning is an **active** process. Do **all** the activities as you work through the Interactive Text so you can be sure you really understand what you have read.

(c) After you have covered the material in the Interactive Text, work through the **Devolved Assessment Kit**.

(d) Before you take the devolved assessment, check that you still remember the material using the following quick revision plan for each chapter.

    (i) Read through the chapter learning objectives. Are there any gaps in your knowledge? If so, study the section again.

    (ii) Read and learn the key terms.

    (iii) Look at the devolved assessment alerts. These show the sort of things that are likely to come up.

    (iv) Read and learn the key learning points, which are a summary of the chapter.

    (v) Do the quick quiz again. If you know what you're doing, it shouldn't take long.

    This approach is only a suggestion. Your college may well adapt it to suit your needs.

Remember this is a **practical** course.

(a) Try to relate the material to your experience in the workplace or any other work experience you may have had.

(b) Try to make as many links as you can to your study of the other Units at Technician level.

(c) Keep this text, (hopefully) you will find it invaluable in your everyday work too!

TECHNICIAN QUALIFICATION STRUCTURE

The competence-based Education and Training Scheme of the Association of Accounting Technicians is based on an analysis of the work of accounting staff in a wide range of industries and types of organisation. The Standards of Competence for Accounting which students are expected to meet are based on this analysis.

The Standards identify the key purpose of the accounting occupation, which is to operate, maintain and improve systems to record, plan, monitor and report on the financial activities of an organisation, and a number of key roles of the occupation. Each key role is subdivided into units of competence, which are further divided into elements of competences. By successfully completing assessments in specified units of competence, students can gain qualifications at NVQ/SVQ levels 2, 3 and 4, which correspond to the AAT Foundation, Intermediate and Technician stages of competence respectively.

Whether you are competent in a Unit is demonstrated by means of:

- *Either* a Central Assessment (set and marked by AAT assessors)

- *Or* a Devolved Assessment (where competence is judged by an Approved Assessment Centre to whom responsibility for this is devolved)

- Or *both* Central *and* Devolved Assessment

Below we set out the overall structure of the Technician (NVQ/SVQ Level 4) stage, indicating how competence in each Unit is assessed. In the next section there is more detail about the Devolved Assessment for Unit 10.

Note that Units 8, 9 and 10 are compulsory. You can choose one out of Units 11 to 14, and then three out of Units 15 to 19.

NVQ/SVQ **Level 3 – Intermediate**

All units are mandatory

Unit of competence

Elements of competence

Unit 5 Maintaining financial records and preparing accounts
Central *and* Devolved Assessment

5.1	Maintain records relating to capital acquisition and disposal
5.2	Record income and expenditure
5.3	Collect and collate information for the preparation of financial accounts
5.4	Prepare the extended trial balance account

Unit 6 Recording cost information
Central *and* Devolved Assessment

6.1	Record and analyse information relating to direct costs
6.2	Record and analyse information relating to the allocation, apportionment and absorption of overhead costs
6.3	Prepare and present standard cost reports

Unit 7 Preparing reports and returns
Devolved Assessment *only*

7.1	Prepare and present periodic performance reports
7.2	Prepare reports and returns for outside agencies
7.3	Prepare VAT returns

Unit 21 Using information technology
Devolved Assessment *only*

21.1	Obtain information from a computerised Management Information System
21.2	Produce spreadsheets for the analysis of numerical information
21.3	Contribute to the quality of the Management Information System

Unit 22 Monitor and maintain a healthy, safe and secure workplace (ASC)
Devolved Assessment *only*

22.1	Monitor and maintain health and safety within the workplace
22.2	Monitor and maintain the security of the workplace

BPP
PUBLISHING

Technician qualification structure

Unit of competence

Elements of competence

Unit 8	Contributing to the management of costs and the enhancement of value

Central Assessment *only*

8.1	Collect, analyse and disseminate information about costs
8.2	Make recommendations to reduce costs and enhance value

Unit 9	Contributing to the planning and allocation of resources

Central Assessment *only*

9.1	Prepare forecasts of income and expenditure
9.2	Produce draft budget proposals
9.3	Monitor the performance of responsiblity centres against budgets

---

Unit 10	Managing accounting systems

Devolved Assessment *only*

10.1	Co-ordinate work activities within the accounting environment
10.2	Identify opportunities to improve the effectiveness of an accounting system
10.3	Prevent fraud in an accounting system

Unit 22	Monitor and maintain a healthy, safe and secure workplace (ASC)

Devolved Assessment *only*

22.1	Monitor and maintain health and safety within the workplace
22.2	Monitor and maintain the security of the workplace

Unit 11	Drafting financial statements (Accounting Practice, Industry and Commerce)

Central Assessment *only*

11.1	Interpret financial statements
11.2	Draft limited company, sole trader and partnership year end financial statements

---

Unit 12	Drafting financial statements (Central Government)

Central Assessment *only*

12.1	Interpret financial statements
12.2	Draft central government financial statements

Unit 13	Drafting financial statements (Local Government)

Central Assessment *only*

13.1	Interpret financial statements
13.2	Draft local authority financial statements

Unit of competence   **Elements of competence**

Unit 14	Drafting financial statements (National Health Service)
Central Assessment *only*	

14.1	Interpret financial statements
14.2	Draft NHS accounting statements and returns

Unit 15	Operating a cash management and credit control system
Devolved Assessment *only*	

15.1	Monitor and control cash receipts and payments
15.2	Manage cash balances
15.3	Grant credit
15.4	Monitor and control the collection of debts

Unit 16	Evaluating current and proposed activities
Devolved Assessment *only*	

16.1	Prepare cost estimates
16.2	Recommend ways to improve cost ratios and revenue generation

Unit 17	Implementing auditing procedures
Devolved Assessment *only*	

17.1	Contribute to the planning of an audit assignment
17.2	Contribute to the conduct of an audit assignment
17.3	Prepare related draft reports

Unit 18	Preparing business taxation computations
Devolved Assessment *only*	

18.1	Adjust accounting profit and losses for trades and professions
18.2	Prepare capital allowances computations
18.3	Prepare Capital Gains Tax computations
18.4	Account for Income Tax payable or recoverable by a company
18.5	Prepare Corporation Tax computations and returns

Unit 19	Preparing personal taxation computations
Devolved Assessment *only*	

19.1	Calculate income from employment
19.2	Prepare computations of property and investment income
19.3	Prepare Capital Gains Tax computations
19.4	Prepare personal tax returns

UNIT 10 STANDARDS OF COMPETENCE

The structure of the Standards for Unit 10

The Unit commences with a statement of the **knowledge and understanding** which underpin competence in the Unit's elements.

The Unit of Competence is then divided into **elements of competence** describing activities which the individual should be able to perform.

Each element includes:

(a) A set of **performance criteria.** This defines what constitutes competent performance.

(b) A **range statement.** This defines the situations, contexts, methods etc in which competence should be displayed.

(c) **Evidence requirements.** These state that competence must be demonstrated consistently, over an appropriate time scale with evidence of performance being provided from the appropriate sources.

(d) **Sources of evidence.** These are suggestions of ways in which you can find evidence to demonstrate that competence. These fall under the headings: 'observed performance; work produced by the candidate; authenticated testimonies from relevant witnesses; personal account of competence; other sources of evidence.' They are reproduced in full in our Devolved Assessment Kit for Unit 10.

The elements of competence for Unit 10 *Managing Accounting Systems* are set out below. Knowledge and understanding required for the unit as a whole are listed first, followed by the performance criteria and range statements for each element. Performance criteria are cross-referenced below to chapters in this Unit 10 *Managing Accounting Systems* Interactive Text.

Unit 10:   Managing Accounting Systems

What is the unit about?

This unit relates to the **internal** and **external auditing process** and requires the candidate to be involved from planning through to the reporting stage. The candidate is responsible for the identification of control objectives and their assessment, the selection of a sample and tests, drawing appropriate conclusions from the tests and drafting the reports which give preliminary conclusions and recommendations. The unit requires the candidate to be supervised in the work.

Elements contained within this unit are:

Element 10.1 Co-ordinate work activities within the accounting environment
Element 10.2 Identify opportunities to improve the effectiveness of an accounting system

Knowledge and understanding

The business environment

- The range of external regulations affecting accounting practise (Elements 10.2, & 10.3)

- Common types of fraud (Element 10.3)

- Implications of fraud (Element 10.3)

Management techniques

- Scheduling and planning methods (Element 10.1)

- Time management (Element 10.1)

- Methods of measuring cost effectiveness and systems reliability (Element 10.2)

- Quality management, quality circles (Element 10.2)

- Methods of detecting fraud (Element 10.3)

Management principles and theory

- Principles supervision (Element 10.1)

- Principles of human relations, team building, staff motivation (Element 10.1)

The organisation

- Understanding that the accounting systems of an organisation are affected by its organisational structure, its MIS, its administrative systems and procedures and the nature of its business transactions (Elements 10.1, 10.2 & 10.3)

- An overview of the organisation's business and the critical external relationships (customer/clients, suppliers etc) (Elements 10.2 & 10.3)

- Purpose of the work activity and its relationship with other related work activities (Element 10.1)

- Organisation of the accounting function, relationship between the accounting function and other departments; structure of the accounting function (Elements 10.2 & 10.3)

BPP PUBLISHING

Element 10.1: Co-ordinate work activities within the accounting environment

Performance criteria	Chapters in this Text
1 Work activities are planned in order to optimise the use of resources and ensure completion of work within agreed timescales	2, 5, 6, 8
2 The competence of individuals undertaking work activities is reviewed and the necessary training is provided	3, 10
3 Contingency plans to meet possible emergencies are prepared with management and, if necessary, implemented within agreed timescales	9
4 Work methods and schedules are clearly communicated to all individuals in a way which assists their understanding of what is expected of them	3, 4, 5, 6
5 Work activities are closely monitored in order to ensure quality standards are being met	2, 7, 8
6 Work activities are effectively co-ordinated in accordance with work plans and any contingencies that may occur	2, 6, 9
7 Problems or queries concerning work activities are identified and either resolved or referred to the appropriate person	7, 9, 10

Range statement

1 Work activities: within the accounting function	Throughout
2 Plans include: computer security routines, absence cover, contingency plans for changes in work patterns and demands	9

Evidence requirements

- Competence must be demonstrated consistently over an appropriate timescale with evidence of performance being provided of candidates co-ordinating work activities within the accounting function

Element 10.2: Identify opportunities to improve the effectiveness of an accounting system

Performance criteria	Chapters in this Text
1 Weaknesses and potential for improvements to the accounting system are identified and considered for their impact on the operation of the organisation	7, 8
2 Methods of operating are regularly reviewed in respect of their cost-effectiveness, reliability and speed	8
3 Recommendations are made to the appropriate people in a clear, easily understood format	3, 4, 5, 6, 10
4 Recommendations are supported by a clear rationale which includes explanation of any assumptions made	7
5 The system is updated as in accordance with changes in internal and external regulations, policies and procedures	4

Range statement

1   Recommendations: verbal, written

2   Accounting system: one section of an accounting system

Evidence requirements

- Competence must be demonstrated consistently over an appropriate timescale, with evidence of performance being provided of candidates making recommendations to improve the effectiveness of the accounting function

Element 10.3: Prevent fraud in an accounting system

Performance criteria	Chapters in this Text
1 Existing systems for preventing fraud are evaluated and compared with examples of best practice	11, 12
2 Past examples of control avoidance are analysed and used to inform evaluations of the controls within the system	11, 12
3 Areas of potential fraud within the control avoidance accounting system are identified and the risk graded	11, 12
4 Areas of concern and weakness within the system are reported to management	11, 12
5 Possible methods of avoiding the risks and safeguarding the system are identified	11, 12
6 Recommendations for the prevention of fraud are made to the appropriate people	11, 12

Range statement

1 Examples of best practice: within the organisation, outside the organisation	11, 12
2 Recommendations: verbal, written	11, 12
3 Accounting system: one section of an accounting system	Throughout

Evidence requirements

- Competence must be demonstrated consistently over an appropriate timescale, with evidence of performance being provided of candidates identifying potential areas of risk within an accounting system and suggesting potential solutions

  Sources of evidence (these are examples of sources of evidence, but candidates and assessors may be able to identify other, appropriate sources)

BPP
PUBLISHING

ASSESSMENT STRATEGY

Candidates are asked to address this unit by means of a project plus assessor questioning and employer testimony.

Nature of the project

The project takes the form of a report to management that defines the management accounting system and describes how it has been or might be modified to improve its effectiveness. In doing so, the candidate will need to prove competence in the co-ordination of work activities and the prevention of fraud in that system.

The total length of the project (excluding appendices) should not exceed 4,000 words. An appropriate manager should attest to the authenticity and quality of the project report.

The project should be based on an actual management accounting system, or part-system, within the candidate's workplace in the present or recent past. For candidates not in relevant employment, an unpaid placement such as a voluntary organisation or charity, club or society or a college department may be suitable.

The centre's role

The centre should undertake the following steps:

- make an initial assessment of the project data
- use one-to-one sessions to advise and support the candidate
- use action plans
- encourage workplace mentors to participate (testimony etc)
- ensure the project is the candidate's original work
- use formative assessments to guide the candidate
- undertake summative assessment against performance criteria, range statements and knowledge and understanding
- sign off each performance criterion
- conduct a final assessment interview with documented questioning
- take account of the interview and workplace evidence in the overall assessment

The student's role: project format

The student should ensure that the project:

- covers all performance criteria, range statements and knowledge and understanding
- covers the objectives set out in the Terms of Reference of the project
- is well laid out and easy to read
- shows clear progression from one idea to the next
- cross-refers the main text to any appendices
- uses diagrams and flowcharts appropriately
- starts each section on a fresh page

The student's role: project content

The student should ensure that:

- issues and objectives are clearly identified
- the current situation is clearly analysed
- recommendations are subjected to cost-benefit analysis
- key data is included; superfluous detail is omitted
- methodology is fully described
- a strategic approach is taken
- the project focuses on company needs, not personal feeling.

Part A
Co-ordinating work activities

Chapter 1   Your organisation

Chapter topic list

1   Your organisation

2   How is your organisation divided up?

3   Knowing your place: the organisation chart

4   What is your organisation for?

5   Critical external relationships

Learning objectives

On completion of this chapter you will be able to:

	Performance criteria	Range Statement
• *understand organisation structure and its implications for accounting systems*	n/a	n/a
• *appreciate the organisation's business and its critical external relationshp*	n/a	n/a
• *appreciate the signifiance of the business environment*	n/a	n/a
• *draw organisation charts*	n/a	n/a

Italicised objectives are areas of knowledge and understanding underlying elements of competence for this Unit.

BPP PUBLISHING

1   YOUR ORGANISATION

1.1   Here are some examples of organisations.

- A multinational car manufacturer (eg Ford)
- An accountancy firm (eg Ernst and Young)
- A charity (eg Oxfam)
- A local authority
- A trade union (eg Unison)
- An army

What organisations have in common

1.2   The definition below states what all organisations have in common.

> **KEY TERM**
>
> An **organisation** is: 'a *social arrangement* which pursues collective *goals*, which *controls* its own performance and which has a *boundary* separating it from its environment'.

1.3   Here is how this definition applies to two of the organisations listed in paragraph 1.1.

Characteristic	Car manufacturer	Army
Social arrangement: individuals gathered together for a purpose	People work in different divisions, making different cars	Soldiers are in different regiments, and there is a chain of command from the top to the bottom
Collective goals: the organisation has goals over and above the goals of the people within it	Sell cars, make money	Defend the country, defeat the enemy, international peace keeping
Controls performance: performance is monitored against the goals and adjusted if necessary to ensure the goals are accomplished	Costs and quality are reviewed and controlled. Standards are constantly improved	Strict disciplinary procedures, training
Boundary: the organisation is distinct from its environment	Physical: factory gates Social: employment status	Physical: barracks Social: different rules than for civilians

- Organisations are preoccupied with **performance**, and meeting or improving their standards. Achieving quality targets is an example of performance.

- Organisations contain formal, documented **systems and procedures** which enable them to control what they do.

- Within the organisation different people do different things, or **specialise** in one activity.

- Organisations pursue a variety of **goals**.

- Most organisations obtain **inputs** (eg materials), and **process** them into **outputs** (eg for others to buy).

How organisations differ

1.4   Organisations differ in many ways. Here are some possible differences.

Factor	Example
Ownership (public vs private)	Private sector: owned by private owners/shareholders. Public sector: owned by the government
Control	By the owners themselves, by people working on their behalf, or indirectly by government-sponsored regulators
Activity (ie what they do)	Manufacturing, healthcare
Profit or non-profit **orientation**	Business exists to make a profit. The army, on the other hand, is not profit orientated
Legal status	Limited company or partnership
Size	Size can be measured in many ways, for example number of staff, number of branches, sales revenue each year, number of customers and market share
Sources of **finance**	Borrowing, government funding, share issues
Technology	High use of technology (eg computer firms) vs low use (eg corner shop)

(A mnemonic to help you remember, using the words above in bold is: Organisations Can Achieve Outcomes Like Several Friends Together.)

DEVOLVED ASSESSMENT ALERT

You should be able to state the general business area that your organisation operates within. This is probably one of the first things you do when you tell somebody about your job, anyway.

Be as specific as possible, but bear in mind that if you say you work for a manufacturer of splined-shaft broaching machines it might be helpful to add that your firm is a supplier to the 'building materials' industry or to 'telecommunications companies'. That is, you can define your organisation in terms of its *customers*.

If you work for a non-commercial organisation you ought to explain what its main activity is: 'a charity whose aim is to provide shelter for the homeless'.

Activity 1.1

(a)   What are four ways of classifying and distinguishing organisations?
(b)   How may the size of an organisation be measured?

2 HOW IS YOUR ORGANISATION DIVIDED UP?

2.1 **Within** a typical organisation, there are many different types of activity being carried out.

- **Purchasing materials** and components
- Carrying out **operations** on purchased materials and components, to make them into something
- **Accounting and record keeping,** eg keeping track of costs.
- **Research and development** of new products or technologies.
- Taking **orders** from customers.
- **Planning** and implementing marketing strategies to obtain new customers.
- **Employing** people and paying them.
- **Co-ordinating** all the above to ensure the organisation reaches its goals.

2.2 Clearly in many organisations large numbers of people are involved in different tasks. At BPP Publishing, for example, there are nine authors who write the books, five typesetters who do the typesetting work, a warehouse with five members of staff, and a customer services function (who you can phone, fax, email or contact by post).

2.3 The large numbers of staff and the variety of activities mean that people have to be grouped together in some way. This grouping together is called organisation structure.

KEY TERM

Organisation structure: the framework of formal work relationships between people in an organisation.

Organisational structure

2.4 Organisation structure is a framework which serves several purposes.

- It **links individuals** in an established network of relationships so that authority, responsibility and communications can be controlled.
- It **allocates the tasks** required to fulfil the objectives of the organisation to suitable individuals or groups.
- It gives each individual or group the **authority** required to perform the allocated tasks, while **controlling** their use of resources.
- It **co-ordinates** the objectives and activities of separate units, so that overall aims are achieved without gaps or overlaps in the flow of work.
- It facilitates the **flow of work,** information and other resources through the organisation.

Activity 1.2

Jason, Mark, Gary and Robbie set up in business together as repairers of musical instruments - specialising in guitars and drums. They are a bit uncertain as to how they should run the business, but when they discuss it in the pub, they decide that attention needs to be paid to three major areas: taking orders from customers, doing the repairs (of course) and checking the quality of the repairs before notifying the customers.

Suggest three ways in which they could structure their business.

2.5 Most organisations of any size are split into **departments** and there are many ways of doing this.

(a) **Function**. The firm is organised on the basis of the **type of work done** (eg sales, finance, production).

- Advantage: **logical,** as people are grouped according to their skills
- Disadvantage: **co-ordination**; not related to products or customers

(b) **Geographic area**. Activities are organised on an **area basis** (eg South East England, Scotland), with some activities retained at head office.

- Advantage: local knowledge and flexibility
- Disadvantage: duplication (eg of accounts staff)

(c) **Product or brand**. A product or brand manager is in charge of most of the activities relating to an **individual product**.

- Advantage: directly related to profitability, and product improvement
- Disadvantage: increased overhead costs

(d) **Customer or market segment**. The organisation is based around **groups of customers** (eg 'business customers' and 'domestic customers').

- Advantage: customers drive the business, and so attention is devoted to their needs
- Disadvantage: possible duplication

(e) **Hybrid**. Most organisations contain elements of a number of these structures. Sales staff might be organised by territory, whereas the accounts staff might be centralised on a functional basis.

(f) **Divisionalisation** is the creation of largely **autonomous** business units, with **performance targets** set by head office.

DEVOLVED ASSESSMENT ALERT

Your project report needs a context. Your report should set the scene by describing, for example, the size and structure of the organisation. Use this information to *tailor* your recommendations to the actual circumstances of the organisation.

3 KNOWING YOUR PLACE: THE ORGANISATION CHART

3.1 The **organisation chart** is an aid to designing, expressing and understanding the shape and structure of an organisation.

3.2 The chart is a traditional way of setting out in pictures **the various relationships between individuals and groups** in an organisation in terms of their functions, responsibilities and the bounds of their authority.

(a) The parts, or **departments**, into which the organisation is divided and how they relate to each other formally.

(b) Formal **communication and reporting channels**.

(c) **Structure**

- authority and delegation
- responsibility and accountability

including, for example, how **many levels of hierarchy** there are (how much delegation goes on in the organisation); the people each manager is **responsible** (and accountable) for, and *to*.

3.3 The most common is the **vertical organisation chart**, but a **horizontal chart** may also be used.

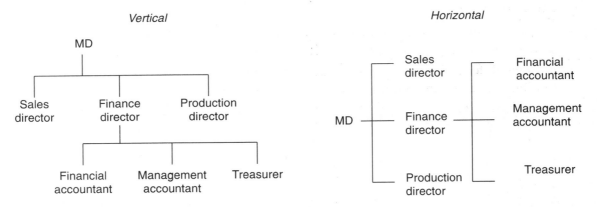

Limitations of organisation charts

3.4 Any organisation chart, of course, only gives an **impression** of how the organisation is run - what actually happens may be very different.

- They are a **static** model, whereas an **organisation is dynamic**, continually changing.
- They show only the **formal and not the informal structure** of communications across departments and ranks and the 'networks' of contacts and friends.
- Other aspects of the organisational life can be more important than its structure.
- They do not tell you what each person actually does, or how well he/she does it.

Examples of organisation structures

Functional structure

> **KEY TERM**
>
> A **function** in an organisation is a broad area covering a group of similar or work related activities.

3.5 **Departmentation by function** allows the division of work into **specialist areas**, for example, all the finance staff are grouped into one department. The main functions in a manufacturing company might be production, sales, purchasing, finance and personnel.

Specialisation can be continued, dividing these into functional sub-departments.

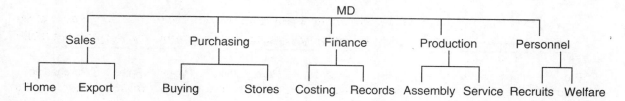

Geographical or territorial structure

3.6 **Departmentation by territory or region** may be a more suitable method for a firm such as an insurance company, estate agent or travel agency, where similar activities are carried out in widely different locations. The organisation can take advantage of local knowledge, and decision-making, with co-ordination from a central Head Office. A disadvantage of this would be the duplication of some jobs, for example in accounting, which would be costly and possibly confusing.

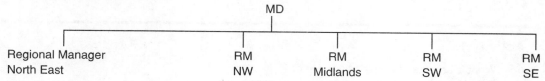

Product-based structure

3.7 Most companies have a mix of products. Department or divisional managers may thus be given responsibility for a product, line or brand of products. For example for a printing firm:

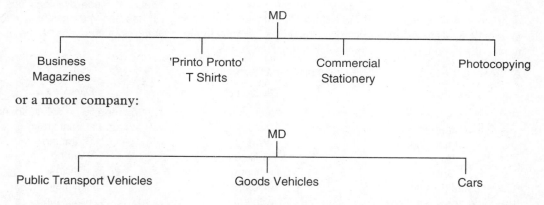

or a motor company:

Individual managers can be held responsible for the profitability of individual products, and this structure also encourages specialisation and expertise of salespersons, service engineers and so on. There are problems of duplication, similar to those found in a territorial structure.

Structure throughout the organisation

3.8 Most firms do not stick to one of the three types of departmentation. They mix and match. For example, sales staff are usually organised by regions. Within product departments, functional areas such as manufacturing and distribution, still operate.

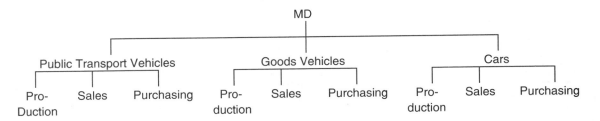

3.9 You can see from the 'family tree'-like charts that the organisation divides its work into different **areas, groups** and **levels.** Departmentation occurs 'below' the Managing Director's level. So the lines and levels do tell us about relationships: how many people have authority and over how many others, how they pass on authority to others, who is responsible for decisions and so on.

3.10 You will also have realised that the accounting function has its own structure. We shall look at this in Chapter 4. For now we are getting an overview of the organisation as a whole.

Activity 1.3

(a) What is an organisation designed to do?
(b) Set out a logical sequence in forming an organisation.
(c) What sort of problems may be shown up by an organisation chart?
(d) What are the limitations of organisation charts?

Activity 1.4

Q plc is a business which is divided into three product divisions. Each of these divisions has been operating from different sites and relatively old-fashioned buildings. It has become possible to acquire an eminently suitable site cheaply, to which Q plc intends to move all the divisions. It has been decided to take the opportunity to reorganise on a functional basis.

At present, the following activities take place in the divisions:

Division A	*Division B*	*Division C*
Purchasing	Purchasing	Commercial (ie sales, finance
Stamping	Machining	and administration)
Machining	Wiring	Stamping
Wiring	Drilling	Wiring
Drilling	Painting	Drilling
Commercial (ie sales, finance	Assembly	Painting
and administration)	Sales	Assembly
	Finance	

Required

(a) Draw an organisation chart showing the revised functional structure for Q plc.

(b) Suggest reasons why the decision to switch from a product organisation structure to a functional organisation structure might have been taken.

4   WHAT IS YOUR ORGANISATION FOR?

4.1 We mentioned in Section 1 that an organisation has goals.

Mission

> **KEY TERM**
>
> **Mission:** 'describes the organisation's basic function in society'.

4.2 **Mission outlines why an organisation exists**. Of course for businesses, making a profit for investors is a primary goal, but this is not true for charities or most public sector organisations. Mission is in part related to 'activity' but it has other elements.

4.3 EXAMPLE

To get an idea of the mission of your organisation, go to the latest Report and Accounts - or other documentation - and look at the mission statement.

The following statements were taken from annual reports of the organisations concerned. Are they 'mission statements'? If so, are they any good?

(a) The **Guinness Group:** Guinness plc is one of the world's leading drinks companies, producing and marketing an unrivalled portfolio of international best-selling brands, such as Johnnie Walker, Bell's and Dewar's Scotch whiskies, Gordon's and Tanqueray gins, and Guinness stout itself - the world's most distinctive beer. The strategy is to focus resources on the development of the Group's alcoholic drinks businesses. The objectives are to provide superior long-term financial returns for shareholders, to create a working environment in which people can perform to their fullest potential and to be recognised as one of the world's leading consumer brand development companies.

(b) **The British Film Institute.** 'The BFI is the UK national agency with responsibility for encouraging and conserving the arts of film and television. Our aim is to ensure that the many audiences in the UK are offered access to the widest possible choice of cinema and television, so that their enjoyment is enhanced through a deeper understanding of the history and potential of these vital and popular art forms.'

Goals and objectives

4.4 Below the mission are goals, aims and objectives.

> **KEY TERMS**
>
> **Goals:** 'The intentions behind decision or actions' (Henry Mintzberg) or 'a desired end result' (Shorter Oxford English Dictionary)
>
> There are two types of goal, non-quantifiable goals or **aims** and quantifiable goals or **objectives.**

4.5 **Aims**

Characteristics	Example
Aims are non-quantifiable goals.	A university's: 'to seek truth'. (You would not see: 'increase truth by 5%')

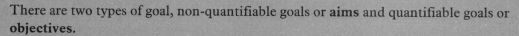

4.6 **Objectives** are quantifiable goals, in other words they are SMART.

Characteristics	Example
Objectives are SMART • Specific • Measurable • Attainable • Realistic • Time-bounded	• Departmental goal: cut costs. • Objective: reduce budgeted expenditure on paper-clips by 5% by December 31 1999

4.7 In practice, people often use the words goals, aims and objectives interchangeably. But remember that some goals fulfil SMART criteria, and others do not, even though they are still meaningful.

DEVOLVED ASSESSMENT ALERT

• It is a good idea to define your terms explicitly when using words like goal, aim and objective which might have rather vague or overlapping connotations. We recommend that you learn and use our definitions.

• Most of the objectives you will be working towards will be SMART - in terms of deadlines and so on. But if 'low morale' is a problem in your department, you might try to 'raise morale'. This is an important aim, although not a SMART objective.

4.8 Objectives can be used in three ways.

• Reference points, directing people's work
• Yardsticks, to measure performance
• Motivators

Levels of objectives

4.9 **Primary and financial objectives**

As accountancy students, you may have got the idea that the purpose of an organisation is to make **profits** for its owners. For a business organisation, other **financial** objectives may include survival (for example, to have sufficient funds to be still functioning in a year's time), growth or cash flow.

4.10 **Secondary objectives.** Remember, however, that as well as the main objective of making profits, there are subsidiary aims.

• Improved **quality** of a product or service (for example, to sell the best 'x' on the market)

• The satisfaction of the **customer** (for example, the shopkeeper who buys 'x' to stock his shop) and/or the **consumer** (for example, the person who uses/eats 'x')

• Gaining a **share of the market** for a product (for example, to sell 30% of all 'x's bought in the country in a year).

4.11 **Non-profit-making organisations,** especially government-run organisations, may have the primary objective of providing a **service** of a certain standard rather than making a profit - for example, the fire department, the police, the armed forces, the hospital and health service, charities and so on.

4.12   In a complex organisation, there should be a **hierarchy of objectives**.

- The objectives of the total **organisation** will be reinterpreted as objectives of each **division**

- The objectives of each **division** will in turn be reinterpreted as objectives of each **department** within the division

- The objectives of each **department** will in turn be reinterpreted as objectives for each **work group** within the department.

4.13 EXAMPLE

Let us take the example of a holiday firm.

Organisational goal	Survive and prosper in the leisure industry
Sales dept goal	Achieve an average of 10% year-on-year growth in holiday sales
High Street office sales target	Achieve £X total sales turnover in the first quarter of the current year

---

Activity 1.5

Long-term and short-term objectives are relative to the context. List some long-term and short-term objectives for your accounts department. Try to dream up a 'mission statement' for it, too.

---

5   CRITICAL EXTERNAL RELATIONSHIPS

5.1   There are various ways in which the **environment** is related to an organisation.

Issue	Example
Resources	The organisation brings in resources such as raw materials from 'outside' suppliers; employees are recruited from an external labour pool.
Opportunities and threats	The organisation **can exploit opportunities** (for example, for a company, new markets, or for a hospital, new medical discoveries). The organisation **must respond to threats** in order to survive (for example, for a company, competitors' actions, restrictive government laws, political unrest).
Outputs	The organisation processes the resources it gets from the environment, and produces **outputs** to the environment such as finished goods, payment to employees, tax payments to the government).

5.2   The organisation is also influenced by **stakeholders**.

Stakeholders, interest and pressure groups

KEY TERM

Stakeholder: a person, group or organisation with an interest in what the organisation does.

5.3   Stakeholders have different objectives and so make different demands over what the organisation does.

5.4   There are three broad types of stakeholder.

- Internal stakeholders (employees, management)
- Connected stakeholders (investors, shareholders, customers, suppliers, financiers)
- External stakeholders (the community, government, pressure groups)

We discuss connected and external stakeholders below.

Investors/shareholders

5.5   A business organisation exists to provide a return to shareholders - but in practice there are many different kinds of shareholders.

Shareholder type	Comment
Institutional investors (eg pension funds, unit trusts)	These generally invest money on behalf of other people.
Venture capital firms	These provide capital to more risky or new businesses. They expect to recover their investment - with profit - once the firm is established.
Private investors	Most private individuals invest via institutional investors, but privatisation issues and the conversion of building societies to banks has increased the number of private shareholders.
Employees and managers	Some firms run schemes enabling employees to acquire shares, perhaps at a reduced 'option' price.

Lenders and bankers

5.6   **Providers of long-term finance**

- **Banks** lend long-term so that borrowers can acquire long term assets.

- **Bonds** are financial instruments promising the **bondholder** a fixed rate of interest. Bond holders can be individuals of institutions.

Such lenders are mainly concerned with the **security** of their loan and their **income**.

5.7   **Providers of short-term finance**

- **Banks** provide overdraft finance, and so have an intimate knowledge of the cash flows of the business.

- Other providers include **factors** and **lease companies**.

Suppliers

5.8   **Suppliers' interests**

- A long-term relationship
- Preference over other suppliers
- A sufficient volume of business
- Prompt payment

Customers

5.9 Businesses have to **satisfy customers** to generate a return. Customers want three things.

- The products and services offered to live up to expectations
- Fair treatment
- Easy redress of any grievances, complaints or replacements for any defective items

Interest groups and regulatory bodies representing customers

5.10 **Regulatory bodies** are government-sponsored organisations set up to regulate particular industries. For **privatised utilities**, regulators are Ofgas, Ofwat, Offer, Oftel and Ofrail. They are not primarily consumer protection organisations, but they do have extensive control over pricing and competition policy.

5.11 The main consumer protection body is the **Office of Fair Trading** which has four roles.

- Promotes competition.
- Encourages the adoption of codes of practice.
- Curbs anti-competitive practices.
- Issues licences under the Consumer Credit Act.

5.12 **Other bodies**

- **Users committees** (eg London Passenger Transport Users Committee)

- **Ombudsmen,** paid for by representatives of an industry to adjudicate between customers and suppliers in cases of dispute (eg the Banking Ombudsman).

- The **Financial Services Authority** is currently taking over most of the **regulatory roles** in the world of finance

5.13 The **Consumers' Association** (CA)

- Publishes *Which?* magazine which investigates products and services identifying 'best buys'

- Represents its members in legal disputes

- Lobbies Parliament

BPP PUBLISHING

Government

5.14 Legal controls affecting

Factor	Example
Personnel	Minimum wage, discrimination, job security, working hours, redundancy payments
Operations	Health and safety at work, product safety standards, working hours
Marketing	sending unsolicited goods, dangerous packaging, misleading advertising, weights and measures
Environment	products or operations which are damaging to health, or pollute water, air or land
Finance	Taxation. Organisations: (i) *collect* tax for the government (PAYE and VAT); and (ii) *pay* tax to the government (corporation tax). There are also legal requirements to produce financial information (for example, annual returns, annual report and accounts).

5.15 The government also shapes the environment of organisations in other ways.

- **The government controls many organisations,** such as the police and fire services and the National Health Service. Local government controls planning and waste management.

- **Political and economic policy.** Control over interest rates, taxation and public spending influences the economic environment of companies in the UK.

Activity 1.6

(a) Give some examples of organisational objectives.
(b) What is a corporate mission?
(c) What do you understand by the term 'hierarchy of objectives'?
(d) Briefly explain the ways in which an organisation affects or is affected by its environment.

Activity 1.7

How might a supervisor of an accounts section be involved in the critical external relationships of an organisation?

DEVOLVED ASSESSMENT ALERT

How to improve 'critical external relationships' could be one of the issues raised in your project.

Key learning points

- Organisations can be classified and distinguished in a variety of ways (eg size, activity).

- **Organisation structure** is shaped by **divisions of labour, authority and relationships**.

  o Many organisations have a formal organisation structure with an informal organisation operating inside it at the same time.

  o As a business grows **tasks have to be divided up** - departmentation may be functional, geographical, product-based, shift-based, etc.

- **Organisation charts** can be a useful aid to designing, describing and understanding the shape and structure of an organisation, though they have certain limitations.

- Organisations have goals. These are arranged in a hierarchy with the **corporate mission** at the top and department or section **objectives** at the bottom. The objectives should support the mission.

- There are a wide **variety of factors that influence the way an organisation works**: not only its own objectives, but also its commercial, political and legal, technological, social and ethical environment.

- **Critical external relationships** include investors, customers, suppliers and the government.

Quick quiz

1   Why are organisations useful?

2   List some of the different activities in the organisation.

3   What is the purpose of organisation structure?

4   What is functional structure?

5   What is 'mission'?

6   What is a SMART objective?

7   What is a stakeholder?

8   List four types of shareholder.

9   What are banks concerned with?

10 What are customers concerned with?

Answers to quick quiz

1   They achieve more than people do individually.

2   Purchasing, operations, marketing, management

3   To group people together on some basis.

4   People who do similar jobs are grouped together.

5   The organisation's basic purpose.

6   Specific, measurable, accountable, realistic, time-bounded.

7   A person, group or organisation with an interest in what the organisation does.

8   Institutions, employees, venture capitalists, individuals.

9   Security and income.

10 Quality, delivery, the product.

Answers to activities

Answer 1.1

(a) Four classifications are: by type of activity, by size, according to whether it is profit orientated or non profit orientated, and according to legal status and ownership.

(b) Size can be measured in terms of number of staff, number of branches, geographical spread, financial characteristics, number of customers served, and in comparison with competitors.

Answer 1.2

The group has identified three major functions of their business (sales, repairs and quality control) and two main product areas (guitars and drums). They might decide to structure the business in the following ways.

(a) Have one 'general manager' (whose responsibilities may include quality control) and three 'operatives' who share the sales and repair tasks.

(b) Divide tasks by function: have one person in charge of sales, one quality controller and two repairers (perhaps one for drums and one for guitars).

(c) Divide tasks by product: have a two-man drums team (who share sales/repair/control tasks between them) and a similar guitars team.

Since there are only four individuals, each (we assume) capable of performing any of the functions for either of the products, they may decide to have a looser social arrangement. They may prefer to discuss who is going to do what, as and when jobs come in. A larger organisation would not have this luxury.

Answer 1.3

(a) An organisation is designed to link individuals in an established set of *relationships*; to enable them effectively to *plan* and *make decisions*; and to enable them to achieve their *own goals* as a necessary step towards achieving the overall *objectives of the organisation*.

(b) An organisation may be formed as follows.

   (i) Formulate objectives, policies (a guiding framework for behaviour and decision-making) and plans (how to go about achieving objectives).

   (ii) Identify the *activities* that will carry out the plans.

   (iii) Classify and group those activities, for example by forming 'departments'.

   (iv) Give the groups *authority* to carry out their activities.

   (v) Establish *relationships* between groups, so that there is a structure of authority and communication.

(c) A chart may show up problems such as insufficient delegation, poor communication, co-ordination or control, too many people under one person's control, or unclear lines of authority.

(d) The limitations of organisation charts include the following.

   (i) They are a static model, whereas an organisation is 'dynamic', continually changing. Charts can become quickly out of date.

   (ii) They show only the formal and not the informal organisation structure, and can therefore be misleading; they do not include informal communications across departments and ranks.

   (iii) They *only* describe the structure of the organisation, not other important aspects of organisational life.

   (iv) They do not tell you what each person actually does, or how well he/she does it. Remember also that people on the same level of the chart do not necessarily have the same authority.

Answer 1.4

> ***Tutorial note.*** There are a variety of ways in which the organisation could be structured. This is only one suggestion. It is possible that the purchasing and stock control functions would be under much closer supervision of the accounts department. Nor do we know how the separate manufacturing operations will be organised. The three different products could still be organised in different manufacturing departments.

(a) Organisation chart

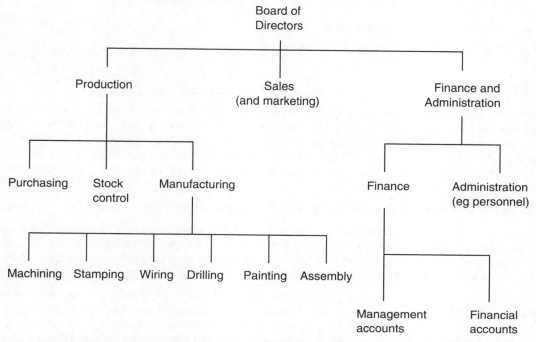

(b) Many of the reasons for changing organisation structure are those which are disadvantages of product organisation structures in any circumstances .

Principal disadvantages of product organisation structures are as follows.

(i) Duplication of functions such as sales order administration, accounting, personnel and other administrative functions. This leads to higher costs.

(ii) Loss of other economies of scale in production and administration.

(iii) If selling and marketing are decentralised, there can be a loss of opportunities for cross-selling different products to the same market.

(iv) Conflict between different products in the market place.

In the case of Q plc, it appears that the product organisation structure was the result of the company's geographical split into three locations. Where this is the case, a product structure might make some sense, to ensure that time is not wasted on paper work going to and from a head office. However, given that Q plc is to relocate to a single site the 'geographical imperative' leading to a product departmentation structure no longer holds.

The advantages of moving to a functional structure for Q plc are as follows.

(i) Economies of scale. For example, the accounts department is likely to be in one place, and so staff time can be used more efficiently.

(ii) The pooling of administrative resources may lead to better management information systems, as there could be a more efficient division of labour.

(iii) On the production side, manufacturing planning can be enhanced, as production can be switched between different machines if production flows are uneven. There would be fewer bottlenecks.

(iv)   In purchasing, it may be possible to take advantage of quantity discounts on raw materials, if this is a centralised function for each of the three products.

(v)   Centralisation in one spot could make decision-making easier as all of the relevant personnel are on site, and management can react immediately to problems and opportunities.

Answer 1.5

For an accounts department:

Mission: 'Our mission is to ensure that the business's financial transactions are recorded and processed completely, accurately and securely and that relevant information is given to management.'

Long-term objective: 'Computerise the sales ledger'.

Short-term objective: 'Do that bank reconciliation by lunchtime!'

Answer 1.6

(a)   One of the main purposes of a commercial organisation is to make profits for its owners. Other objectives may include survival, growth and cash flow. Subsidiary to the main objective of making profits, there are aims such as improved quality of a product or service, the satisfaction of the customer and/or the consumer, and gaining a share of the market. Non-profit-making organisations, especially government-run organisations, may have the purpose of providing a service of a certain standard rather than making a profit.

(b)   'Missions' are objectives formulated at the top of the organisation hierarchy and are long-term in nature.

(c)   Where there is a hierarchy of objectives, the objectives of the total organisation will be reinterpreted as objectives of each division; the objectives of each division will in turn be reinterpreted as objectives of each department within the division; and the objectives of each department will in turn be reinterpreted as objectives for each work group within the department.

(d)   The organisation brings in resources (inputs) from the environment, processes the resources, and produces outputs to the environment - finished goods, services, satisfied customers, trained employees and so on. The organisation has to take account of various 'interest' groups in the environment, including customers, the government, the general public, suppliers, shareholders and employees. The environment provides opportunities which the organisation can exploit and threats which the organisation must respond to in order to survive.

Answer 1.7

Although not directly involved in sales or marketing, you are still involved in the organisation's critical relationships.

Customers: offering/refusing credit; chasing payment; accurately processing sales orders and remittance advices.

Suppliers: paying on time.

The government: dealing with tax authorities and making statistical returns.

Chapter 2   Management and supervision

Chapter topic list

1   Managers: what they are for

2   Some principles of management and supervision

3   The management hierarchy

4   Supervisors and what they do

5   What do you manage: jobs or people?

Learning objectives

On completion of this chapter you will be able to:

	Performance criteria	Range Statement
• *understand the principles of supervision*	10.1.1, 10.1.6	n/a
• *understand the role of supervisors in co-ordinating work* activities	1.1.6	n/a
• understand the techniques of monitoring work activities	10.1.5	n/a

Italicised objectives are areas of knowledge and understanding underlying elements of competence for this Unit.

1 MANAGERS: WHAT THEY ARE FOR

KEY TERM

Management can be defined as: 'getting things done through other people'.

What managers should do

1.1 Here are some possible **management** tasks.

Task	Comment
Planning for the future	Selecting objectives and the designing the strategies and procedures for achieving them.
Organising the work (who is to do the work and when)	Establishing a **structure of tasks** to be performed to achieve the goals, **grouping these tasks into jobs** for individuals, creating **groups of jobs** within departments, **delegating authority** to carry out the jobs and providing **systems of information**.
Commanding	Giving instructions to subordinates to carry out tasks.
Co-ordinating	**Harmonising** the activities of individuals and groups within the organisation, reconciling differences of **priority**.
Controlling	**Measuring** the activities of individuals and groups, to ensure that their **performance is in accordance with plans**. Deviations from plan are identified and corrected.

DEVOLVED ASSESSMENT ALERT

In an organisation, managerial work has a purpose: directing the organisation's activities in order to carry out the mission. Your managerial or supervisory job is not simply to follow procedures blindly. You should be looking actively at ways in which your role and department can better satisfy the objectives of the organisation.

Activity 2.1

Using the list above, indicate under which of the five headings the activities below fall.

1 Ensuring that the sales department does not exceed its budget.
2 Deciding which products will form the main thrust of advertising during the next financial year.
3 Ensuring that new working practices are communicated to the workforce.
4 Ensuring that the sales department liases with production on delivery dates.
5 Changing work schedules to reduce idle time.

1.2 *Henry Mintzberg* suggests that in their daily working lives, managers fulfil three **types** of managerial role.

Role category	Role	Comment
Interpersonal, from formal authority and position	**Figurehead** (or ceremonial)	A large part of a Chief Executive's time is spent representing the company, both outside it and within
	Leader	Hiring, firing and training staff, motivating employees, and reconciling individual needs with the requirements of the organisation
	Liaison	Making contacts outside the vertical chain of command. Some managers spend up to half their meeting time with their peers rather than with their subordinates
Informational Managers have: • Access to all their staff • Many external contracts	**Monitor**	The manager **monitors** the environment, and receives information from subordinates, superiors and peers in other departments. Much of this information is of an informal nature.
	Spokesperson	The manager provides information within and outside the organisation
	Disseminator	The manager **disseminates** this information to subordinates
Decisional The manager's formal authority and access to information mean that no one else is in a position to take decisions relating to the work of the department as a whole.	**Entrepreneur**	A manager initiates projects to improve the department or to help it react to a changed environment.
	Disturbance handler	A manager has to respond to pressures, taking decisions in unusual or unexpected situations.
	Resource allocator	A manager allocates scarce resources and authorises decisions taken by subordinates.
	Negotiator	Both inside and outside the organisation takes up a great deal of management time.

1.3 The manager needs to wear the right 'hat' for each task and situation. A manager will wear some hats more than others.

- Senior officials, for example, are more likely to be called upon to at as figureheads than team leaders.

- Supervisors are more concerned with resource allocation and disturbance handling.

Activity 2.2

The *Telegraph Magazine* asked a cinema manager: 'What do you actually do? The answer was as follows.

'Everything, apart from being the projectionist and cleaning the lavatories. My office is also the ticket office. If there is a big queue at the confectionery kiosk, I'll help serve and I'll usher people to their seat if we're really busy. Sometimes I go into the cinema before a show and tell the audience about any special events, such as a director coming to give a talk.

'I get in around lunchtime, deal with messages and ensure that the lights and heating are working. I write orders for posters and publicity pictures, popcorn and ice creams and cope with the correspondence for the 2,000 members on our mailing list. I'll brief the projectionist, ushers and kiosk staff and at about 1.45pm the first matinee customers arrive. Our afternoon audience is mainly elderly people and they take some time to settle, so I'll help them to their seats and only start the film when everyone is comfortable. In the evening, more ushers and bar staff arrive and I'll brief them about the programme, seating and timing. While the film is on, I'm selling tickets for the other screen, counting the takings and planning tomorrow. If I get a moment I try to grab something to eat.'

Which of Mintzberg's roles does this manager take on in his 'average' day?

2 SOME PRINCIPLES OF MANAGEMENT AND SUPERVISION

2.1 The knowledge and understanding for Unit 9 includes 'the principles of supervision'. Traditionally these include the following.

Principle	Comment
Division of work (specialisation of tasks)	Specialisation allows an individual to build up an expertise and thereby be more productive. In manufacturing, there is a trend towards **multi-skilling**.
Authority and responsibility	A supervisor's **official** authority derives from his or her rank or office. **Authority is the right to issue orders**. No manager can give orders unless he/she has the authority to do so.
	With authority goes **responsibility** for exercising it. Responsibility means being accountable for the way authority is exercised.
Discipline	**Discipline** is the enforcement of **standards of behaviour**. Managers and supervisors should set a good example; setting bad examples undermines their authority.
Remuneration	The rewards given to employees should be fair, satisfying both employer and employee alike. Rewards mean more than just financial rewards.
Scalar chain	The scalar chain is the term used to describe the organisation's management hierarchy, ie the chain of superiors from lowest to highest rank.
Fairness	Managers should be fair in all their dealings. Everybody must be judged on their performance, and dealt with accordingly. This means not rewarding the under-achievers, as well as rewarding the achievers.
Initiative	This is one of the most important ideas in modern management thinking: it is essential to encourage and develop this capacity in staff to the full.
Team spirit	Building up a team spirit takes considerable talent: to co-ordinate efforts, encourage enthusiasm and avoid inter-personal conflict.

3 THE MANAGEMENT HIERARCHY

3.1 **Organisational structure** shows how tasks are differentiated and distributed. Management structure is an aspect of this. It shows the distribution of authority and responsibility.

Chain of command

> ### KEY TERM
>
> The **scalar chain** or **chain of command** is the organisation's formal management hierarchy, that is the chain of superiors from lowest to highest rank.

3.2 **Formal communication runs up and down the lines of authority**, eg E to D to C to B to A in the diagram below. If communication between different branches of the chain is necessary (eg D to H) the use of a 'gang plank' of horizontal communication saves time.

Scalar chains: ————

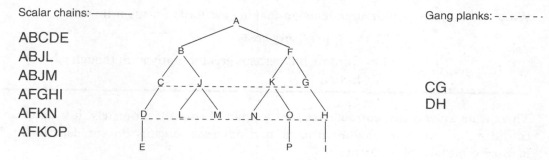

ABCDE
ABJL
ABJM
AFGHI
AFKN
AFKOP

Gang planks: - - - - - - -

CG
DH

3.3 The length of the chains of command is influenced by five things.

- Work practices
- Size of the organisation
- Products and services (type, range, complexity)
- Geographical dispersion
- Controls

3.4 An organisation has many such scalar chains of authority and command, but all of them originate at the **topmost management authority** which in a company is the **board of directors**. Managers at **different levels in the hierarchy are all links** in a chain of command.

3.5 One important problem for efficient and effective management is establishing the most suitable **number of links** in the chains of command.

(a) Short chains of command

- information - good or bad - can, in theory, flow quickly up and down, without going through too many levels.

- Junior managers can influence and obtain insight into senior management decisions.

(b) Long chains of command provide a satisfying career structure and reduce **span of control**.

Span of control

3.6 The **span of control** refers to the number of staff immediately responsible to a particular manager or supervisor. In the diagram under paragraph 3.2, C has a span of control of 1 (because D is the only person directly reporting to C) and J has a span of control of 2. B also has a span of control of 2.

3.7 The number of subordinates and tasks over which a manager has supervisory responsibilities should be restricted to what is physically and mentally possible.

Width of span	Key issues
Narrow	Tight **control** and close supervision and co-ordination of subordinates' activities.
	Time to think and plan; managers are not burdened with too many day to day problems.
	Reduced delegation; a manager can do more of his work himself.
	Better communication with subordinates, who are sufficiently small in number to allow this to occur.
Wide	**Greater decision-making authority** for subordinates.
	Lower supervisory costs.
	Less control, but perhaps **greater motivation** though job satisfaction.

3.8 There is no **universally 'correct' size for the span of control**: ultimately, it is necessary to consider the particular circumstances of any individual organisation or department, but here are some possible influences.

- The nature of the manager's **work load**

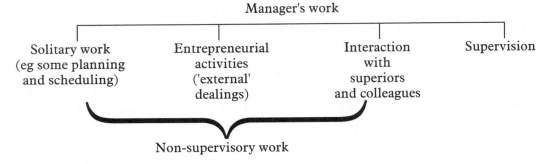

The more non-supervisory work in a manager's work load the narrower the span of control should be or the greater the delegation of authority to subordinates should be.

- The **geographical dispersion** of the subordinates.

- **Subordinates' work:** if subordinates do the same simple job a wide span is possible.

- The nature of **problems** that a supervisor might have to help subordinates with.

- The degree of **interaction between subordinates** (with close interaction, a wider span of control should be possible).

- The **competence and abilities** of both management and subordinates.

- Whether **close group cohesion** is desirable. Small groups will be more cohesive, with a better sense of team work. This would call for narrow spans of control.

- The amount of **help that supervisors receive** from other departments (such as the personnel department or the production planning department).

Project and matrix management

3.9 A golden rule of older management theory is that one person should have one boss. However, in many modern organisations this is impractical.

3.10 A project, such as the development of a new product, for example, may be inter-disciplinary, and require the contributions of an engineer, a marketing person and a production expert, who would each be appointed to the team from their separate departments, whilst still retaining membership and status within their own departments.

Level in departmental hierarchy	Department				
	A	B	C	D	E
1	X	Ⓧ	X	X	Ⓧ
2	Ⓧ	X	X	X	X
3	X	X	Ⓧ	X	X
4	X	X	X	Ⓧ	X

(a) Members of the project team (circled) would provide formal lateral lines of communication and authority, superimposed on the functional departmental structure. **Most projects are temporary arrangements:** project teams are drawn together to accomplish one task and then disbanded.

3.11 **Matrix organisations are permanent arrangements,** in which two (or more) lines of authority overlap. For example, a section leader in a regional accounts department might have to report both to a **financial controller** at head office and to a **regional general manager,** so that functional and geographic organisation run at the same time.

(a) **Advantages**

- Greater flexibility and co-operation from everyone involved
- Co-ordination between business functions at local level

(b) **Disadvantages**

- Dual authority threatens a conflict between managers. A subordinate must know to which superior he is responsible for each aspect of his duties.

- One individual with two or more bosses is more likely to suffer stress at work.

Activity 2.3

Six months ago Dawn Reeves, your friend in another section of the accounts department, was promoted to a first line supervisory position. She undertook her new duties enthusiastically and the performance of her section has improved. Dawn, however, is not as happy as she used to be when she was an ordinary member of the section. 'I'm not sure I'm the type to be a supervisor,' she confided to you recently. 'There seems to be so much to do, but not a lot of it is what I call proper work.' This seems to be an ideal opportunity to talk to Dawn about 'managerial roles'.

(a) Note, in brief, what you would say to Dawn about managerial roles in general. Try to draw your answer from your *own* experience (and *observation* of others) rather than merely listing the traditional roles outlined in this Interactive Text.

(b) List the key roles which Dawn should play in her current job.

 BPP PUBLISHING

DEVOLVED ASSESSMENT ALERT

Inappropriate spans of control may be a problem in your section. Perhaps you feel there are too many people reporting to one person. One way of dealing with this may be to appoint section leaders. For example, if there are three people looking after cash, say, one person could be asked to look after that mini-section. You would have one person reporting to you rather than three - even though you have increased the number of management levels.

4 SUPERVISORS AND WHAT THEY DO

4.1 This diagram in Paragraph 3.2 in this chapter showed a pyramid, with A at the apex and others below.

4.2 This suggests that there are different levels of management. A **finance department** in an organisation might be headed by the finance director (at A), supported by a chief **financial accountant** (B) and chief **management accountant** (F). C, J, K and G are lower down in the hierarchy; they might be assistant accountants.

4.3 The **supervisor is the lowest level of management.**

KEY TERM

'A **supervisor** is a person selected by middle management to take charge of a group of people, or special task, to ensure that work is carried out satisfactorily ... the job is largely reactive dealing with situations as they arise, allocating and reporting back to higher management.' (Savedra and Hawthorn).

4.4 **Features of supervision**

(a) A supervisor is usually a 'front-line' manager, dealing with the levels of the organisation where the bread-and-butter work is done. The supervisor's **subordinates are non-managerial employees**.

(b) A supervisor does not spend all his or her time on the managerial aspects of his job. A supervisor does **technical/operational work**.

(c) The supervisor monitors and controls work by means of **day-to-day, frequent and detailed information**: higher levels of management plan and control using longer-term, less frequent and less detailed information.

(d) The **managerial aspects and responsibilities of a supervisor's job are often ill-defined**, and have no precise targets to measure achievement against.

What do supervisors do?

4.5 As a supervisor's job is a junior management job, the tasks of supervision can be listed under similar headings to the tasks of management.

4.6 **Planning**
- Planning **work** so as to **meet work targets** or schedules set by more senior management
- Planning work **methods and procedures**
- Preparing **budgets** for the section
- Planning **staff training** and staff development

4.7 **Organising and overseeing the work of others**
- **Ordering** materials and equipment
- Authorising overtime
- **Allocating work and equipment** to staff
- Monitoring **performance standards** for staff
- Deciding **job priorities**

4.8 **Controlling: making sure the work is done properly**
- Keeping **records** of time worked, time spent on each job, time spent idle
- **Disciplining** staff (for late arrival at work and so on)
- Ensuring that the **quality of work** is sustained to the required levels
- Ensuring that **safety standards** are maintained
- **Co-ordinating** the work of the section with the work of other sections
- Ensuring that **work targets are achieved**, and explaining the cause to senior management of any failure to achieve these targets

4.9 **Motivating employees, and dealing with others:**
- Dealing with **staff problems**
- **Reporting to a senior manager**
- Dealing with **customers**
- Helping staff to **understand** the organisation's goals and targets
- **Training staff**, and identifying the need for more training

4.10 **Communicating**
- **Telling employees about plans, targets and work schedules**
- **Telling managers** about the work that has been done, and the attitudes of staff to the work and work conditions
- **Filling in reports** (for example absentee reports for the personnel department, on appraisal forms)
- **Collecting information** and distributing it to the other persons interested in it.

4.11 **'Doing'**
- Doing operations work
- Standing in for a senior manager when he or she is on holiday or otherwise absent
- Giving advice to others to help solve problems

Activity 2.4

Look at the job of the supervisor (or similar position) in your office (your own job, if you are in such a position).

(a) Identify the (i) managerial and (ii) technical aspects of the job, and list as many as you can think of of the duties they entail.

(b) Get hold of a copy of the **job description** of a supervisory job (or have a look at one in the organisation manual). Does it bear any relation to the list you compiled yourself? Is it a realistic description of the actual work of the supervisor? Is the 'supervisory' part of the job well-defined (as compared with the technical part)? Are there targets or standards, and training requirements?

(c) Consider your own experience of promotion to a supervisory post (or ask your supervisor). What preparation, training, coaching, and/or advice was given by the manager for this first step into managerial work - or was it 'sink or swim'?

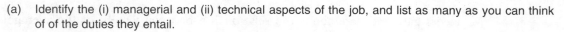

BPP
PUBLISHING

4.12 **Role conflict** is where an individual has to act in more than one role at the same time, and finds those roles incompatible. A supervisor may find himself in situations of role conflict.

(a) Supervisors often have a dual role in doing **technical** work as well as **'supervision'** or managing. They are closer to their staff in this sense than managers, and have frequently been promoted from the ranks of the section, so that there is some ambiguity between the roles of **colleague** and **superior** in relation to staff.

(b) **'In-the-middle'.** Supervisors are at the lowest level of management, which puts them directly between management (and the expectations and objectives set by senior executives and their immediate superiors) and the non-managerial workforce who probably have different priorities.

5 WHAT DO YOU MANAGE: JOBS OR PEOPLE?

5.1 Is there a right way of being a manager or supervisor? Probably not, but two early approaches suggested otherwise. These approaches are scientific management and human relations. The topic **human relations** features in the knowledge and understanding in this Unit, but you cannot really understand human relations without looking at **scientific management** first.

Scientific management: planning work

5.2 FW Taylor pioneered the **scientific management** movement about 100 years ago. He argued that management should be based on 'well-recognised, clearly defined and fixed principles, instead of depending on more or less hazy ideas.'

5.3 **Scientific management in practice**

(a) **Work study techniques** broke each job down into its smallest and simplest component parts in order to achieve the greatest efficiency.

(b) **Planning the work and doing the work were separated.** Workers lost any control over what they did, and all knowledge was assumed to reside in the heads of work study analysts.

(c) **Workers were paid incentives** on the basis of acceptance of the new methods and output norms as the new methods greatly increased productivity and profits.

Some people felt the Taylor approach was de-humanising.

5.4 EXAMPLE

It is useful to consider an application of Taylor's principles to shovelling work at the Bethlehem Steel Works.

(a) Managers gathered data about the relationship between weight of the average shovel load and the total load shifted per day. From these facts, management was able to decide on the ideal shovel size for each type of material handled in order to optimise the speed of shovelling work done. Thus, scientific technique was applied to deciding **how work should be done**.

(b) By **organising work a day in advance,** it was possible to minimise the idle time and the moving of men from one place in the shovelling yard to another. Once again, scientific method replaces 'seat-of-the-pants' decisions by supervisors.

(c) **Workers were paid for accepting the new methods** and 'norms' and received 60% higher wages than those given to similar workers in other companies in the area.

(d) **Workers were carefully selected and trained** in the art of shovelling properly; anyone falling below the required norms consistently was given special teaching to improve his performance.

(e) **The costs of implementing this method were more than repaid by the benefits.** The labour force required fell from 400 - 600 men to 140 men for the same work.

Reactions to scientific management

Human relations: promotion of job satisfaction

5.5 In the 1930s, a critical perception of scientific management emerged. Elton Mayo was pioneer of a new approach called **human relations**. This concentrated mainly on the concept of 'Social Man' (Schein): **people are motivated by 'social' or 'belonging' needs,** which are satisfied by the social relationships they form at work.

5.6 Attention shifted towards people's 'higher' psychological needs for growth, challenge, responsibility and self-fulfilment. **Herzberg** suggested that only these things could **positively motivate** employees to improved performance.

5.7 The human relations approaches contributed an important awareness of the influence of the human factor at work on organisational performance.

(a) Most theorists offered guidelines to enable practising managers to satisfy and motivate employees and so (theoretically) to obtain improved productivity.

(b) However, as far as the practising manager is concerned there is still **no proven link between job satisfaction and motivation,** or either of these **and productivity** or the achievement of organisational goals.

Other ideas about management

Diagnosing organisational problems

5.8 Handy proposed a **diagnostic role** for managers. Management is responsible for maintaining the 'health' of the organisation.

- **Identify the symptoms** in the situation (eg low productivity, high labour turnover).
- **Diagnose the 'disease'** or cause of the trouble.
- **Decide how it might be dealt with** by developing a strategy for better health.
- **Start the treatment.**

DEVOLVED ASSESSMENT ALERT

Diagnosing problems is a key to improving the effectiveness of a system.

Management as 'coaching' and support

5.9 Those who are directly involved in doing the work are those who have the greatest knowledge of the process's inefficiencies and efficiencies. **Supporting the workforce** involves four activities.

- **Soliciting their expertise** and allowing them to take some operational decisions.
- **Supporting operations** and helping them become efficient.
- Providing **counselling** and advice.

- Bringing the **organisation's resources** to bear on problems identified by the workforce.

Management as the promotion of organisational learning

5.10 Many organisations innovate. **Innovation** can occur in new product design, production, marketing, service delivery, organisation structure and culture.

5.11 **Implications for managers**

- **No one individual** or group of individuals can, even in principle, be the source of **all knowledge** about an organisation's activities.

- People should be able to **communicate their insights** to others in the organisation, creating a pool of knowledge from which the **whole** organisation can draw.

- Creativity does not only reside in individuals, but in groups.

DEVOLVED ASSESSMENT ALERT

Applications in an accounts department can include 'brainstorming' or training meetings where the team generates ideas as to how they can work better.

Which is the right way?

5.12 The scientific management school and the human relations school were both interested in **increasing productivity** on the shop floor, but their opinions on the proper way to motivate workers were diametrically opposite. It might seem, therefore, that one must be right and the other wrong. However, this is not necessarily true, since they were looking at the work situation from two entirely different angles. Modern thinking suggests that the right managerial approach will vary with the situation, and managers should consider all aspects of the job, the work people and the work group. This is called the **contingency** approach.

Corporate culture

KEY TERM

Culture in an organisation is the sum total of the beliefs, knowledge, attitudes of mind and customs to which people are exposed.

5.13 All organisations will generate their own cultures, whether spontaneously or under the guidance of positive managerial strategy. The culture will consist of three elements.

(a) The **basic, underlying assumptions which guide the behaviour of the individuals and groups** in the organisation, such as belief in quality, freedom to make decisions, freedom to make mistakes, and the value of innovation and initiative at all levels.

(b) **Beliefs expressed by the organisation and its members**. These beliefs and values may emerge as sayings, slogans or mottos such as 'we're getting there', 'the customer is always right', or 'the winning team'. They may not be explicit.

(c) **Visible artefacts** - the style of the offices or other premises, dress rules, display of 'trophies', the degree of informality between superiors and subordinates.

DEVOLVED ASSESSMENT ALERT

You can probably see some sense - something applicable to your job - in each of the approaches described. You should feel free to take from each approach whatever you find useful for you and your circumstances.

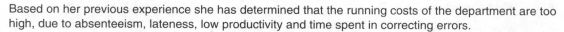

Activity 2.5

Harriet has just been appointed to take charge of part of a management accounting department concerned with processing information from the operating division of a large company.

Based on her previous experience she has determined that the running costs of the department are too high, due to absenteeism, lateness, low productivity and time spent in correcting errors.

Investigation of the design of the jobs in the department reveals that each employee is trained in a task which is made as simple as possible. The equipment used is maintained by a service department. Strict discipline ensures that clerks do not carry on conversations during working hours, and that tasks are performed in exactly the order and method laid down.

Harriet has decided that performance can be improved by changing the job design.

Assuming that Harriet's superiors approve the changes, that correct training is provided and that resistance by the clerks to change is properly overcome, you are required:

(a)   to describe six changes which might achieve improved job satisfaction;
(b)   to explain four problems which may make it difficult to change the design of such jobs.

DEVOLVED ASSESSMENT ALERT

When recommending changes to an accounting system, you have to bear in mind the effect on the organisation. This must include its culture. If your recommendations go against the established way of doing business, you will have to fight hard to justify them.

Key learning points

- Managers **forecast** and **plan**, **organise**, **motivate** and **command**, **co-ordinate**, **control** and **measure**. Communication is essential for all of this.

- A **supervisor is a junior manager** who gets more actively involved in the actual work of his or her section than more senior managers.

- Particularly important principles of management are **authority** and **responsibility**, **discipline**, **scalar chains**, fairness, initiative and team spirit.

- The nature of a supervisor's job is affected by the chains of command in the organisation and the span of control.

- **Matrix organisation** structures challenge classical ideas of one person, one boss.

- **Scientific management** concentrates on the tasks to be performed.

- The **human relations** approach focuses on people. Other theories attempt to reconcile these views.

- Organisation **culture** is the sum of its beliefs, knowledge, attitudes and customs.

Quick quiz

1   What does a manager do?

2   What is meant by 'organising'?

3   List some of the characteristics of the work of a supervisor.

4   One of the most important tasks of a supervisor is communication. What might this involve?

5   What is horizontal communication?

6   Would you agree that managers and supervisors should have an intimate knowledge of the work that their staff are doing at all times?

7   What is a chain of command?

8   What is a span of control?

9   What influences the width of a manager's span of control?

10 What are the weaknesses of scientific management?

11 What are the principles of human relations?

12 What are the characteristics of organisation culture?

Answers to quick quiz

1   Writers have identified a number of elements of management including the following.

    (a)   Formulating policy
    (b)   Forecasting and planning
    (c)   Organising
    (d)   Motivating
    (e)   Controlling and measuring
    (f)   Communicating
    (g)   Staffing
    (h)   Leading

2   Organising means determining what activities are necessary to achieve the objectives of the business and then dividing the work and assigning it to different groups and individuals.

3   A supervisor is a 'front line' manager, dealing directly with people who do the bread-and-butter work. A supervisor does not spend all his time managing other people. Much of his time will be spent doing operational work himself. However, a supervisor *is* responsible for getting things done: supervisory work is really management work, but at a lower level in the organisation than that of managers.

4   (a)   Telling employees about plans, targets and work schedules.

    (b)   Telling managers about the work that has been done.

    (c)   Filling in reports (eg absentee reports for the personnel department, job appraisal forms).

    (d)   Collecting information and distributing it to the other persons interested in it.

5   Horizontal communication takes place when people at the same management level in different departments communicate with each other directly.

6   The answer depends partly upon the precise work involved and the nature of the management post. In general the job of the manager or supervisor is to co-ordinate, control, provide information, motivate, and so on rather than to interfere in the detailed operations: in other words, to do whatever is necessary to *enable* others to do the work. The manager or supervisor *may* do some of the detailed work, too, but this is in his or her role as the operative for some of the team's work, it is not part of 'managing' the team.

7   A chain of command in an organisation is a line of authority from the top of the management hierarchy down to employees at the very bottom.

8   The span of control refers to the number of subordinates responsible to each superior. In other words, if a manager has five subordinates, the span of control is five.

9   The extent of a manager's span of control is determined by the following factors.

    (a)   The amount of non-supervisory work in his or her workload.

(b)   The geographical dispersion of the subordinates.

(c)   Whether subordinates' work is all of a similar nature (wide span possible) or diversified.

(d)   The nature of problems that a supervisor might have to help subordinates with.

(e)   The degree of interaction between subordinates (with close interaction, a wider span of control should be possible).

(f)   The competence and abilities of both management and subordinates.

(g)   Whether close group cohesion is desirable. Small groups will be more cohesive, with a better sense of team work. This would call for narrow spans of control.

(h)   The amount of help that supervisors receive from staff functions (such as the personnel department or the production planning department).

10   The scientific management approach may lead to the de-humanisation of the individual worker, who may be manipulated and programmed like a machine. To get the best out of people it is generally necessary to give them a *whole* job, rather than a series of unrelated activities.

11   Human relations theorists argued that motivation to work, productivity and the quality of output are all related to the 'psychology of the work group' - that is, social relations among the workers, and the relationship between the workers and their supervisor/boss.

12   *Culture* in an organisation is the sum total of the beliefs, knowledge, attitudes of mind and customs to which people are exposed. The culture will consist of: the *basic, underlying assumptions* which guide the behaviour of the individuals and groups in the organisation, for example customer orientation, or belief in quality; *overt beliefs* expressed by the organisation and its members, which may emerge as sayings like 'the customer is always right', or in jokes and stories about past successes and *visible artefacts* - the style of the offices or other premises, dress 'rules' and the degree of informality between superiors and subordinates.

Answers to activities

Answer 2.1

1 = controlling; 2 = planning; 3 = commanding; 4 = co-ordinating; 5 = organising.

Answer 2.2

Your answer may well be that the cinema manager takes on all of Mintzberg's roles, although **figurehead** and **negotiator** play a very minor part in his day.

Answer 2.3

(a)   You are asked to draw upon your experience and observation of what supervisors actually do and from this draw conclusions about what their roles are. Mintzberg's list in paragraph 1.3 might get you thinking.

(b)   Dawn should be told that in her present job as supervisor she is not expected to act in all these roles at once, but that some of them are to be found within her scope as a supervisor.

    (i)   Liaison - Dawn's section communicates with the organisation as a whole through her, and it is part of her job to ensure that the assistance which her section requires is obtained from the organisation.

    (ii)   Leader - she seems to be performing well in her role as leader of the section - the increase in output appears to be linked with her new duties, which must mean that she is motivating her team.

    (iii)   Disturbance handler and resource allocator - these two roles include most of the work of supervision.

BPP PUBLISHING

Answer 2.5 _____

(a) Job satisfaction could be improved in the following ways.

    (i) It appears that each employee performs a single task and this is likely to lead to monotony, poor concentration and frustration. Allowing employees to swap jobs after a period of time would add variety to each employee's work and make the department as a whole more flexible.

    (ii) Harriet could attempt to widen jobs by increasing the number of operations in which the job holder is involved. This lengthens the time-cycle of repeated operations and thus reduces monotony.

    (iii) Harriet could attempt to build greater responsibility, breadth and challenge of work into a job. At present it seems that work is conducted according to a rule book: allowing the employee greater freedom to decide how the job should be done will encourage innovation and give employees more sense of responsibility.

    (iv) Communication between employees is not encouraged and this may mean that one part of the department does not know what the other is doing. This, in turn, is likely to lead to misunderstandings and errors and cause a general sense of failure. The ban on conversations should therefore be relaxed and communication about work could be encouraged.

    (v) Teamwork is a further possibility, growing naturally out of the changes outlined above. If these are implemented there is likely to be more overlap between the individual employee's work. If a group has collective responsibility for the whole group's output they will be more inclined to put in the required effort (for the sake of the group) and take an interest in the work of the department as a whole.

    (vi) Participation in decisions that affect their jobs may help the employees to feel that they have some control over what they are expected to do and encourage commitment to the work.

(b) Problems in changing the design of such jobs may be as follows.

    (i) Opposition from other departments. If the present working conditions are typical of the organisation, then changes in one part of it may cause resentment elsewhere.

    (ii) The relative abilities of staff. Rotating jobs, for example, may not be possible if different jobs require different abilities.

    (iii) The timescale of the changes. Some of the changes proposed would require the staff to learn new skills and this will take time and slow down the work of the department as a whole.

    (iv) The nature of the work. The work itself may not lend itself to some of the changes proposed. Swapping jobs round, for example, may confuse the people whom the department serves, who may be used to dealing with a particular person. Sharing responsibilities may reduce control over certain areas where duties have been segregated deliberately so that different employees check each other's work.

Chapter 3   Human relations

Chapter topic list

1   Interpersonal relationships

2   Different personalities at work

3   How are people motivated?

4   Improving motivation

5   Working in teams

6   Leading the team

7   Using communication skills

Learning objectives

On completion of this chapter you will be able to:

	Performance criteria	Range Statement
• *understand the principles of human relations, team building and motivation*	n/a	n/a
• understand some of the issues involved in reviewing competence of individuals	10.1.2	
• understand how to make verbal recommendations	Units 10.2 and 10.3	1 1
• understand some of the issues involved in how to communciate	10.1.4	1

Italicised objectives are areas of knowledge and understanding underlying elements of competence for this Unit.

BPP
PUBLISHING

1 INTERPERSONAL RELATIONSHIPS

KEY TERM

Interpersonal behaviour is behaviour between people. It includes two way processes such as communicating, delegating, negotiating, resolving conflict, persuading, selling, using and responding to authority, as well as a person's manner with other people.

1.1 Desirable interpersonal behaviour includes:

- **Perceiving** other people
- **Listening to** and **understanding** other people
- **Behaving** in a way which builds on this understanding
- Being **sensitive** to the impression one gives, in the light of the roles one is expected to play

Role theory

1.2 Many people behave in any situation according to the roles they are expected to perform, and the role tends to influence the type of interpersonal relationships that people have.

Activity 3.1

Managers could exert a powerful influence over team members if they could establish themselves as role models. What kind of example could they set that might be helpful for the team members and for the organisation?

Interpersonal skills

1.3 **Interpersonal skills** are those skills which are needed by an individual in order to do three things.

- Understand and manage the roles, relationships, attitudes and perceptions operating in any situation in which two or more people are involved.
- Communicate clearly and effectively.
- Achieve his or her aims from an interpersonal encounter (ideally, allowing the other parties to emerge satisfied too).

1.4 Interpersonal skills may include the following abilities.

- Interpret other people's **body language** (and to control your own, to reinforce the message you want to give).
- Identify what **roles** you and others are in, as these roles interact with each other.
- **Listen** attentively and actively to people.
- **'Read between the lines'** of a message, by recognising where attitudes, bias, or deliberate ambiguity are distorting the real message being given.
- Put **others at their ease**, to persuade, to smooth over difficult situations - ie diplomacy.

- Use **communication media** effectively: to speak articulately, write legibly and in an appropriate vocabulary, or draw diagrams where required.

- Communicate and show **enthusiasm** - ie leadership or inspiration.

1.5 The above list is by no means exhaustive. There are many types of skill brought into play in encounters between people, especially if their purpose is not just informing but persuading, disciplining, dealing with problems or sharing emotions.

2 DIFFERENT PERSONALITIES AT WORK

Personality

2.1 In order to identify, describe and explain the differences between people, psychologists use the concept of personality.

> **KEY TERM**
>
> **Personality** is the total pattern of characteristic ways of thinking, feeling and behaving that constitute the individual's distinctive method of relating to the environment.

2.2 Traits and types

(a) **Traits** are consistently observable properties, or the tendency for a person to behave in a particular way. If you say someone is generally sweet-tempered or undemonstrative, you are identifying traits in their personality.

(b) People who possess a particular trait might be likely to possess certain other compatible or related traits: **trait clusters**. Taken as a whole the trait cluster forms and identifiable **personality type**.

2.3 Self and self-image

Personality develops from experience whereby the individual interacts with his or her environment and other people.

(a) **Self-image.** People tend to behave, and expect to be treated, in accordance with their self-image but this may not be accurate.

(b) **Personality development.** People tend, as they mature, to become more actively independent, to take on more equal or superior and to develop self control and self awareness. Some psychologists consider that classical, efficiency-seeking organisations actively **prevent** people from maturing, by encouraging passive compliance with authority.

2.4 Personality and work behaviour

Managers can consider the following aspects of personality in a work situation. An individual should be 'compatible' in three ways.

BPP PUBLISHING

Compatibility	Comments
With the task	Different personality types suit different types of work. A person who appears unsociable and inhibited will find sales work, involving a lot of social interactions, intensely stressful - and will probably not be very good at it.
With the systems and management culture of the organisation	Some people hate to be controlled, but others accept and even exploit their place in the hierarchy.
With other personalities in the team	**Personality clashes** are a prime source of conflict at work. An achievement-oriented personality, for example, tends to be a perfectionist, is impatient and unable to relax; such a person will clearly be frustrated and annoyed by laid-back sociable types working (or not working) around him.

2.5 Where incompatibilities occur the manager or supervisor will have to achieve three things.

(a) **Restore compatibility,** for example by giving people different jobs more suited to their personality type or changing management style to suit the personalities of the team.

(b) **Achieve a compromise.** Individuals should be encouraged to **understand the nature** of their differences. Others have the right to be themselves (within the demands of the team). It may be necessary for some to **modify their behaviour** if necessary.

(c) **Remove the incompatible personality.** In the last resort, obstinately difficult or disruptive people may simply have to be weeded out of the team.

Activity 3.2

Look at the following list and number the qualities in priority order. 1 is very important, 2 is quite important, 3 is unimportant.

- Good appearance
- Ability to do the job
- Ability to answer questions clearly
- A pleasant speaking voice
- Being objective

- A pleasant personality
- The ability to reason
- Being interested in further training
- Being used to working in a team
- Being a good listener

Perception

2.6 The ability to assess the personality of others - with very little information - is an essential part of social behaviour, enabling individuals to interact with each other effectively.

2.7 The way in which we perceive other people is obviously going to be crucial to how we will relate to them and communicate with them in any context. There are two important forms of bias in the perception of other people that tend to operate in any situation:

(a) **The halo effect** is a term used to describe the way that **first impressions,** based on immediately obvious characteristics like dress, manner or facial expression, colour later perceptions of other features of those people, whether to positive or negative effect.

(b) **Stereotyping.** We group together people who share certain characteristics, and then attribute traits to the group as a whole, assuming that all members of the group are the same in all characteristics. The grouping may be done according to nationality, occupation, social position, age, sex or physical characteristics.

Activity 3.3

In general terms, organisations will make certain generalised assumptions about the personalities of the individuals they wish to employ. They may have an idea of the character traits or types that are considered desirable in whatever business they are in, or in whatever role the individual is to fill. You only have to look in job advertisements to see the recurrence of the desired characteristics: extrovert, steady, lively, responsible, hard working and so on.

However, research has not been able to show a significant correlation between personality (on the basis of test results) and performance.

(a) The extrovert may be active, cheerful, social and not averse to risk - but may also be unreliable, easily bored, irresponsible and fickle.

(b) Neurotics tend to be depressive, anxious, obsessive and emotional, and take too many days off sick - but they may also be conscientious, highly disciplined and they do not fret under authority. Moreover, the ability to display and share emotion can be a healthy and desirable quality.

Which of these would *you* rather have working in your section?

2.8 One of the commonest mistakes that managers make is to want to 'clone' themselves: to assume that what motivates them is (or should be) what motivates everybody else or, worse, to assume that anybody whose approach and attitude to work is not the same as their own is 'wrong' or inappropriate.

3 HOW ARE PEOPLE MOTIVATED?

3.1 In chapter 1 we saw that an **organisation has goals,** which can only be achieved by the efforts of the people who work in the organisation. **Individual people also have their own 'goals'** in life, and these may not be consistent with those of the organisation. A major consideration for supervisors and management is the problem of motivating the employees to work in such a way that the organisation achieves its goals. When the employees goals support the organisation's goals there is said to be **goal congruence.**

Activity 3.4

What factors in yourself or your organisation motivate you to:

(a) Turn up to work at all?
(b) Do an average day's work?
(c) 'Bust a gut' on a task or for a boss?

Go on - be honest!

KEY TERMS

Motivation is 'a decision-making process through which the individual chooses the desired outcomes and set in motion the behaviour appropriate to acquiring them'. (Buchanan and Huczynski).

Motives: 'learned influences on human behaviour that lead us to pursue particular goals because they are socially valued'. (Buchanan and Huczynski).

3.2 In practice, the words **motives** and **motivation** are commonly used in at least three ways.

- **Goals or outcomes** that have become desirable for a particular individual. We say that money, power or friendship are motives for doing something.

- The **mental process of choosing desired outcomes,** deciding how to go about them (and whether the likelihood of success warrants the amount of effort that will be necessary) and **setting in motion** the required behaviour.

- The **social process** by which **other people motivate us** to behave in the ways they wish. Motivation in this sense usually applies to the attempts of organisations to get workers to put in more effort.

Need theories

Maslow's hierarchy of needs

3.3 Maslow outlined seven needs, as in the diagram below, and put forward certain propositions about the motivating power of each need.

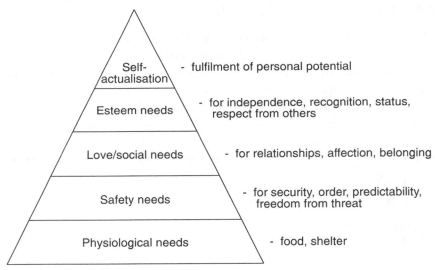

- Each level of need is **dominant until satisfied**; only then does the next higher level of need become a motivating factor.

- A **need which has been satisfied no longer motivates** an individual's behaviour. The need for self-actualisation can rarely be satisfied.

Activity 3.5

Decide which of Maslow's categories of need the following fit into.

(a) Receiving praise from your manager
(b) A family party
(c) An artist forgetting to eat
(d) A man washed up on a desert island
(e) A pay increase
(f) Joining a local drama group
(g) Being awarded the OBE
(h) Buying a house

3.4 Problems with Maslow's hierarchy

- An individual's behaviour may be in response to **several needs**. Work, after all, can either satisfy or thwart the satisfaction of a number of needs.

- The **same need may cause different behaviour** in different individuals.

- It ignores the concept of **deferred gratification** by which people are prepared to ignore current suffering for the promise of future benefits.

- **Empirical verification is hard to come by.**

Herzberg

3.5 **Herzberg's** two-factor theory identified **hygiene factors** and **motivator factors**.

(a) **Hygiene factors** are based on a **need to avoid unpleasantness.**

If inadequate, they cause **dissatisfaction** with work. They work analogously to sanitation, which minimises threats to health rather than actively promoting 'good health'. Unpleasantness demotivates: pleasantness is a steady state. Hygiene factors (the conditions of work) include:

- Company policy and administration
- Salary
- The quality of supervision
- Interpersonal relations
- Working conditions
- Job security

(b) **Motivator factors** are based on a **need for personal growth**.

They actively create job satisfaction and are effective in motivating an individual to superior performance and effort. These factors are:

- Status (this may be a hygiene factor too)
- Advancement
- Gaining recognition
- Responsibility
- Challenging work
- Achievement
- Growth in the job

3.6 A lack of motivators at work will encourage employees to concentrate on bad hygiene factors (such as to demand more pay). Stemming from his fundamental division of motivator and hygiene factors, Herzberg encouraged managers to **change the job** itself (the type of work done, the nature of tasks, levels of responsibility) rather than conditions of work.

Expectation theories

Expectancy theory - Vroom

3.7   Vroom suggested that people will decide how much they are going to put into their work, according to two factors.

(a) **Valence:** the value that they place on the outcome for themselves (whether the positive value of a reward, or the negative value of a punishment)

(b) **Expectancy:** the strength of their expectation that behaving in a certain way will in fact bring out the desired outcome.

$$Expectancy \times Valence = Force\ of\ motivation.$$

3.8   Put more simply, if you work hard to get promoted but then find that you do not get promoted you will be less highly motivated to work hard in future.

Targets: goal theory

3.9   Goal theory is currently the most popular.

- **Difficult goals lead to higher performance** than easy goals, so long as they have been *accepted* by the person trying to achieve them.

- **Specific goals lead to higher performance** than general 'do your best' goals. Specific goals seem to create a precise intention, which in turn helps the person to shape their behaviour with precision.

- **Knowledge of results (feedback) is essential** if the full performance benefits of setting difficult and specific goals are to be achieved.

What are *your* goals at work?

4   IMPROVING MOTIVATION

DEVOLVED ASSESSMENT ALERT

In your project report you are expected to make suggestions for improving performance in an accounting section, and motivation may be a possible area for improvement.

4.1   Ways of increasing the motivation of staff

- **Pay and incentive schemes** are frequently regarded as powerful motivators.

- Herzberg and others recommended **job enrichment**. This is dealt with later in this chapter.

- Various writers have suggested that **leadership style**, and **participation by subordinates in decision-making** will improve motivation.

Pay as a motivator

4.2   **Pay satisfies several of the needs in Maslow's hierarchy.** Not only does it indirectly provide food and shelter, it can be a **mark of status and esteem**.

4.3 Pay can be used as a motivator. However:

(a) Many people are motivated by **other needs** in Maslow's hierarchy.

(b) **Satisfaction** with pay is often connected with notions of what is **fair in relation to what other people** in the organisation are earning.

(c) **Performance-related pay schemes have not been very successful in practice.** Some evidence suggests that if people are assessed and rewarded as individuals they are less likely to co-operate or help fellow team members.

DEVOLVED ASSESSMENT ALERT

It is quite likely that you have *no control at all over the pay of the staff* you supervise, so we shall not explore this topic further, except to remind you that you can reward people by saying 'thank you' and praising them, as well as with money.

The job as motivator

4.4 The job itself can be a motivator, or it can be a cause of dissatisfaction.

4.5 **Job design**

KEY TERM

Job design is the incorporation of the tasks the organisation needs to be done into a job for one person.

Job design can influence motivation by giving wider **responsibility**.

(a) **Job specialisation** tends to reduce breadth of responsibility.

• How many **different tasks** are contained in the job and how broad and narrow are these tasks?

• To what extent **does the worker have control over the work**?

(b) **Regulation of behaviour.** Co-ordination requires that organisations formalise behaviour so as to predict and control it; this tends to reduce responsibility.

(c) **Training and indoctrination** can push responsibility lower down the organisation.

• Training refers to the process by which job related skills are taught.

• Indoctrination is the process by which organisational values are acquired.

Job simplification

4.6 One of the consequences of mass production was what might be called a micro-division of labour, or **job simplification**.

4.7 **Advantages of job simplification**

Advantage	Comment
Little training	A job is divided up into the smallest number of sequential tasks possible. Each task is so simple and straightforward that it can be learned with very little training.
Replacement	If labour turnover is high, this does not matter because unskilled replacements can be found and trained to do the work in a very short time.
Flexibility	Since the skill required is low, workers can be shifted from one task to another very easily. The production flow will therefore be unaffected by absenteeism.
Control	If tasks are closely defined and standard times set for their completion, production is easier to predict and control.
Quality	Standardisation of work into simple tasks means that quality is easier to predict. There is less scope for doing a task badly, in theory.

4.8 **Disadvantages of job simplification**

- The work is **monotonous** and makes employees tired, bored and dissatisfied. The consequences will be high labour turnover, absenteeism, spoilage, unrest.

- **People work better** when their work is **variable**, unlike machines.

- An individual doing a simple task feels like a small cog in a large machine, and has no **sense of contributing to the organisation's end product** or service.

- Excessive specialisation **isolates** the individual in his or her work and inhibits not only social contacts with 'work mates', but knowledge generation.

- In practice, excessive job simplification leads to **lower quality, through inattention**.

4.9 Herzberg suggest three ways of improving job design, to make jobs more interesting to the employee, and hopefully to improve performance.

- Job enrichment
- Job enlargement
- Job rotation

Job enrichment

> **KEY TERM**
>
> **Job enrichment** is planned, deliberate action to build greater responsibility, breadth and challenge of work into a job. Job enrichment is similar to **empowerment** although the emphasis of job enrichment is on the individual rather than on the team.

4.10 **Enriching a job**

- Give the job holder **decision-making capabilities of a 'higher' order**. What is, mundane detail at a high level can represent significant job interest at a lower level.

- Give the **employee greater freedom** to decide how the job should be done.

- Encourage employees **to participate** in the planning decisions of their superiors.

- Give the employee regular **feedback**.

4.11 Job enrichment alone will not **automatically** make employees more productive. 'Even those who want their jobs enriched will expect to be rewarded with more than job satisfaction. Job enrichment is not a cheaper way to greater productivity. Its pay-off will come in the less visible costs of morale, climate and working relationships'. (Handy).

Job enlargement

> **KEY TERM**
>
> **Job enlargement** is the attempt to widen jobs by increasing the number of operations in which a job holder is involved.

4.12 Reducing the number of repetitions of the same work should reduce the dullness of a job. Job enlargement is therefore a **'horizontal' extension** of an individual's work, whereas job enrichment is a 'vertical' extension.

(a) Just giving an employee tasks which span a larger part of the total production work should **reduce boredom**.

(b) Enlarged jobs can provide a **challenge and incentive**. A trusted employee might be given added responsibilities, such as **checking the quality of output**. An employee who is responsible for his own work quality, might easily see a challenging responsibility in such a job. Such views are becoming more widespread with the introduction of Total Quality Management (TQM). Another possibility is **on the job training** of new recruits.

(c) Enlarged jobs might also be regarded as 'status' jobs within the department, and as stepping stones towards promotion.

Job rotation

4.13 **Job rotation** might take two forms:

(a) An employee might be **transferred to another job** after a period of, say, two to four years in an existing job, in order to give him or her a new interest and challenge, and to bring a fresh person to the job being vacated.

(b) **Job rotation might be regarded as a form of training**. Trainees might be expected to learn a bit about a number of different jobs, by spending six months or one year in each job before being moved on. The employee is regarded as a 'trainee' rather than as an experienced person holding down a demanding job.

Job rotation is not widely practised.

Job optimisation

4.14 A **well designed job** should therefore provide the individual with several advantages.

- **Scope** for setting his own work standards and targets
- **Control** over the pace and methods of working
- **Variety** by allowing for inter-locking tasks to be done by the same person
- **Voice**: a chance to add his comments about the design of the product, or his job
- **Feedback** of information to the individual about his performance

DEVOLVED ASSESSMENT ALERT

You can enrich people's jobs by allowing them to have a say over *how* they do the work, or by giving them wider responsibilities. Ask yourself how you could apply these ideas to the people in your workplace.

Participation, morale and culture

4.15 **Participation.** Many people want more interesting work and to have a say in decision-making. These expectations support the movement towards greater **participation** at work.

4.16 The methods of achieving increased involvement have largely crystallised into two main streams.

(a) **Immediate participation** is used to refer to the involvement of employees in the **day-to-day** decisions of their work group.

(b) **Distant participation** refers to the process of including company employees at the top levels of the organisation which deal with long-term policy issues including investment and employment. Major firms in the EU are required to have **works councils**.

4.17 Participation can involve employees and make them feel committed to their task, given the following conditions (5 Cs).

Condition	Comment
Certainty	Participation should be genuine.
Consistency	Efforts to establish participation should be made consistently over a long period.
Clarity	The purpose of participation is made quite clear.
Capacity	The individual has the ability and information to participate effectively.
Commitment	The manager believes in participation.

4.18 However, remember that some people do **not** want extra responsibility at work and are happiest performing predictable, undemanding tasks.

Conclusions on motivation

4.19 **Motivation's consequences for management**

(a) Individuals **vary in the kind of needs** they have and the satisfactions they want. Managers may be able to improve staff motivation and performance by studying these needs and providing opportunities for staff to fulfil them through their work.

(b) Supervisors and managers should continually seek to motivate through **empowerment** of staff. There are desirable qualities to work.

- A **clear meaning and purpose** in relation to the objectives of the organisation

- Being as **self-contained as possible,** so that the employee will be doing a 'complete' job

- **Opportunities for making decisions** or participating in decisions which affect work and targets (eg in deciding the methods for doing work)

- **Regular feedback** of information to the employee about his performance
- Avoidance of monotony and repetitiveness.

5   WORKING IN TEAMS

5.1   Organisations enable the activities and skills of the people within them to be combined so that the output of the whole is greater than the sum of the parts. This is relevant **within** organisations, too, especially large organisations. A team is more than just a collection of individuals - it has a specific purpose and even a sense of an identity, and in a work context it has a task to perform. A team is a type of group.

Groups and teams

> **KEY TERM**
>
> A **group** is 'any collection of people who perceive themselves to be a group'. Unlike a random collection of individuals, a group of individuals share a common sense of identity and belonging.

5.2   Groups have certain attributes that a random 'crowd' does not possess.

(a)   **A sense of identity**. There are acknowledged boundaries to the group which define it.

(b)   **Loyalty to the group,** and acceptance within the group are generally expressed through acceptance of the 'norms' of behaviour and attitude that bind the group together and exclude others from it.

(c)   **Purpose and leadership.** Most groups have an express purpose, whatever field they are in: most will, spontaneously or formally, choose individuals or sub-groups to lead them towards the fulfilment of those goals.

5.3   A **primary working group** is the immediate social environment of the individual worker, in other words, the people he/she works with most of the time.

5.4   A **formal group** used for particular objectives in the work place is called a **team**. Although many people enjoy working in teams, their popularity in the work place arises because of their **effectiveness in fulfilling the organisation's work**.

Teams

> **KEY TERM**
>
> A **team** is a 'small number of people with complementary skills who are committed to a **common purpose**, performance **goals** and approach, for which they hold themselves basically accountable'.

5.5   **Team roles**

Teams can fulfil a variety of roles:

Type of role	Comments
Organising work	Combines skills of different individuals.
	Avoids complex communication between different business functions.
Control	Fear of letting down the team or breaking its unwritten rules can be powerful motivator.
	Teams can be used to resolve conflict
Knowledge generation	Teams can generate ideas.
Decision-making	Decisions can be evaluated from more than one viewpoint.
	Teams can be set up to investigate new developments.

Teamworking

5.6   Teamworking allows work to be shared among a number of individuals, so it is done faster than by individuals working alone, but without people losing sight of their 'whole' tasks or having to co-ordinate their efforts through lengthy channels of communication.

5.7   A team may be called together temporarily, to achieve specific task objectives (**project team**), or may be more or less permanent, with responsibilities for a particular product, product group or stage of the production process (a **product or process team**). There are two basic approaches to the organisation of team work; **multi-skilled teams** and **multi-disciplinary teams**.

Multi disciplinary teams

5.8   **Multi-disciplinary teams** bring together individuals with **different skills and specialisms**, so that their skills, experience and knowledge can be **pooled** or exchanged.

Multi skilled teams

5.9   A **multi-skilled team** may simply brings together a number of individuals who can perform **any of the** team tasks (eg each individual has many skills). These tasks can then be shared out in a more flexible way between group members, according to who is available and best placed to do a given job at the time it is required.

Activity 3.6

Before reading on, list five 'types' of people that you would want to have on a project team, involved (say) in organising an end-of-term party.

Membership of the team

5.10   Deciding who is to belong to a team involves considering several matters.

(a) The technical specialist **skills needed**. A team might exist to combine expertise from different departments. An accountant might belong to a team which is putting forward a bid for a building contract, to give some idea of cost.

(b) Individuals' **power** in the wider organisation

(c) Individuals' access to **resources**

(d) The **personalities** and goals of the individual **members** of the team: these help to determine the group's and goals

(e) The **blend** of the individual skills and abilities of its members

5.11 **Belbin**, in a study of business-game teams at Carnegie Institute of Technology in 1981, drew up a list of the most effective character-mix in a team. This involves eight necessary roles which should ideally be balanced and evenly 'spread' in the team. An effective group will have all these roles represented; one person may play more then one role.

Member	Role
Co-ordinator	Presides and co-ordinates; balanced, disciplined, good at working through others.
Shaper	Highly strung, dominant, extrovert, passionate about the task itself, a spur to action.
Plant	Individualistic, but intellectually dominant and imaginative; source of ideas and proposals.
Monitor-evaluator	Analytically (rather than creatively) intelligent; dissects ideas, spots flaws; possibly aloof, tactless - but necessary.
Resource-investigator	Popular, sociable, extrovert, relaxed; source of new contacts; responds to challenge.
Implementer	Practical organiser; scheduling, planning; trustworthy and efficient, but not excited by unproven ideas.
Team worker	Most concerned with team maintenance – supportive, understanding, diplomatic; popular but uncompetitive – contribution noticed only in absence.
Finisher	Chivvies the team to meet deadlines, attend to details; urgency and follow-through important, though not always popular.

The **specialist** joins the team to offer expert advice when needed.

5.12 Effective teams therefore need a mix of people who have two main abilities.

- Getting things done
- Getting along with other people

Contribution patterns

5.13 **Analysing the functioning of a team**

You may have an opportunity to analyse a team you work with.

(a) Assess who (if anybody) is performing each of Belbin's **team roles**. Which is the team's plant? co-ordinator? monitor-evaluator? and so on.

(b) Analyse the frequency and type of individual members' contributions to group discussions and interactions. This is a relatively simple framework, which can revolutionise the way you behave in groups - as well as your understanding of the dynamics of a given team.

Team development

5.14 You probably have had experience of being put into a group of people you do not know. Many teams are set up in this way and it takes some time for the team to become effective.

5.15 Four stages in this development were identified by Tuckman.

Step 1. Forming

The team is just coming together, and may still be seen as a collection of individuals. Each member wishes to impress his or her **personality** on the group. The individuals will be trying to find out about each other, and about the aims and norms of the team. There will at this stage probably be a **wariness about introducing new ideas**. The **objectives** being pursued may as yet be **unclear** and a leader may not yet have emerged.

Step 2. Storming

This frequently involves more or less open **conflict** between team members. There may be **changes** agreed in the original objectives, procedures and norms established for the group. If the team is developing successfully this may be a fruitful phase as more realistic targets are set and **trust** between the group members increases.

Step 3. Norming

A period of **settling down**: there will be agreements about work sharing, individual requirements and expectations of output. Norms and procedures may evolve which enable methodical working to be introduced and maintained.

Step 4. Performing

The team sets to work to execute its task. The difficulties of growth and development no longer hinder the group's objectives.

Activity 3.7

Read the following statements and decide to which category they belong (forming, storming, norming, performing).

(a) Two of the group arguing as to whose idea is best.
(b) Desired outputs being achieved.
(c) Shy member of group not participating.
(d) Activities being allocated.

Building the team

5.16 Not all teams develop into mature teams; they may stagnate in any one of the stages. There are certain constraints involved in working with others.

(a) **Too much discord.** Conflicting **roles and relationships** (where an individual is a member of more than one group) can cause difficulties in communicating effectively.

(b) **Personality problems** will develop if one member dislikes or distrusts another; is too dominant or so timid that the value of his ideas is lost; or is so negative in attitude that constructive communication is rendered impossible.

(c) **Rigid leadership** and procedures may strangle initiative and creativity in individuals.

(d) **Differences of opinion** and political conflicts of interest are always likely.

(e) **Too much harmony.** Teams work best when there is room for disagreement.

(f) **Corporate culture and reward systems.** Teams will fail if the company promotes and rewards the individual at the expense of the group.

(g) **Too many meetings.** Teams should not try to do everything together. This wastes time in meetings, and team members are exposed to less diversity of thought.

(h) **Powerlessness.** People will not bother to work in a team or on a task force if its recommendations are ignored.

It falls to the supervisor or manager to build the team. There are three main issues involved in team building.

Issues	Comments
Team identity	Get people to see themselves as part of this group
Team solidarity	Encourage loyalty so that members put in extra effort for the sake of the team
Shared objectives	Encourage the team to commit itself to shared work objectives and to co-operate willingly and effectively in achieving them.

Effective teams

5.17 Some teams work more effectively than others, for a variety of reasons, and we can identify ways of evaluating whether a team is effective. Here are some examples

Quantifiable factors

Factor	Effective team	Ineffective team
Labour turnover	Low	High
Accident rate	Low	High
Absenteeism	Low	High
Quality of output	High	Low
Commitment to targets and organisational goals	High	Low
Understanding of individual roles	High	Low
Communication between team members	Free and open	Mistrust
Interest in work decisions	Active	Passive acceptance
Opinions	Consensus	Imposed solutions
Job satisfaction	High	Low

Activity 3.8

Neville is in charge of a group of twelve people involved in complex work. The group has been working together amicably and successfully for a considerable time. Its members value Neville's leadership and the back-up given him by Olivia. She is very keen on getting the job done and is good at encouraging the others when there are problems.

Much of the success of the group has been due to Peter, who is very creative at problem solving, and Rosalinde who has an encyclopaedic knowledge of sources of supply and information. Quentin is particularly reliable and efficient; he has reduce the scheduling of the team's work to a fine art. Sheila is invaluable at sorting out disagreements and keeping everyone cheerful. The remaining members of the group also have roles which are acceptable to themselves and to the others.

Recently Olivia resigned for family reasons. Because the workload has been increasing, Neville recruited four new people to the group. Neville now finds that various members of the group complain to him about what they are expected to do, and about other people's failings. Peter and Rosalinde have been unusually helpful to Neville but have had several serious arguments between themselves and with others, usually about priorities.

Relating your answer to the theories of team working, you are required:

(a) to analyse the situation before and after the changes
(b) to recommend how Neville should ensure that the group reverts to its former cohesiveness.

6 LEADING THE TEAM

KEY TERM

Leadership is the process of influencing others to work *willingly* towards a goal, and to the best of their capabilities. The essence of leadership is *followership:* it is the willingness of people to follow that makes a person a leader.

6.1 Leadership comes about in a number of different ways.

- A manager is **appointed** to a position of authority within the organisation. He relies mainly on the authority of that position.

- Some leaders (for example in politics or in trade unions) might be **elected**.

- Other leaders might **emerge** through their personal drive and social skills. Unofficial spokesmen for groups of people are leaders of this style.

Theories of leadership: superman?

6.2 Early writers believed that leaders were 'born, not made'. Studies on leadership concentrated on the personal **traits**, (eg intelligence, initiative, self assurance) of existing and past leadership figures. However, the trait approach does not take account of the individuality of the **subordinates** and other factors in the **leadership situation**.

Leadership styles: the Ashridge model

6.3 More recent work on leadership has concentrated on what leaders do and how they do it. The Ashridge model is an example. The research unit at Ashridge Management College identified four styles of leadership, (tells, sells, consults, joins) in the table on the next page.

Style	Characteristics
Tells (autocratic)	The manager makes all the decisions, and issues instructions which must be obeyed without question.
Sells (persuasive)	The manager still makes all the decisions, but believes that subordinates have to be motivated to accept them in order to carry the out properly.

Style	Characteristics
Consults	The manager confers with subordinates and takes their views into account, but has the final say.
Joins (democratic)	Leader and followers make the decision on the basis of consensus.

(a) The studies found, in an ideal world, subordinates preferred the **consults** style of leadership. Those managed in that way had the most favourable attitude to work, but managers were most commonly thought to be exercising the **tells** or **sells** style.

(b) In practice, consistency was far more important. The least favourable attitudes were found amongst subordinates who were **unable to perceive a consistent style** of leadership in their boss.

(c) It may however be appropriate to vary the style of leadership according to the prevailing circumstances. This is called a **contingency approach** and reflects the view that there is a variety a single best solutions to a given type of problem. Many managers will, for instance, use a **consults** style for preference, but will use a **tells** style for dealing with a sudden crisis, such as a flu epidemic, or, at a higher level, a collapse of sales, because urgent measures are needed.

Activity 3.9

Ruth Parker is 42 years old, married, with two children aged 13 and 9. She returned to work on a part time basis two years ago. As her manager you have offered her, and she has accepted, promotion (on a full time basis) to what will be her first managerial position.

She will be in charge of a well established team of six (all in their mid-twenties) who carry out a processing function which is basically routine work but which does give rise to some (often complex) problems. Their work requires accuracy and occasionally there are high volumes, particularly during holiday periods.

As a parent, Ruth has a lot of managerial experience. She is good at solving problems by making decisions swiftly and implementing them efficiently. She rarely feels the need to consult with other people.

Her predecessor as head of the section believed in allowing people to develop themselves through implementing their own solutions. He accustomed the section to operating with a minimum of managerial interference.

The labour turnover in the section is very low.

You recognise that Ruth's choice of managerial style may give rise to difficulties.

(a) Identify and explain these difficulties.
(b) Suggest how Ruth should approach her choice of managerial style.

The trouble with theories

6.4 Most theories provide some useful pointers but they cannot be applied uncritically.

(a) Many theories **do not take relevant organisational conditions** into account, and for a manager or supervisor to model his own behaviour on a formula in a completely different situation will not necessarily be helpful.

(b) The **manager's personality may not be flexible** enough to utilise leadership theories by attempting to change styles to suit a situation. A manager may not be able to be participative in some circumstances and authoritative in others where his personality and personal goals are incompatible with that style.

(c) The **demands** of the task, technology, organisation culture and other managers **constrain** the manager in the range of 'styles' and leadership behaviours open to him.

(d) **Consistency is important** to subordinates. If a manager tries to practise a flexible approach to leadership, subordinates may simply perceive him to be 'fickle', or may suffer insecurity and distrust the 'changeful' manager.

7 USING COMMUNICATION SKILLS

Communication processes in the organisation

7.1 In any organisation, the communication of information is necessary for four purposes.

(a) **Management decision-making**

(b) **Interdepartmental co-ordination.** All the interdependent systems for purchasing, production, marketing and administration must co-operate in accomplishing the organisation's aims.

(c) **Individual motivation and effectiveness.** People must know what they have to do and why.

(d) **Control.** Results must be reported for comparison with targets.

Direction of communication

7.2 Communication direction

(a) **Vertical** ie up and down the scalar chain (from superior to subordinate and back).

(b) **Horizontal or lateral:** between people of the same rank, in the same section or department, or in different sections or departments.

(c) **Diagonal.** This is interdepartmental communication by people of different ranks.

Barriers to communication

7.3 **General faults in the communication process**
- **Distortion** or omission of information by the sender.
- **Misunderstanding** due to lack of clarity or technical jargon.
- **Non-verbal signs** (gesture, posture, facial expression) contradicting the verbal message, so that its meaning is in doubt.
- **'Overload'** - a person being given too much information to digest in the time available.
- **People** hearing **only what they want** to hear in a message.
- **Differences** in social, racial or educational **background**, compounded by age and personality differences, creating barriers to understanding and co-operation.

(Mnemonic using words in bold above: Distorted Messages Never Overcome Personal Differences.)

7.4   **Communication difficulties at work**

Problem	Comment
Status (of the sender and receiver of information).	• A senior manager's words are listened to closely and a colleague's perhaps discounted. • A subordinate might mistrust his or her superior and might look for 'hidden meanings' in a message.
Jargon	People from different job or specialist backgrounds (such as accountants and personnel managers) can have difficulty in talking to one another.
Suspicion	People discount information from those they do not respect.
Priorities	People or departments have different priorities or perspectives so that one person places more or less emphasis on a situation than another.
Selective reporting	Subordinates may give superiors incorrect or incomplete information (eg to protect a colleague, to avoid 'bothering' the superior); a senior manager may only be able to handle edited information because he does not have time to sift through details.
Timing	Information which has **no immediate** use tends to be forgotten.
Opportunity	Opportunities for people to say what they think may be lacking.
Conflict	Where there is conflict between individuals or departments, communications will be withdrawn and information withheld.
Personal differences	such as age, educational/social background or personality mean that people have different views as to what is important or different ways of expressing. sometimes views may be discounted because of who they are, not what they say.
Culture	(i) **Secrecy.** Information might be given on a need-to-know basis, rather than be considered as a potential resource for everyone to use. (ii) **Can't handle bad news.** The culture of some organisations may prevent the communication of certain messages. Organisations with a 'can-do' philosophy may not want to hear that certain tasks are impossible.

DEVOLVED ASSESSMENT ALERT

You may have to show that you can communicate effectively with your staff.

7.5   **Improving the communications system**

(a)   **Establishing better communication links** in all directions.

57

- **Standing instructions** should be recorded in easily accessible manuals which are kept fully up-to-date.

- Management **decisions** should be sent to all people affected by them, preferably in writing.

- Regular **staff meetings,** may be appropriate.

- **A house journal** may be helpful.

- **Appraisal schemes** give opportunities for detailed discussion of a worker's progress, prospects and potential.

- Use **new technology** such as e-mail - but not so as to overload everybody in messages of no importance.

(b) Use the **informal organisation** to supplement this increased freedom of communication.

7.6 **Clearing up misunderstandings** about message content.

(a) **Redundancy** - issuing a message in more than one form (eg by word of mouth at a meeting, confirmed later in minutes)

(b) **Reporting by exception** should operate to prevent **information overload** on managers.

(c) **Train** managers who do not express themselves clearly and concisely. Necessary jargon should be taught in some degree to people new to the organisation or unfamiliar with the terminology of the specialists.

7.7 **Skills in the selected medium of communication** (Use this as a checklist.)

Oral	Written	Visual/non verbal
Clear pronunciation	Correct spelling	Understanding and control over 'body language' and facial expressions
Suitable vocabulary	Suitable vocabulary	Drawing ability
Correct grammar	Correct grammar	
Fluency	Suitable style	
Expressive delivery		

7.8 **General skills in sending messages**

- **Selecting and organising your material:** marshalling your thoughts and constructing your sentences and arguments.

- **Judging the effect of your message** on the particular recipient in the particular situation.

- **Choosing appropriate language and media.**

- **Adapting your communication style** accordingly: putting people at their ease, smoothing over difficulties, or being comforting/challenging/informal/formal as the situation and relationship demand.

- **Using non-verbal signals** to reinforce (or at least not to undermine) your spoken message.

- **Seeking and interpreting feedback.**

7.9   **Skills in receiving messages**

- **Reading** attentively and actively: making sure you understand the content, looking up unfamiliar words and doubtful facts if necessary; evaluating the information given: is it logical? correct? objective?

- **Extracting relevant information** from the message, and filtering out inessentials.

- **Listening** attentively and actively; concentrating on the message - not on what you are going to say next, or other matters; questioning and evaluating what you are hearing.

- **Interpreting the message's underlying meaning**, if any, and evaluating your own reactions: are your reading into the message more or less than what is really there?

- **Asking questions** in a way that will elicit the information you wish to obtain. This will usually involve **open** questions

- **Interpreting non-verbal signals**, and how they confirm or contradict the spoken message.

- **Giving helpful feedback**, if the medium is inappropriate (eg a bad telephone line) or the message is unclear, insufficient or whatever.

Key learning points

- People are different so there **is no foolproof set of golden rules** to follow that will enable you to deal successfully with everybody at all times.

- There are various theories about what motivates people. Maslow identifies a **'hierarchy of needs'** that must be fulfilled; Herzberg distinguishes between what causes dissatisfaction and what encourages superior effort; others have introduced the factor of people's expectations into the equation; **goal theory** is the important modern approach.

- Various methods of increasing motivation have been suggested, such as empowerment (job enrichment, job enlargement and job rotation), rewards and participation.

- Most work is done in **teams**. This raises issues of **team development and effectiveness**. The effectiveness of a team depends upon the personalities of individual members, the nature of their task, and the environment in which they do it, motivation, leadership, the processes and procedures involved in the task, and how far high productivity coincides with individual satisfaction.

- Some pointers to group efficiency or inefficiency are quantifiable measures; others are qualitative and more difficult to measure. Groups can sometimes be too cohesive ('group think').

- A variety of **leadership styles** can be identified: dictatorial, autocratic, consultative, democratic.

- The essence of leadership is **followership**.

- **Communication** is important for the supervisor so that staff know what is expected of them and managers are informed of what is going on.

Quick quiz

1   What is the halo effect?

2   What is the link between personality and performance at work?

3   What is motivation?

4   What did Maslow mean by 'esteem needs', 'social needs' and 'self-actualisation' needs? Where do these needs come in Maslow's hierarchy?

5   Distinguish between what Herzberg called 'hygiene factors' and 'motivator factors'.

6   What are the three fundamental elements of goal theory?

7   What is the difference between job enrichment and job enlargement?

8   What is the chief value of job rotation?

9   What conditions are necessary in order for participation to be an effective motivator?

10 List four stages of group development.

11 List four leadership styles.

Answers to quick quiz

1   The halo effect is a term used to describe the way that our first judgements about people - based on immediately obvious characteristics like dress, manner or facial expression - affect our later perception of other features of those people, whether to positive or negative effect. Information subsequently gathered that does not agree with the first assessment tends to be filtered out.

2   Research into this question has not been able to show any significant correlation between personality on the basis of test results and performance. The important point is that managers and supervisors must realise and accept that different people will behave in different ways.

3   Depending on the context, the words motivation may mean: goals, that have become desirable for a particular individual ('motivating factors'); the mental process of choosing desired outcomes, deciding how to go about them, assessing whether the likelihood of success warrants the amount of effort that will be necessary, and setting in motion the required behaviours; or the social process by which the behaviour of an individual is influenced by others. 'Motivation' in this last sense usually applies to the attempts of organisations to get workers to increase their productivity.

4   *Esteem needs* are needs for status, recognition, respect and appreciation, the desire to excel. *Social needs* are needs for friendship, affection and acceptance. *Self-actualisation needs* are needs for an individual to realise his own full potential and for self-development. Social needs come above safety and physiological needs, but below esteem needs and self-actualisation needs.

5   Hygiene factors are essentially preventative. They prevent or minimise dissatisfaction but do not give satisfaction, in the same way that sanitation minimises threats to health, but does not give 'good' health. Motivator factors create job satisfaction and are effective in motivating an individual to superior performance and effort.

6   Goal theory suggests the following.

    (a)   *Difficult* goals lead to higher performance than easy goals, so long as they have been *accepted* by the person trying to achieve them.

    (b)   *Specific* goals lead to higher performance than general 'do your best' goals. Specific goals seem to create a precise intention, which in turn helps the person to shape their behaviour with precision.

    (c)   Knowledge of results (*feedback*) is essential if the full performance benefits of setting difficult and specific goals are to be achieved.

7   Job *enlargement* is the attempt to widen jobs by increasing the number of operations in which a job holder is involved. Job *enrichment* is planned, deliberate action to build greater responsibility, breadth and challenge of work into a job.

8   Job rotation is probably best regarded as a form of training.

9   Participation may be effective if the following conditions are satisfied.

(a)　If it is *genuine*. It is very easy for a boss to pretend to invite participation from staff but end up issuing orders.

(b)　If efforts to establish participation are *consistent*, that is, continuous, energetic and long-lived.

(c)　If the *purpose* of the participation is made clear. If employees are consulted to make a *decision*, their views should carry the decision. If, however, they are consulted for advice, their views need not necessarily be accepted.

(d)　If the individuals have the *abilities and the information* to join in decision-making effectively.

(e)　If the individuals *want* to participate. Some people expect and want authoritarian management and fear responsibility.

10　The four stages are as follows.

(a)　During the *forming* stage the group is just coming together, and may still be seen as a collection of individuals.

(b)　The second stage is called *storming* because it frequently involves more or less open conflict between group members.

(c)　The third stage (*norming*) is a period of settling down.

(d)　The fourth stage is *performing* . At this stage the group sets to work to execute its task. This stage marks the point where the difficulties of growth and development no longer hinder the group's objectives.

11　The research unit at Ashridge Management College identified four styles: tells, sells, consults, joins.

Answers to activities

Answer 3.1

You may have your own views on examples managers could set. Basically, successful managers provide an aspirational model: showing junior staff that it is possible for them to achieve organisational success and the lifestyle that may go with it. A manager may also model the roles of popular leaders, a person who combines work and home/leisure life, a person who does not panic in a crises, a person who is developing their skills and so on. Models are, after all, in the eye of the beholder!

Answer 3.2

You probably felt as we did that none of the qualities listed were unimportant. You probably had similar priorities to ours, as follows.

1 = b, c, e, g, j.　　2 = a, d, f, h, i.

However, priorities might change if the qualities were considered in relation to a particular role, and some might, in fact, be quite unimportant.

Answer 3.5

Maslow's categories for the listed circumstances are as follows.

(a)　Esteem needs
(b)　Social needs
(c)　Self-actualisation needs
(d)　He will have physiological needs
(e)　Safety needs initially; esteem needs above in a certain income level
(f)　social needs or self-actualisation needs
(g)　Esteem needs
(h)　Safety needs or esteem needs

Answer 3.6

For your ideal team, you might have listed: a person with originality and ideas; a 'get up and go' type, with energy and enthusiasm; a quite logical thinker who can be sensible about the ideas put forward; a plodder who will be happy to do the routine leg-work; and a leader who can organise the others and help them reach agreement on ideas.

Answer 3.7

Categorising the behaviour of group members in the situations described results in the following: (a) storming, (b) performing, (c) forming, (d) norming.

Answer 3.8

(a)   Belbin's picture of the most effective character-mix in a team involves eight necessary roles which should ideally be balanced and evenly 'spread' in the team. These are covered in paragraph 5.11.

In the situation described we can see several of these roles being played out by the people concerned.

Co-ordinator	Neville
Shaper	Olivia
Plant	Peter
Resource investigator	Rosalinde
Implementer	Quentin
Team worker	Sheila

Prior to the resignation of Olivia the group was clearly at the *performing* stage in Tuckman's terms (see below) but has now reverted to forming and storming. A particular problem is the conflict between Peter and Rosalinde. both of whom seem to want to take on the 'shaper' role formerly occupied by Olivia.

(b)   Four stages in the development of a group are: forming, storming, norming and performing. Briefly, the first stage is the coming together of the group, the second a phase of conflicts, the third a settling down period and the fourth the point where the group can execute its task unhindered by the problems of growth and development.

Assuming that these theories apply, the group clearly faces an unsettled period. Neville has a number of options for dealing with this.

(i)   He can simply allow the development to continue without interference. The problem with this is that it may take time and the group will be underperforming until its development is complete.

(ii)   He can encourage the group to develop more quickly. For example, either Peter or Rosalinde should be formally appointed to Olivia's former role. This will end the bickering between them and establish a clear hierarchy, to the benefit of the whole group. The unlucky candidate may leave as a result, but it may be possible to find a satisfactory compromise. However, he can allow some of the others to find their own roles.

(iii)   Neville himself should get more involved in the day to day work of the group for a time. This will serve two purposes.

(1)   He will be able to establish a new leadership style more appropriate to the needs of his new group (a contingency approach to leadership).

(2)   He will gain a fuller understanding of the present abilities and desires of old group members and become acquainted with those of the new members. This will help him to reassess roles and responsibilities.

Answer 3.9

(a)   Two main issues immediately present themselves. Firstly, the management styles of Ruth and her predecessor are very different. This might be a problem for the team, and for Ruth. Secondly, the people she is to manage are members of quite a closely integrated team.

Both these factors could cause potential difficulties as Ruth and the team get used to each other.

Management style

Ruth uses a **tells** style, in the terminology adopted by the Ashridge studies. Basically, the manager makes the decisions and issues instructions to subordinates who carry them out. Its strength is that it facilitates quick decisions, and there are defined lines of responsibility. Communication is generally one-way, so subordinates might have valuable information which is being ignored.

The team, on the other hand, have been used to something quite different. Subordinates have been given little direction and allowed to establish their own objectives and make their own decisions.

Ruth does not really know the ropes, and so she will be forced, in some cases, to rely on her team's technical expertise. This she might find uncomfortable, as she is not naturally a team player. Moreover, Ruth will be forced to delegate in periods when she is faced with highest demands from her family (eg in school holidays). Motivating the team on a personal level is important in peak periods and when complex problems must be solved.

Both the job and her own personal circumstances will force Ruth to moderate her natural 'tells' leadership style.

(b)   Ruth is probably aware of her own natural managerial style. She should be made aware that the team's previous manager took a rather different approach, and there are occasions where team maintenance and consideration is important.

Ruth should endeavour to be consistent. This does not mean that she should not be flexible when the circumstances demand it. Nor does it mean that she cannot alter her style over time. It would be best for her to start off with a consistent style: a basis on which to build, as it were.

The team can also be expected to adjust its expectations of a manager in due course, so it will be a process of learning and change for them as well.

BPP
PUBLISHING

Chapter 4 The organisation and role of the accounting function

---

Chapter topic list

1   Accounting systems and the organisation

2   External regulations

3   The accounts department and other departments

4   Structuring the accounting function

5   The office

6   Information systems

7   Office procedures

Learning objectives

On completion of this chapter you will be able to:

	Performance criteria	Range Statement
• *understand how the accounting systems of an organisation are affected by its organisational structure, its MIS, its administrative system and the nature of its business transactions*	n/a	n/a
• *understand the organisation of the accounting function, its relationship with other departments and its structure*	n/a	n/a
• *understand the range of external relationships affecting accounting practice*	n/a	n/a
• ensure that work methods are clearly communicated to all individuals in a way which assists their understanding of what is expected of them	10.1.4	1
• ensure the system is updated in accordance with changes in external regulations	10.2.5	1

Italicised objectives are areas of knowledge and understanding underlying elements of competence for this Unit.

BPP PUBLISHING

1 ACCOUNTING SYSTEMS AND THE ORGANISATION

1.1 An organisation's accounting systems are affected by the nature of its business transactions and the sort of business it is.

Factor	Example
Size	A **small business** like a greengrocer will have a simple, accounting system, where the main accounting record will probably be the till roll. A **large retail business**, such as a chain of supermarkets, will have elaborate accounting systems covering a large number of product ranges and sites.
Type of organisation	A **service business** might need to record the time employees take on particular jobs. Accounting on a **job or client basis** might also be a feature of service businesses.
	A **public sector organisation**, such as a government department, may be more concerned with the **monitoring of expenditure** against performance targets than recording revenue.
	A **manufacturing company** will account both for unit sales and revenue, but needs to keep **track of costs** for decision-making purposes and so forth.
Organisation structure	In a business managed by **area**, accounts will be prepared on an area basis.
	In a functional organisation, the accounts staff are in a separate self-contained department of their own.

Area organisation

1.2 Some organisations are spread over many different **countries**, and organised by area. Here is how the accounting function will be specifically affected by geography.

Difference	Comment
Different currencies	**Recording information.** Customers might want to pay in local currency, but the business might have to pay for imported supplies in a different currency.
	Reporting information. If you wanted to *compare* the performance of a Belgian subsidiary company with that, say, of a subsidiary in Uruguay, you would have to convert the results to a common currency such as US dollars.
Different legal and accounting requirements	In some countries, the state regulates the keeping of accounts, down to minute detail. In the UK, on the other hand, companies can prepare accounts as they wish, subject to the Companies Act, and financial reporting standards.
Different ways of doing business (for example, the length of credit normally allowed)	The emphasis of the accountant's job differs from country to country. In a country in which payments are made by cash, management of debtors is likely to take up far less time and effort than in a country where extended credit periods are the norm.
Different economic conditions	Some countries have very high rates of inflation; this can affect accounting practice.

DEVOLVED ASSESSMENT ALERT

If your company operates on an area basis, you will probably find that the accounting information, such as monthly management accounts, is structured by area. In other words reports for regions are aggregated together to build up a picture of the performance of the whole company. In a functional organisation structure, however, you would separately analyse costs and revenues for each department.

Product-division structure

1.3 When an organisation has a product-based structure, accounting information must be grouped in a particular way to highlight revenue earned and costs incurred by a particular product. It is possible, then, that the product divisional basis will affect the **account coding system** of the company.

Revenue	Recording accounting information relating to revenue is usually easy. Each product has a price, and it is relatively simple to record unit sales. Invoices may be analysed by product group.
Costs	Some costs, such as materials, can be traced to individual products. Overheads are more difficult to deal with.

Cost information is not just a feature of a product-division structured organisation, as this information is necessary for decision making in any organisation.

1.4 In a product-division structure, administrative functions are carried out by individual product divisions. However, there will still be some areas (eg research and development) which are shared by all divisions, and it might not be easy to allocate these common costs.

2 EXTERNAL REGULATIONS

2.1 The knowledge and understanding for Unit 9 states that you should know about the range of external regulations affecting accounting practice, but *not in detail*. Anyway, you should have covered these areas in doing other Units.

Financial accounting regulations

2.2 For an unincorporated business, any form of accounting information is adequate if it gives the owner(s) of the business a basis for planning and control, and satisfies the requirements of external users such as the Inland Revenue.

2.3 Limited companies are more closely regulated. The regulations on accounts come from a number of sources.

- **Company law** enacted by the UK Parliament, and also EU law
- **Financial Reporting Standards** issued by the Financial Reporting Council.
- The requirements of the **Stock Exchange**
- **Tax law** may have an impact

Company law

2.4 Limited companies are required by law to publish **accounts annually** for distribution to their shareholders.

- A copy of these accounts must be lodged with the Registrar of Companies and is available for inspection by any member of the public.

- The published accounts should show a 'true and fair view'. This is a complex concept which you will learn about elsewhere.

- The Companies Act also contains set formats for company accounts and states what information must be disclosed.

Non-statutory regulations

2.5 The **Financial Reporting Council** (FRC). The FRC is independent of the accountancy profession and draws its membership from a wide spectrum of accounts preparers and users. Its chairman is appointed by the Government. The FRC guides the standard setting process. The **Accounting Standards Board** (ASB) is responsible for the issue of **Financial Reporting Standards** (FRSs). Prior to publication, the ASB circulates its proposals in the form of a financial reporting exposure draft (inevitably referred to as a FRED) and invites comments. Some **Statements of Standard Accounting Practice** (SSAPs) issued by the ASB's predecessor are still in force.

2.6 **FRSs**

(a) FRSs lay down prescribed accounting treatments in areas where a variety of approaches might be taken.

(b) The aim is to ensure that users can compare the accounts of different companies.

2.7 The **Urgent Issues Task Force** (UITF). The UITF is an offshoot of the ASB. Its role is to assist the ASB in areas where an accounting standard or Companies Act provision already exists, but where unsatisfactory or conflicting interpretations have developed. As its name suggests, the UITF is designed to act quickly.

International accounting standards

2.8 The International Accounting Standards Committee (IASC) attempts to co-ordinate the development of international accounting standards. It includes representatives from many countries throughout the world, including the USA and the UK.

2.9 International standards are not intended to override local regulations. In the UK, however, the ASB will support international standards by incorporating them within the UK standards, although not every IAS has so far been incorporated in this way.

The Stock Exchange regulations

2.10 The Stock Exchange is a market for stocks and shares, and a company whose securities are traded in this market is known as a 'quoted' or 'listed' company.

Such a company commits itself to certain procedures and standards, including matters concerning the disclosure of accounting information, which are more extensive than the disclosure requirements of the Companies Acts.

Auditing regulations

2.11 Company legislation also requires that the accounts of a limited company must be **audited**.

> **KEY TERM**
>
> An **audit** may be defined as an 'independent examination of, and expression of opinion on, the financial statements of an enterprise'.

In practice, a limited company must engage a firm of chartered or chartered certified accountants to examine its accounting records and its financial statements in order to form an opinion as to whether the accounts present a 'true and fair view' and comply with the Companies Act: At the conclusion of their audit work, the auditors issue a report addressed to the owners of the company (its **members** or **shareholders**) which is published as part of the accounts. Audit work is governed by Auditing Standards which are issued by the Auditing Practices Board.

> **DEVOLVED ASSESSMENT ALERT**
>
> As a working accountant within an organisation many of these need not concern you since they are about the way **auditors** do their jobs. However, one of the tasks an auditor generally undertakes is to **report to your organisation** on problems in the accounting system and possible improvements in areas like debt collection, cash control, checking procedures, avoidance of fraud and so on. If you work for an organisation that has auditors, therefore, it is quite likely that their work will have an impact on your work.

2.12 You are **required** by law to provide auditors with any information that they need to do their job.

Taxation regulations

2.13 Taxation regulations will affect the work of the accounts department of any organisation that runs a PAYE system or is registered for VAT.

(a) A substantial amount of payroll work consists of keeping records (P11s) and submitting returns (P11D, P14, P35 etc) to the Inland Revenue and the DSS. You probably learnt all about this at Foundation stage.

(b) VAT returns must be submitted at regular intervals and can also involve considerable administrative effort.

2.14 Regulations such as these have a significant impact on the **timing** of accounting work, since returns are required every month for payroll and (usually) every three months for VAT, and the **information must be ready in time** to comply with these requirements.

Other external influences

2.15 Cost and management accounting is not subject to any statutory rules. There may, however, be circumstances in which outsiders can influence the **timing** of the production of management information, and its format, or affect the procedures adopted in the accounts department.

Investors	People who have invested in the business may be entitled to know how well it is doing.
Banks	Banks often make it a condition of their loan that they be supplied with regular monthly management accounts, or cash flow projections and the like.
Suppliers	They insist on having their bills paid early, especially if they are larger than the organisation they are supplying and the organisation is dependent upon them. This may disrupt the normal operating cycles of the purchases section.
Customers	Can also sometimes have an impact on the operation of an accounting system. Tesco, for example, have encouraged many of their small suppliers to install sophisticated *electronic data interchange systems*.
Bench-marking	Some industries have standard formats for management reports so that companies can be compared anonymously under a scheme of inter-firm comparison or benchmarking.
Privatised utilities	Former public sector bodies like British Gas have their costs and revenues closely scrutinised by their regulators.

Activity 4.1

Review the accounting information produced by your department. Identify all the different users, internal and external. How have they influenced the information presented?

3 THE ACCOUNTS DEPARTMENT AND OTHER DEPARTMENTS

3.1 In very broad terms, accounting work can be seen as a mixture of two types of work.

(a) Handling the **financial operations aspects of running** an organisation.

- Handling receipts and payments - ie managing the **cash flows** of the business

- Acting as a collection and reporting agency for the **government** (payroll, VAT)

- Receiving and checking invoices from **suppliers**

- Sending out invoices to **credit customers** and chasing up late payers; keeping a record of debts owed to the organisation

- **Borrowing** money and repaying loans

- Keeping the financial position of the organisation - cash flows, gearing and debt - in good order

- Through **internal controls**, preventing errors or fraudulent practices, and that the assets of the business are safeguarded.

(b) **Providing information** (and advice if required) to the managers of other departments to help them do their work better. The accounts department has to liase with other departments all the time. **Performance reports** enable managers and others to judge how well the organisation is doing.

- **Planning information**: for instance information for budgets is often provided by accountants.

- **Control information** helps other managers to identify problem areas and take control decisions. Budgetary control variance reports are an example of this.

- **Information to make one-off decisions**. Sometimes, a decision has to be taken by management, and some knowledge about the financial consequences of each choice needs to be available. Accountants can provide such information (eg information about the costs and likely cash benefits of capital expenditure proposals).

3.2 In each case, **input information** from **other departments** is necessary to carry out the accounting activity. The **procedures** for communication with other departments may be set out in manuals or schedules of duties for example, before an invoice for raw material supplies is paid, the accounting department will need to check the details of the invoice against the **purchase order form** (co-ordination with the purchasing department) and the **goods received note** (co-ordination with the stores department).

3.3 The role of **budget officer** is also involves other departments: the accountant is responsible for ensuring that the formal procedures laid down in the budget manual are properly carried out by the various managers responsible for particular aspects of the work.

DEVOLVED ASSESSMENT ALERT

You may have to *recommend* some new or revised procedures in your project report. You should, however, remember that not all procedures are necessary and that they can outlive their usefulness.

Other departments and sections

3.4 Accounting management provides a good example of the **need for close co-ordination** between managers and sections, and this need is particularly acute in financial accounts work because of the **internal controls dividing up responsibilities**.

Department	Accounts section	Relationship
Purchases dept (PD)	Purchase ledger (PL)	PD advises PL of purchase orders
		PD indicates valid invoices
	Cashier (C)	C informs PD and PL of payment
Personnel dept	Payroll	Personnel gives details of wage rates, starters and leavers, to payroll
Sales dept (SD)	Sales ledger (SL)	SD advises SL of sales order
Credit control (CC)		SL might give CC information about overdue debts
		SL might give details about debtors ageing and other reports
Operations, stock controllers	Cost accounting staff	Operations might give details of movements of stock, so that the accounts staff can value stock and provide costing reports
Senior management	Financial accounting and cost accounting staff	The accounts department as a whole produces management information for decision making and control

BPP
PUBLISHING

DEVOLVED ASSESSMENT ALERT

No organisation is the same and it is likely that the different departments or sections in your organisation will have different names and duties from those identified above. So bear in mind:

(a) other departments in the organisation who give you information

(b) the departments you give information to, your 'internal customers' in other words.

Importance of the relationship

3.5   The accounts department is crucial to the organisation.

- If it provides the wrong information, managers will make bad decisions

- It if confuses the data, important transactions might slip through the net, and fraud may result

- There is a legal duty to ensure that accounting records are in good order

Activity 4.2

The Modern Company is concerned to provide the best possible working conditions for its staff. Each department has one or two representatives on a staff liaison committee that meets regularly to consider matters of common interest regarding working conditions, social activities and so on.

Many representatives are now reporting that there is a keen interest by most but not all staff, in requesting the management to consider the introduction of 'flexitime', whereby staff attendance flexible within given times and a minimum number of hours worked each month.

You are the representative from the accounts and wages section and the chairman of the committee has asked you to help her to consider the implications of this request. In readiness for your first working meeting with her:

(a) prepare an outline of how you envisage this flexitime might be organised;

(b) discuss what control systems you might wish to introduce;

(c) explain how you think the chairman and you might communicate your initial proposals to all staff.

4   STRUCTURING THE ACCOUNTING FUNCTION

4.1   In UK companies, the head of the accounting management structure is usually the **finance director**. The finance (or financial) director has a seat on the **board of directors** and is responsible for routine accounting matters and also for broad financial policy matters.

4.2   In many larger companies the finance director has one or more deputies below him.

(a) Some responsibilities of the **Financial Controller**

- Routine accounting
- Providing accounting reports for other departments
- Cashiers' duties and cash control

(b) Management accounting is such an important function that a **Management Accountant** is often appointed with status equal to the financial controller and separate responsibilities.

- Cost accounting
- Budgets and budgetary control
- Financial management of projects

(c)   A very large organisation might have a **Treasurer** in charge of treasury work.

  •   Raising funds by borrowing
  •   Investing surplus funds on the money market or other investment markets
  •   Cash flow control.

4.3   Sections in the accounts department

  •   The **financial accounts** section is divided up into sections, with a supervisor responsible for each section (eg for credit control, payroll, purchase ledger, sales ledger etc).

  •   Similarly, **management accounting** work is divided up, with a number of cost accountants as supervisors of sections responsible for keeping cost records of different items (eg materials, labour, overheads; or production, research and development, marketing).

  •   Some companies that spend large amounts on **capital projects** might have a section assigned exclusively to capital project appraisal (payback appraisal, DCF appraisal, sensitivity analysis, the capital budget).

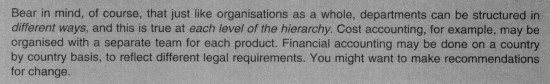

DEVOLVED ASSESSMENT ALERT

Bear in mind, of course, that just like organisations as a whole, departments can be structured in *different ways*, and this is true at *each level of the hierarchy*. Cost accounting, for example, may be organised with a separate team for each product. Financial accounting may be done on a country by country basis, to reflect different legal requirements. You might want to make recommendations for change.

4.4   An organisation is shown in the diagram on the next page. This organisation is typical of a functional organisation structure, where people are grouped together by the type of work they do. In an area structure, accounts staff might be dispersed throughout the different regions of an organisation. Management accounting work is often decentralised to departments because it provides vital information for management control purposes.

4.5   Many organisations have an **internal audit department**. This functions as an internal financial control. One of its responsibilities is to prevent fraud and error. For this reason it should be separate from the finance department and the chief internal auditor should report to the audit committee of the board of directors, bypassing the Financial Director.

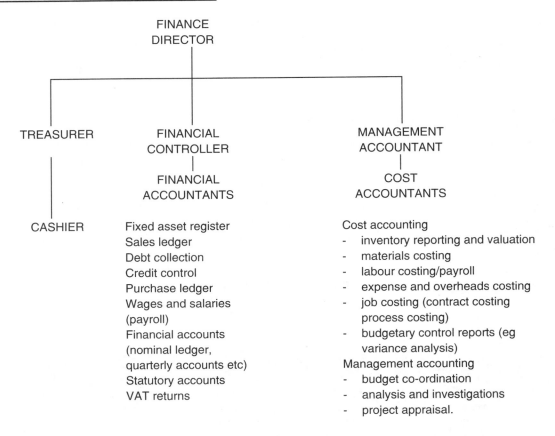

The structure of a section

4.6 Taking just one section of the accounts department, here is a possible structure.

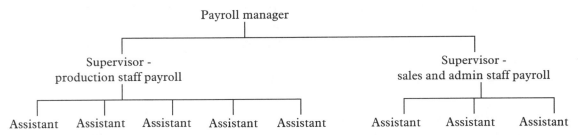

(a) In this example we are envisaging a business which has a large number of weekly paid production staff. The five **assistants** would be carrying out tasks like extracting information from production records about normal time, overtime, piecework rates and so on.

(b) On the sales and administration side the employees are monthly paid and there are fewer of them. Only three assistants are needed to deal with timesheets, bonuses and so forth.

(c) There may be significant differences between jobs that look as if they are fairly similar on the organisation chart. For this reason you may find that individual jobs are described more fully in the **job descriptions** for the people involved.

Job descriptions

> **KEY TERM**
>
> A **job description** attempts to describe the contents of the job and work performed, the responsibilities involved, skill and training required, working conditions (if appropriate - this is more likely to mean location), relationships with other jobs and personal requirements of the job, including skill, experience and social aptitudes.

4.7 Purpose of job description

Purpose	Comment
Organisational	The job description defines the job's place in the organisational structure
Recruitment	The job description provides information for identifying the sort of person needed (person specification)
Legal	The job description provides the basis for a contract of employment
Performance	Performance objectives can be set around the job description
Operational	Job descriptions clarify what people are expected to do, thereby avoiding confusion and conflict.

4.8 Contents of a job description

(a) **Job title** (eg Assistant Financial Controller). This indicates the function/department in which the job is performed, and the level of job within that function.

(b) **Reporting to** (eg the Assistant Financial controller reports to the Financial Controller), in other words the person's immediate supervisor.

(c) **Subordinates** directly reporting to the job holders.

(d) **Overall purpose** of the job, distinguishing it from other jobs.

(e) **Principal accountabilities or main tasks**

  (i) Group the main activities into a number of broad areas.

  (ii) Define each activity as a statement of accountability: what the job holder is expected to achieve (eg **tests** new system to ensure they meet agreed systems specifications).

(f) The current movement towards multi-skilled teams means that **flexibility** is sometimes expected.

Activity 4.3

Broadside Retail Services of Leeds has a vacancy for an assistant accountant. The post is located in the financial accounting section of the company's large finance department which, among other things, is responsible for the preparation of interim and published accounts and the maintenance of the computerised nominal ledger records from which these accounts are compiled. The person appointed to the post is responsible for updating these records and this entails the supervision of a number of clerks. For these reasons the Chief Accountant is seeking to recruit a qualified accounting technician.

(a) Prepare a draft of an appropriate advertisement for the post and indicate what you consider would be the most appropriate media of communication to prospective applicants.

(b) Specify the types of information that you consider should be incorporated in the job description of the post.

4.9 Here is a job description in outline. In practice the 'main duties/responsibilities' section should probably be expanded into a job summary and job content list.

JOB DESCRIPTION

1 Job title: Accounts Assistant

2 Department: Payroll - Production Staff

3 Responsible to: Supervisor, Production Staff Payroll

4 Age range: over 18 (no upper limit)

5 Supervises work of: N/A

6 Has regular co-operative contact with: Production department supervisors and clerical staff; fellow accounts assistants

7 Main duties/responsibilities: Calculating wages due to production staff and statutory and other deductions. Analysing labour costs for management information purposes

8 Location: Head office, accounts department

9 Employment conditions: Salary: £12,000 per annum
                                      Hours: 9 am - 5 pm (1 hour for lunch)
                                      Holidays: 4 weeks per annum

Prepared by: Sue James, Production Staff Payroll Supervisor   **Date**: 20 November 19X5

Preparing job descriptions

4.10 Job descriptions might be prepared by any of the following people.

(a) **The job holder's manager or supervisor.** The manager should have a good understanding of the job, and how it fits into the work of the section or department as a whole. However, managers might not know the job in detail, and it might be easy to confuse the job itself with the current holder of the job.

(b) **The job holder** knows the job best, but he does not have the advantage of the manager's overview.

(c) **A specialist in preparing job descriptions.** A specialist has the advantage of being experienced in preparing job descriptions, and in being detached from the job (and so less likely to make subjective judgements). However, he will lack a detailed knowledge of the work, and must rely on others to obtain the information he requires.

(d) **A committee.** A committee of job analysts has the advantage of limiting personal bias, but it is likely to be cumbersome.

DEVOLVED ASSESSMENT ALERT

If you are preparing job descriptions for your project, you are restricted to options (a) or (b). Probably the most useful approach is to prepare job descriptions yourself initially and then allow the current job-holders to comment. There is clearly a problem to be sorted out if you do not agree with your staff about what their jobs involve!

5 THE OFFICE

5.1 You may work in superbly modern, fully-equipped, user-friendly offices. On the other hand, you may not. Practical matters like this are not trivial; they can have a profound influence on the way work is performed and its efficiency or otherwise. Here are some matters to think about.

5.2 **Location of accounting staff**

(a) **Receipts**.

(i) By **post**. The location of the accounts receivable group and cashier's section dealing with receipts is unlikely to be significant if most payments arrive by post.

(ii) **'Over the counter'**. In order to account for the receipts as soon as possible, and to minimise the movement of cash before it is banked, it might be appropriate to have an accounts receivable section in a location where customers can come to pay in person. Some large organisations make these arrangements: for example, customers can pay a gas bill or electricity bill at their local gas or electricity showroom.

(iii) **Telephone**. More and more firms are taking orders over the phone by obtaining credit card details. These are frequently managed in *'call centres'*, which do not have to be in any particular location as long as telecommunications links are suitable. The accounts department may instead have to deal with *Mastercard* or *Visa*.

(b) **Geography**. Depending on the size of the organisation and the number of customers it has, there might be several accounts receivable groups and cashiers' offices **spread around the country**.

(c) **Paperwork**. Even with computerisation of accounting records, financial accounting work involves passing large amounts of paper between sections for checking - for example, goods received notes, purchase orders and suppliers' invoices.

(d) **Information**. Information providers should not be remote from the managers for whom the information is intended.

(e) **Treasury managers** might need to be close to the London money markets.

(f) Managers should ideally have an office close to their staff. Supervisors should preferably be in the same room as their staff.

5.3 **Environment**. Accountants, like other office workers, will work better in a good office environment. The supervisor might have some responsibility for maintaining standards. Issues include light, heat, security and health safety. There must be sufficient space for storing records such as copy invoices, ledgers and purchase orders. Accounting records should be retained for a minimum of 6 years for legal reasons.

Activity 4.4

The TAA Group is a manufacturing organisation with several factories and distribution centres. Over the years office accommodation of differing standards has been added to each site as required and in some cases existing buildings close to a location have been leased. The opportunity has now arisen for land to be acquired adjacent to the main factory. This would be sufficient for the building of an office block to accommodate all selling and administrative departments for the group.

(a) Consider the case for locating all the accounting functions for the group centrally in this new building.

(b) What guidelines would you follow in determining the location and layout of the space allocated to the accounting staff?

BPP
PUBLISHING

Equipment and supplies

5.4 You may need to ensure **adequate supplies** for the smooth, efficient and secure functioning of the accounts department.

Item	Comment
Stationery	Accounts departments typically use pre-printed stationery (eg invoices and cheques) and internal forms.
Seating	Bad furniture can cause health problems and make it hard to work.
Filing	Trays and filing cabinets ensure that material is properly sorted.
Safes	Cash and confidential information need to be locked away. Some departments have sophisticated entry-code systems for this purpose.
Calculators/ adding machines	Not everything can be computerised, although some of the tasks of adding machines can be taken over by a spreadsheet. A basic adding machine does produce a 'tally roll' able to record and provide an audit trail of each calculation as you do it.
Communications	Most offices have internal phones and fax machines. Some have direct lines, some are accessed via a switchboard.
	Email will be set up in most networked systems. As a supervisor you need from time to time to ensure that the right equipment is provided and that the facilities are not abused.
Computers	Most accounts staff have PCs for their own personal use as well as for use in the management information system.

6 INFORMATION SYSTEMS

6.1 You should already be familiar with computers from your earlier studies and quite probably also from your personal work experience, and so only a few comments on accountancy and computers are appropriate here. IT options available to management are increasingly varied.

Hardware

6.2 Most small accounting sections to have one or several office PCs for processing sales ledger, purchase ledger, nominal ledger, payroll and cash book transactions.

6.3 **Increasingly PCs are linked to each other in a network**, so that the computers can exchange data. These **networks** provide greater flexibility for data processing and can improve the quality of the information service provided to management. The network may have a **file server** which provides additional services such as e-mail and database storage, for users of the network.

6.4 Some organisations with **large quantities of routine processing** might prefer to use a **remote mainframe computer**, but input the data into the computer direct from the originating office. For example, sales ledger staff could key in sales details to a computer file from their own office. The file could then be processed by the mainframe computer and the sales ledger files updated and output (eg invoices) produced for despatch to the sales ledger office.

6.5 **Batch processing** remains possible, of course. In some supermarkets, for example, bar code data is read to a storage medium, and the file is updated at the day's end.

78

6.6 **Real time systems** provide the opportunity for the master file to be updated immediately. There need be no delay between preparing data for input and the actual processing of the data. **'Interactive' processing** allows the user to receive output information from a computer and immediately use this information to key in further input data for processing.

6.7 In terms of hardware, mainframes are used for very large volumes of transaction processing and as enterprise servers (see above). Their advantages are supposed to be greater reliability, functionality and security than networked systems. Most small to medium sized businesses use networked PCs.

Software

6.8 Software is the generic term for computer programs - the instructions which enable a computer to carry out particular processes.

6.9 An accounts department needs a variety of standard software packages, including word processing and spreadsheets, as well as transaction processing software.

6.10 The software used will depend on the size of the accounts department and the volume of processing.

- Some large organisations, such as banks, have **bespoke** software packages written especially for them.

- Other firms will be able to use **off-the-shelf** packages, such as Sage.

Files and applications

6.11 An application is a program developed to work on a particular task, for example processing sales information. Some firms have separate applications for different types of data or processing tasks. For example, the payroll system may be entirely separate from stock control - indeed, there is no reason why they should be connected.

6.12 In other systems, different applications are **integrated**.

> **KEY TERM**
>
> **Integrated systems** can be defined as a number of systems which, although capable of autonomous operation, may be linked closely to form a comprehensive and single view to the user. The use of common files or records by the individual systems is a feature of integration.

6.13 **Advantages of integrated processing**

(a) Each part of the system can be used **separately,** or in a **combination** of the parts, or as a **total** system.

(b) A transaction item only has to be **entered once** to update all parts of the system. **Duplication of effort** is avoided, and so is the need to store the same data in several different places (**data redundancy**).

(c) Integration of data means that all departments in a company are using the same information and inter-departmental disagreements based on differences about 'facts' can be avoided.

BPP PUBLISHING

(d) **Managers** throughout the organisation should have access to fully **up-to-date information** drawn from sources right across the organisation, not just from one source. This ought to improve the breadth of vision and quality of management decisions.

(e) Integration will require **standardisation** and better defined and documented system design. For example it should bring about standard ways of naming files and of constructing spreadsheets.

The diagram below might make all this more clear. It deals with stock control, sales order and purchases applications.

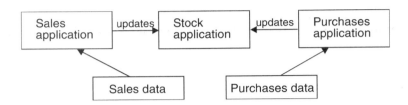

6.14 In other systems, **a database approach** is used in which all the data is coded and held on one file which can be accessed easily.

DEVOLVED ASSESSMENT ALERT

Your office accounting system may contain a variety of computer applications. You should keep in mind the variety of computer systems.

- Accounting systems process data to produce accounting information in standard reports.

- You may use packages such as EXCEL to analyse the data or do special work. Do you have to waste time by re-inputting? Perhaps you could recommend that software be installed which enables you to import data directly into a spreadsheet program.

Transactions processing and management information

6.15 An organisation's information systems might be used to perform a number of tasks **simultaneously**.

- **Initiating transactions** (for example automatically making a purchase order if stock levels are below a specified amount)

- **Recording transactions** as they occur (for example a sale is input to the sales ledger system)

- Producing **reports**

- Responding to **enquiries**

Transactions processing

6.16 Transactions processing systems, or data processing systems, are the lowest level in an organisation's use of information systems. They are used for **routine tasks** in which data items or transactions must be processed so that operations can continue. Handling sales orders, purchase orders, payroll items and stock records are typical examples.

6.17 Transactions processing systems provide the raw material which is often used more extensively by **management information systems** or **decision support systems** to produce **management information**.

Management information

> ### KEY TERM
>
> A **management information system (MIS)** is a system to **convert data** from internal and external sources into **information** and to communicate that information, in an appropriate form, to **managers** at all levels in all functions to enable them to make timely and effective decisions for planning, directing and controlling the activities for which they are responsible.

6.18 An MIS is good at analysing and summarising **regular formal information** gleaned from normal commercial data. For example, an MIS could provide managers with information relating to sales.

- Gross profit margins of particular products
- Success in particular markets
- Credit control information (aged debtors and payments against old balances)

6.19 It may be less efficient at presenting information which is relatively **unpredictable**, or **informal**, or unstructured. So, for example, an MIS could not provide information relating to the sudden emergence of a new competitor into the market.

7 OFFICE PROCEDURES

7.1 It would take too long to list all the clerical work procedures in accounting. However, the following list of clerical activities in the accounting department might act as a basis for a more detailed checklist of the procedures carried out in your own department. Further ideas about the work of different sections can be found in the BPP Unit 9 *Devolved Assessment Kit*.

7.2 **Financial accounting procedures**

(a) **Recording transactions** in a **book of prime entry** (a day book) or the **journal** (or the equivalent in a computer system)

(b) Recording **receipts and payments** in the cash book, with analysis columns to indicate the nature of the receipt or payment

(c) Keeping a **petty cash book** and using the imprest system

(d) Making **bank reconciliation** statements, to reconcile the cash book with bank statements

(e) **Posting transactions** from books of prime entry

- To individual customer accounts in the sales ledger
- To individual supplier accounts in the purchase ledger
- To accounts in the nominal ledger

(f) Preparing the **payroll** for wage-earning and salary-earning staff

(g) Keeping an **asset register**

(h) **Collecting debts**: issuing monthly statements and reminders: recording bad debts

(i) Checking and approving the **credit-worthiness** of credit customers

(j) Conducting an annual **stocktake**

7.3 Cost accounting procedures

- Recording **expenditures** (and revenues) according to a **cost** (or revenue) classification - as a direct cost or as a charge to a cost centre

- **Pricing** materials issued from stores

- Recording and costing **labour times**

- Allocating, apportioning and absorbing **overheads**

- Preparing **statements** of costs such as unit costs, job costs and contract costs

- Preparing **budgets**

- Preparing and distributing **performance reports** and variance statements

7.4 Much of this work is done on a routine basis. For example, bank reconciliations might be prepared each day, management accounts each month and so forth. The **cycle of operations** describes the routine tasks of the section and how they fit into each other. For example, bank reconciliations are generally prepared before the balance sheet cash figure can be determined at the month end.

Activity 4.5

All the accounting tasks for your organisation are carried out in the one open-plan office accommodating about twenty staff. Although most customers pay by cheque through the mail, occasionally some customers call in to the office to settle their accounts by cash. Only the financial director has his own private office. Whenever he can he takes a wide interest in the work of his staff and tries to provide a broad experience for AAT trainees.

He is now proposing that you concentrate more on management accounting duties and relinquish your current cash handling responsibilities. Specifically these are:

Task 1   Receipt of cash and cheques from customers and subsequent payment into the bank.
Task 2   Full control of petty cash (about 10-15 payments per week).

In discussing this proposal with you, the financial director suggests someone in the office to take over the tasks. You consider her to be eminently suitable. To help her you both eventually decide that you will make a note of the procedures for reference. It is also suggested that this could be the pilot for the preparation of a procedures manual for the office.

(a) Prepare a draft outline for incorporation into a procedure manual of task 1 ie receipts of cash and cheques and subsequent payment into the bank.

(b) Briefly discuss the control activities that you would stress to your colleague to be aware of when dealing with task 2 (ie petty cash procedures).

Key learning points

- An organisation's **accounting systems** are affected by the nature of its business transactions and the sort of business it is.

- Accounting work can be seen as a mixture of the financial aspects of **running an organisation** and **providing information** and advice to other departments.

- Accounting work is affected by **external regulations** relating to financial accounting, company law, auditing, tax and other influences on the business.

- The **structure** of accounting departments and the sections within them can be as varied as the structure of organisations as a whole.

- Detailed responsibilities of individuals may be set out in **job descriptions**.

- The **physical environment** in which work is done can have a profound influence on the way the work is done.

- The choice of **equipment**, both mundane items such as stationery and more sophisticated items such as computers, influence the effectiveness of the accounts department.

Quick quiz

1   What impact will size, organisation structure and geography have on the organisation of the accounting function?

2   What difference is there between information and operational work for accountants in terms of relationships with other parts of the organisation?

3   Why should *any* external regulations affect accounting practice?

4   Briefly, what impact does company law have on accounting systems?

5   How could the Urgent Issues Task Force affect the work of an accounts department?

6   Besides the government and the accountancy bodies, who else has an influence on accounting practices, and in what way?

7   Do any external regulations affect cost and management accounting practice?

8   List ten sections that there might be in an accounts department.

9   If job descriptions are useful why do many organisations not bother to prepare them?

10 Briefly, what matters need to be considered relating to the location of parts of the accounting department?

11 What problems could arise for an accounting section if office equipment is not properly managed?

12 Briefly describe the computerisation options available in a modern accounting department.

13 List five typical financial accounting procedures.

14 List five typical cost accounting procedures.

Answers to quick quiz

1   A *small* business will have a simple accounting system, whereas a *large* business will have elaborate accounting systems of some technological complexity covering a large number of product ranges and sites. The *structure* of the organisation will determine the way in which accounting information is aggregated, summarised and reported. There are a number of ways in which the accounting function will be affected by *geography*: different currencies, different legal standards and requirements for recording accounting information, different ways of doing business might mean that the emphasis of the accountant's job differs from country to country.

2   Operations work for the most part involves *obtaining* input information from other departments for processing by the accounts department. Information work involves the output of information to other departments, although it may also be necessary to obtain extra input information from those departments first.

3   Some organisations are very little affected by external regulations, except for their tax affairs. However, one of the prices that a limited company pays for its limited liability is that its dealings are open to public scrutiny: it has to lodge a copy of its financial accounts with the Registrar of Companies so that they are available for inspection by the public. Accounting regulations and standards are meant to ensure that what is published in this way is understandable by the public.

4   The Companies Act contains set formats for company accounts and lists of what information must be disclosed. In normal circumstances, company accounts should adhere to these requirements in every detail, and the accounting system needs to be set up in such a way that it can provide the information needed. The Companies Act requires companies (generally meaning you and your department) to provide auditors with any information that they need to do their job.

5   The role of the Urgent Issues Task Force is to assist the Accounting Standards Board in areas where an accounting standard or Companies Act provision already exists, but where unsatisfactory or conflicting interpretations have developed. If the UITF issued a ruling on a matter and your company happened to be one of those that had adopted an accounting practice that was contrary to this ruling, your company's approach would have to be changed. This might require all sorts of re-analysis of data and so on. UITF rulings generally only apply to large companies listed on the Stock Exchange.

6   Depending on the organisation, influential parties may include the International Accounting Standards Committee (IASC), the Stock Exchange, people who have invested in the business, such as banks, and sometimes suppliers or customers. Each of these may be able to influence what information has to be made available, in what way, and at what time intervals.

7   Generally, no. However there may be a standard way of accounting for something in certain industries. Also, former public sector bodies like British Gas have their costing methods very closely scrutinised by government watchdogs, because they still at present have a monopoly which could otherwise be abused.

8   There are endless possible answers to this question. Here are some suggestions (we only asked for ten).

Analysis and investigations section	Management accounting section
Budget co-ordination section	Materials costing section
Budgetary control section	Nominal ledger, section
Cost reports section	Payroll section
Credit control section	Process costing section
Debt collection section	Project appraisal section
Expense and overheads costing section	Purchase ledger section
Financial accounts section	Sales ledger section
Fixed asset register section	Statutory accounts section
Inventory reporting and valuation section	Treasurers section
Job costing/contract costing section	VAT section
Labour costing section	

9   Job descriptions are useful for job evaluation, in the recruitment of staff, in helping new employees to understand the scope and functions of their job; in helping the organisation's managers to recognise weaknesses in the organisation structure, in identifying training needs and for work study when surveys of current practice are conducted.

        However, job descriptions are not *essential* for any of these tasks, and they are not the only way of doing them. They take time to prepare, and have to be kept up-to-date, and so demand time and effort. Some jobs, particularly general management jobs, are very difficult to describe because they entail responding to whatever situation may happen to arise.

10   The location of accounting staff within an organisation is often of some significance.

        (a)   When an organisation receives payments 'over the counter' the location decision is important. In order to account for the receipts as soon as possible, and to minimise the movement of cash before it is banked, it might be appropriate to have an accounts receivable section in a location where customers can come to pay in person.

        (b)   The location of different sections of accounting staff in relation to each other will be a factor to consider in deciding office layout. It will usually be convenient to locate some sections close together, to minimise the transfer of paper and to make the checking of queries (and audit work) quicker and simpler.

        (c)   Much accounting work, especially cost and management accounting, is concerned with providing information to others. A close rapport ought to exist between accountants who provide the information and the managers they serve, and locating them close together is one very useful way of improving this rapport.

(d)   Managers should ideally have an office close to their staff. Supervisors should preferably be in the same room as their staff.

11   Here are some suggestions. You may have thought of others from practical experience.

(a)   Running out of forms or other stationery may hold up work, or lead to vital controls being neglected.

(b)   If workspace is inadequate, or becomes so because of untidiness or neglect it is more than likely that documents will be lost and time will be wasted searching for them or doing work twice.

(c)   Lack of proper storage facilities is again likely to lead to difficulties in locating documents and wasted time. Problems of confidentiality may occur. There is also the danger of theft.

(d)   Sharing telephones between several people that frequently need to use the telephone or be contactable by telephone is inefficient. Queues to use photocopiers or fax machines, or machines that are always breaking down also waste time. For more expensive items of equipment, of course, there is a cost-benefit calculation to be done: does the cost of wasted time exceed the cost of an extra machine? If, say, a computer printer is idle for long periods and much in demand at other times this is a case for rescheduling workloads, not for buying new equipment.

12   Most small accounting sections have one or several PCs, for processing sales ledger, purchase ledger, nominal ledger, payroll and cash book transactions. These may be networked within the same office or spread between different offices. An organisation with *large* quantities of routine processing might prefer to use a remote mainframe computer, but input the data into the computer direct from the originating office. More 'traditional' batch processing remains possible, with data being sent off to the computer centre for subsequent bulk processing. Real time systems on the other hand provide the opportunity for data to be input from a remote terminal via data link, and the master file updated immediately.

Smaller applications will use a combination of standard spreadsheet packages (Lotus 1-2-3, Microsoft Excel and the like) and 'off-the-shelf' accounting packages (Sage, Pegasus, and so on). Larger applications will require tailor-made systems.

13   Here is a summary of the procedures listed in the BPP *Managing Accounting Systems* Tutorial Text. There are, of course, very many possible answers.

(a)   Recording transactions in a book of prime entry or the journal (or the equivalent in a computer system):

(b)   Recording receipts and payments in the cash book, with analysis columns to indicate the nature of the receipt or payment.

(c)   Keeping a petty cash book and using the imprest system.

(d)   Making bank reconciliation statements.

(e)   Posting transactions from books of prime entry to the sales ledger, purchase ledger; or nominal ledger.

(f)   Preparing the payroll.

(g)   Keeping an asset register.

(h)   Collecting debts. Issuing monthly statements and reminders. Recording bad debts.

(i)   Checking and approving the credit-worthiness of credit customers.

(j)   Conducting an annual stocktake.

14   There are, of course, very many possible answers.

(a)   Recording expenditures (and revenues) according to a cost (or revenue) classification.
(b)   Pricing materials issued from stores.
(c)   Recording and costing labour times.
(d)   Allocating, apportioning and absorbing overheads.
(e)   Preparing statements of unit costs, batch costs, departmental costs etc.
(f)   Preparing budgets.
(g)   Preparing and distributing performance reports and variance statements.

Answers to activities _____

Answer 4.2 _____

(a) *Organisation of flexitime*

Flexitime systems enable certain employees to work a certain number of hours at times of their own choosing (within certain guidelines to ensure that the office is adequately staffed at all times). An example is as follows.

(i) Staff might be required to work, on average, a thirty-five hour week (excluding lunch hours) over a four week period (subject, of course, to holidays).

(ii) The office opens at 8am and closes at 6pm (ie it is open for 10 hours a day). The office is open Mondays to Fridays.

(iii) The latest time staff can arrive is 10am. The earliest they can leave is 4pm.

(iv) Lunch will be taken between 12 noon and 2pm.

(v) Staff have to take at least half an hour for lunch.

(vi) Staff must have no more than 14 hours owing to them at a particular time and must use it up when this limit is reached. Staff must *owe* no more than seven hours.

(b) *Control systems over flexitime*

(i) Records should be kept of the hours actually worked and the use and/or abuse of the flexitime system. A signing in book or a clocking on system may be a means of ensuring that the procedures are adhered to. This would be used:

(1) to record arrival time;
(2) to record the timing and duration of the lunch break;
(3) to record departure time.

Periods of absence from the office on company business must be agreed in advance.

(ii) The clock or signing in book would be input to a system which ensured that the other flexitime rules were adhered to.

(iii) To ensure that there is an adequate number of staff in the office at all times, an employee who wishes to take time off in lieu of flexitime must agree with the supervisor in advance when this is to be taken.

(iv) Flexitime decisions must be taken with the interests of other employees as well in mind, so that the 8am to 10am period is covered as is the 4pm to 6pm period.

(v) The supervisor must be prepared to distinguish between flexitime hours built up and genuine overtime which should be authorised and paid accordingly.

(vi) The supervisor might care to check the signing in book, if this is used, and to check that staff's actual attendance is in conformance with their records.

(vii) The supervisor must be prepared to take disciplinary action in the case of any abuse of flexitime. This might include requiring the employee to attend at normal office hours (eg from 9am to 5pm) thereby withdrawing the flexitime privilege.

(c) *Communicating the proposals to staff*

Introducing flexitime is quite a significant change in working methods, although it might be welcomed by many members of staff (eg for working parents who need to collect children from school). Those who wish to work normal office hours might continue to do so, but some staff may dislike the prospect of working when many others have gone, or being required to work either earlier (eg 8am to 9am) or later (eg 5am to 6am) than normal is to ensure the office is staffed.

It may be the case that the idea was generated by the staff themselves or their trade union.

First of all, the firm's managers should discuss the proposals with staff. It is unlikely that any scheme suggested will be immediately acceptable to all parties. Initially, then, staff will be informed in broad terms of the proposal and asked for their comments. Wide-ranging discussion will identify all the various options.

Once the proposal has been discussed and amended by management and employees' representatives, the final details will be communicated to staff. Then a vote can be taken, if this is necessary.

There are a variety of communication media which could be used for the initial proposal requesting comments and the final details of the agreement.

(i)   Staff newsletter
(ii)   Noticeboards
(iii)   Staff meetings
(iv)   Union newsletter
(v)   Individual letter sent to each member of staff

It is probable that the first stage of the communications process (where an outline is suggested and comments are requested) would use staff or union newsletter and noticeboards. However, when the details of the scheme have to be explained, a staff meeting would be best to answer any questions people have. A formal description of the details of the scheme will be sent as a matter of course to each member of staff.

Answer 4.3

Tutorial note. Your advertisement should have included the following essential data: who is offering the job; what the job is; what the salary is; whether there are any other benefits; what qualifications are needed; what the job consists of; whether there are career prospects; how to apply for the job.

(a)

BROOKSIDE RETAIL SERVICES

ASSISTANT ACCOUNTANT

£XX, 000

Brookside Retail Services, a fast-growing company based in Leeds, needs an Assistant Accountant to join its large accounts department and to be responsible for maintaining the company's computerised nominal ledger records and for the preparation of interim and published accounts.

The successful applicant will be a qualified accounting technician probably aged XX to XX, with some previous experience of working with computerised financial accounting systems. Experience in the supervision of staff would be an advantage.

Career prospects for a hard-working and well-motivated accountant are outstanding and conditions of employment are all that could be expected from a successful company.

For further information about the job and for an application form, please telephone or write to:

John Smith
Personnel Manager
Brookside Retail Services
(Address)
(Telephone number)

The most appropriate media to advertise the job vacancy should be those which are most likely to reach the target audience of qualified accounting technicians, probably in the Leeds area only.

The two media which would seem to be most suitable are:

(i)   an advertisement in *Accounting Technician* the magazine of the AAT. This magazine is sent to accounting technicians throughout the country. An advertisement in another professional accountancy magazine such as *Accountancy Age* might also be considered appropriate;

(ii)   a 'space' advertisement in one or more local newspapers in the Leeds area, which will be read by local residents, including accounting technicians.

(b)   The following information might be expected to be included in the job description.

Job title: Assistant accountant

Department: Accounts department

Job code number: 1234

Job summary

The job holder is responsible for the preparation of the company's interim and published accounts and for the maintenance of the computerised nominal ledger records from which these accounts are compiled.

The computer system consists of a multi-user system of [type of computer] using [type of software].

(i)   *Main duties*

(1)   To maintain up-to-date nominal ledger records on the computerised nominal ledger system.

(2)   To provide for the security of the nominal ledger accounts by maintaining suitable back-up files.

(3)   To supervise the work of the three data input clerks who input data to the nominal ledger system.

(4)   To provide the management accountant with data for the budgetary control system.

(5)   To assist the senior accountant in the preparation of the interim and published accounts.

(ii)   *Responsible for*

(1)   the section budget for the nominal ledger section of the accounts department;

(2)   three data input clerks in the nominal ledger section;

(3)   liasing with the computer sales agency which provides software and hardware for the computer system.

(iii)   *Co-operative relationships*

To co-operate with the management accountant for budgetary control.

(iv)   *Reporting to*

Senior accountant

(v)   *Experience required for the job*

(1)   Working experience with financial accounting microcomputer systems.
(2)   Professional qualification as an accounting technician.

Prepared by: J. Smith, Senior Accountant

Agreed by: W Brown, Chief Accountant

Date:

Answer 4.4 _____

(a)   We are not told the precise arrangements made by TAA for sales and distribution: there may be particular information requirements of the managers at the different locations, in which case the cost and management accounting functions at least may need to remain decentralised, or a skeleton accounting staff may be retained on site for day to day collection and processing of accounting data.

In general terms, however, the centralisation would have advantages.

(i)   The accounting function would be moving into a new and more suitable accommodation from its current housing in 'add-on' accommodation 'of differing standards'.

(ii)   Specialist staff and equipment (such as computers) will be used more extensively and therefore more economically, and with less duplication of effort.

(iii)   Procedures and information formats could be standardised.

(iv)   Staff and equipment can be used more flexibly to cope with fluctuating work loads.

(v)   A greater degree of supervision, consultation and communication within the function is facilitated.

On the other hand:

(i)   the operations to which the accounting information relates are geographically dispersed. There may be delays in the collection and provision of data from and to diverse locations, with some loss of control by factory managers;

(ii)   centralisation and standardisation may overlook the conditions and characteristics peculiar to different factories and local areas, and the information provided to them may not be appropriate to their needs;

(iii)   staff *not* centralised to the new Head Office may resent being overlooked, or losing a measure of their responsibility. Directives from Head Office may be regarded with suspicion.

No conclusion as to the best course of action for TAA can be reached without further information about the business and its products, its structure and organisation. Centralisation, however, is capable of bringing substantial benefits to the group, if it is carefully planned and handled.

(b)   *Guidelines for location and layout of space*

(i)   *Location.* In determining the best layout to facilitate work flow, attention should be given to:

(1)   the proximity of people and sections who regularly work together, such as cashiers and ledger clerks;

(2)   the proximity of supervisors and their subordinates, for the sake of communication and control;

(3)   the accessibility of people whose services and/or advice are required by the section as a whole (such as secretarial support staff);

(4)   particular requirements dictated by the activities and equipment used (for example floor strength and power sources for computers and natural light for offices).

(ii)   *Layout.* Decisions will have to be made about potential staff growth, and the availability and cost of a number of options in terms of decor, furniture and type of layout. The most popular modern option in space planning is the 'open plan' office, which facilitates workflow, equipment sharing and flexible arrangements. Guidelines for the layout of the office include:

(1)   economical use of space, in terms of flexible arrangements of furniture and equipment, economies on heating and lighting (for example by not having separate offices) and sharing of equipment;

(2)   efficient work flow, that is, movement of people and documents and communication without unnecessary expense of time and effort;

(3)   ease of supervision. Where control is necessary, supervisors should be able to oversee subordinates' work and be available to give guidance;

(4)   respect for status. If the culture of the department attaches importance to the status symbol of private offices for managers, these should be provided, or morale may suffer;

(5)   provision for security. The cashier's office and the computer room would need security measures with restrictions on entry. Activities such as payroll should also be in private offices, rather than in the general open plan area;

(6)   safety of the occupants. Gangways and fire exits must be kept clear, furniture should be arranged to avoid knocks and falls and to facilitate exit.

Answer 4.5

Tutorial note. Your answer should, of course, describe the procedures in your own office.

(a)   **OFFICE MANUAL**

Task: Receipts of cash and cheques and payment into the bank

Frequency: Daily

Part A: Co-ordinating work activities

Staff responsible: Senior Accounting Assistant

Supervisor: Senior Accounting Officer

Daily receipt of cheques

(i)   Attend at post room at 0900 and in early afternoon following the arrival of the second post. Open post under supervision of the Deputy Company Secretary. Separate out and inspect all cheques for correctness. Where necessary restrictively cross cheques using rubber stamp.

(ii)   Place cheques in a secure case and carry to the accounts office.

(iii)   Using analysis paper, prepare a list of all cheques received, including date, customer name, customer reference and the amount. Total the list. Where details are not clear, the cheque should be noted on a separate exception list for subsequent checking. Include on the list items brought forward from previous day's exception list.

(iv)   Total the amounts on the cheques and agree the total with the total on the list.

(v)   When completed, the list should be photocopied and a copy supplied to the sales ledger accounting section. The top copy should be filed in the loose-leaf cash diary folder.

(vi)   Items on the exception list should be checked with the sales ledger section and retained for the following day's list.

(vii)   Prepare cheques for banking.

Cash receipts

(i)   Count money and agree to copy statement or invoice provided by the customer. If no copy statement or invoice is provided, check details with the sales ledger section.

(ii)   Issue a numbered receipt for the agreed amount, entering the statement or invoice reference and the amount. Different receipt books are used on consecutive days.

(iii)   Retain money in the Cash Sales box in the safe until banking is carried out.

(iv)   Each day just before the close of business, pass the receipt book to the sales ledger section for writing up in the appropriate accounts, and collect the other receipt book which is to be placed in the safe.

Banking

(i)   On request, a member of the security section will attend at the office each afternoon (times to be varied) for collection of the package to be taken to the bank. If cash in excess of £500 is to be carried, two carriers should be requested.

(ii)   Details of each cheque and cash should be entered on paying-in slips and the total agreed with the total on the cash diary list.

(iii)   Details of cash paid in should be agreed with the cash receipt book.

(iv)   Any cash received after the banking procedures commence will be retained for banking on the following day.

(b)   The following control activities are important in dealing with petty cash procedures.

(i)   Physical security should be ensured by keeping petty cash in a separate locked box which is kept in a strong locked cupboard or safe.

(ii)   Numbered vouchers from voucher booklets will be issued by the petty cash clerk.

(iii)   A list of authorised signatories, showing specimens of their signatures and relevant authority limits should be kept by the petty cash clerk.

(iv)   Payments should only be made against properly authorised numbered vouchers, which should also be signed by the employee receiving the cash.

(v)   Petty cash payments should be recorded regularly (at least daily) in an analysis book.

(vi)   The analysis book should be balanced off and agreed with the amount of cash in the box frequently, and not less than once weekly.

Chapter 5 Making plans and making decisions

Chapter topic list

1   Planning

2   Types of plan

3   Steps in planning

4   Making and communicating decisions

Learning objectives

On completion of this chapter you will be able to:

	Performance criteria	Range Statement
• plan work activities to optimise the use of resources and ensure completion of work within agreed timescales	10.1.1	1
• clearly communicate decisions regarding work methods and schedules	10.1.4	1

BPP PUBLISHING

1 PLANNING

1.1 Because organisations have goals they want to achieve, they need to direct their activities by:

- Deciding **what** they want to achieve: setting **objectives**

- Deciding **how and when** to do it and who is to do it: **planning**

- **Checking** that they do achieve what they want, by **monitoring** what has been achieved and **comparing** it with the plan

- Taking action to **correct any deviation**: **controlling**

1.2 The overall framework for this is a system of **planning and control**.

Where there is a deviation from standard, a decision has to be made as to whether to adjust the plans or the standard, or whether it is the performance itself that needs correction.

1.3 EXAMPLE

The **Barings debacle** occurred when securities trader Nick Leeson, in charge of Barings Bank's Singapore office, ran up losses of £830m. A report severely criticised the management of Barings Bank for **failing to control their operations properly**.

(a) Mr Leeson apparently was given job responsibilities which made it easy for him to cover his tracks. In other words, there was poor segregation of duties.

(b) Senior managers apparently did not understand the business, failed to define who was responsible and failed to monitor the situation adequately.

1.4 We will look more closely at control in Chapter 7.

2 TYPES OF PLAN

2.1 We have already discussed **mission** and **objectives** for the organisation as a whole, but there are other types of plan you need to know about as they indicate the direction in which your department is going.

Strategies

2.2 **Strategies** follow on from the determination of long-term goals and objectives. Strategies are plans of activity (mainly long-term) and plans for the allocation of resources which will achieve the organisation's goals and objectives. For example, the computerisation of an accounts department is a **strategy** to help **achieve** the objective of a more efficient accounts department.

2.3 **Policies.** These are general statements or 'understandings' which provide guidelines for management decision-making. Here are some examples:

- Offer five year guarantees on all products sold and give money back to customers with valid complaints.

- Promote managers from within the organisation, wherever possible, instead of recruiting managers to senior positions from 'outside'.

2.4 A **budget** is a formal statement of expected results **set out in money values**.

- The budget indicates what **resources will be allocated** to each department or activity in order to carry out the planned activities.

- The budget gives detailed objectives from departments.

- Budgets are numerical statements and, as such, tend to **ignore qualitative aspects** of planning and achievement.

- Budgets are used to **control** activities.

2.5 A **programme** is a co-ordinated group of plans for the achievement of a particular objective. It has a clear, separate identity within the organisation and its planning structure.

Activity 5.1

Dial-a-Video Limited offers home delivery video rental service to subscribers. From a catalogue, subscribers choose which video they would like. They phone Dial-a-Video Limited. The video is delivered by a despatch rider, who calls at several homes in an area. The Chairman, Rajiv Bharat, says: 'I hope to expand the business. I've discovered a market segment for those who'll pay extra for art movie videos. I've had to knock the marketing and production directors' heads together to develop a plan for building a distribution system for this market. We charge £5 per video per 24 hours including delivery'.

What sort of plans can you see here?

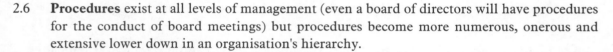

KEY TERM

A **procedure** is a logical sequence of required actions for performing a certain task.

2.6 **Procedures** exist at all levels of management (even a board of directors will have procedures for the conduct of board meetings) but procedures become more numerous, onerous and extensive lower down in an organisation's hierarchy.

KEY TERM

A **rule** is a specific, definite course of action that **must** be taken in a given situation.

2.7 Unlike a procedure, a rule does not set out the sequence of events.

2.8 The following are **rules** but not procedures.

- Employees in department X are allowed ten minutes exactly at the end of their shift for clearing up and cleaning their work-bench.

- Employees with access to a telephone must not use the telephone for personal calls.

2.9 **Advantages of rules and procedures**

Advantage	Description
Reduction of inter-personal tension	They take away from subordinates the feeling that their superiors, in issuing orders, hold power over them.
Efficiency	Procedures prescribe an efficient way of getting a job done.

Advantage	Description
Certainty	They remove the need to exercise discretion in routine tasks.
Simplicity	Staff will find jobs easier to do when they are familiar with established procedures.
Standardisation of work	Prescribed procedures ensure that a task of a certain type will be done in the same way throughout the organisation.
Continuity	The work will be done the same way even when a different person starts in a job or takes over from the previous holder.
Documentation	A **written record** of required procedures can be kept in a procedures manual. People unfamiliar with how a job should be done can learn quickly and easily by referring to the manual.
Reduction of inter-departmental friction	For example, work done by the warehousing department of a factory will affect the work of the sales force, delivery and distribution department and production department. Established procedures limit disputes between departments about who should do what, and when, and how.

2.10 Problems with rules and procedures

Problem	Description
Close supervision increases tension	Employees learn what is the **minimum** level of behaviour expected from them and tend to work at this minimum level of behaviour. This creates a requirement for close supervision which may increase tension within the work group.
Red tape	Too many rules and procedures can reduce the efficiency with which business is conducted.
Conflict	Occasionally, **overlapping areas of authority** might lengthen the time it takes to get things done.
Conformism	**Individual initiative may be stifled** which may hamper the best possible service.
Can't cope with the unusual	Procedures cannot cope with the **unexpected** or exceptional case.
Bad design	Procedures may be too complicated, or difficult to understand, or may have unexpected consequences. Many procedures, especially when form filling is considered, collect information which is not really needed.

Activity 5.2

Albert Spencer is the owner of ten retail mini-markets spread over a radius of 25 miles from his home town. He employs a manager at each location who, in addition to other duties, is required to carry out simple clerical procedures. These cover both the routine administration of the branch and the provision of data for processing at Spencer's head office. Typical tasks include such things as the certification of hours worked by staff, paying in cash receipts daily to the bank and stock administration.

At a meeting of Mr Spencer and his managers, several expressed concern that despite verbal instructions they were not certain of just how, and when, they should complete the records. It was eventually agreed that a member of the head office accounting staff should prepare a simple procedures manual to be issued to all managers.

(a) Briefly outline and discuss the contents you would expect to be included in such a manual.

(b) What form of presentation and layout would you recommend for the manual?

(c) What advantages for the *control* of the business would you expect to be gained by the introduction of such a manual?

---

3 STEPS IN PLANNING

3.1 Different parts of the organisation may have different approaches to planning.

3.2 **Steps in planning** for improvements in an accounts section might be as follows:

Step 1. Identify the **purpose of the section** and of each job within it, by consultation with superiors and the wider corporate plan (to ensure that the job's aim contributes to the section's aim, which contributes to the branch's aim, which contributes to the area division's aim and so on).

Step 2. Identify **the section's key results** (objectives which *must* be achieved if the section is to fulfil its aims) and **key tasks** (those things that *must* be done on time and to the required standard if the key results are to be achieved). Another term for this process is 'prioritising' - ie considering tasks in the order of their importance for the objective concerned.

Step 3. **Develop performance standards** ie indicators that the job is being done 'well' and contributing to the fulfilment of objectives. Effective standards usually relate to specific targets for cost, time taken, quantity and quality of output, or all of them together, ie X staff should process Y items per hour, under normal conditions, with an error rate of no more than 1%.

Step 4. Set **short-term objectives** for key tasks, so that progress towards longer-term goals can be monitored at suitable intervals for control action to be taken.

Step 5. Identify or forecast the future **resource needs**.

Step 6. On an operational work planning level, **organise and schedule** tasks, and **allocate** them to people within appropriate timescales so that the flow of work within and through the section is smooth and continuous as far as possible. See Chapter 6.

Step 7. **Communicate the plan** to staff so that they know what they have to do and why.

Step 8. **Monitoring and control**. Ensure control information tells:

- Whether short-term goals are being met, and performance is therefore on target to meet its objectives.

- Whether performance standards are being maintained.

- The extent of any shortfall or deviation.

- What needs to be done to correct the activity or adjust the plans and standards themselves.

4 MAKING AND COMMUNICATING DECISIONS

4.1 As you have now seen, both planning and control involve frequent decisions. Planning requires you to decide what to do in the first place and control requires you to decide what control action (if any) is necessary to keep to the planned course.

BPP PUBLISHING

4.2   **Types of decision**

Type of decision	Comment
Routine planning decisions	Typically, budgeting and scheduling.
Short-run problem decisions	Decisions of a non-recurring nature. For example, a manager might have to deal with a staff problem.
Investment or disinvestment decisions	For example, should an item of equipment be purchased? Should a department be shut down? Decisions of this nature often have long-term consequences, and are taken at a fairly senior level.
Longer-range decisions	Decisions made once and reviewed infrequently, but which are intended to solve a continuing solution to a continuing or recurring problem.
Control decisions	Decisions about what to do when performance is disappointing and below expectations.

Types of problems

4.3   Decisions are needed to **resolve problems**, when there is a *choice* about what to do. Problems vary, not just according to what they are about, but to other factors too.

- Difficulty
- Frequency
- Quantifiability
- Consequences
- Responsibility

We will go into a little more detail about these issues.

4.4   **Difficulty**. Some problems are difficult to resolve, and call for three things.

- Careful judgement
- A lot of thought
- Technical skill or experience on the part of the manager

4.5   **Frequency**.

(a) **Problems which recur regularly** can be dealt with in a **routine or standardised way,** with the help of **regulations and procedures.**

　　(i)   If a member of staff is continually late for work, a disciplinary code of practice should be available to give guidance to the employee's supervisor about what steps to take

　　(ii)   If a supplier is late with a delivery, there should be procedures in the purchasing department for chasing up the delivery

(b) Problems of a **non-recurring and non-foreseeable nature** cannot easily be provided for in a book of regulations and procedures, and a **higher decision-making ability** is usually needed from managers to deal with them.

4.6   **Quantifiability**. Quantifiable problems are problems where the inputs and likely outcome of each decision option can be given numerical values. Many problems are, at best, only partly quantifiable.

4.7   **Consequences**. The outcome of a decision might be measured in several ways.

- Money terms - eg revenue, costs, profits

- Units of output or work - eg number of items produced or sold, hours of work

- Productivity or efficiency - ie units of work produced per unit of input resource employed, such as 'invoices processed per hour of accounts assistant's time'.

- Impact on customers or competitors

4.8 **Responsibility**. Decisions can only be made by people who have the authority to do so. Expenditure authorisation limits are an example of this.

4.9 **Stages in making a decision**

Step 1. **Recognise the problem**. The decision maker needs to be informed of a problem in the first place. This is sometimes referred to as the **decision trigger**.

Step 2. **Define the problem**. Consider a company with falling sales.

- The *fall in revenue* would be the *trigger*. Further information would be needed to identify where the revenue deficiencies were occurring.

- The problem can therefore be defined. If our company discovers that sales of product X in area Y are falling, the problem can be defined as 'decline of sales of product X in area Y due to new competitor: how can the decline be reversed?' (Some 'problems' may be more vague, however.)

Step 3. **Identify possible courses of action**. If our company wishes to review the price of product X in area Y, information will be needed as to the effect of different prices on demand for the product.

Step 4. **Make the decision**. The decision is made after evaluating the alternatives.

Step 5. **Communicate the decision,** for example, if a sales director decides to lower the price of product X and institute an intensive advertising campaign, nothing will happen unless the advertising and the manufacturing department are told.

Step 6. **Implement the decision**. Implementation may need substantial planning and review. Information is needed to ensure that implementation is going according to plan. Introducing new software is an example.

Step 7. **Monitor the effects of the decision**. For example, if you have introduced new procedures, you need to check they are having the desired effect.

DEVOLVED ASSESSMENT ALERT

Evaluating courses of action is quite significant for your devolved assessment. A 'recommendation' is almost a decision - it just has not been implemented.

Before you make your recommendations you have to evaluate its effects on other departments. For example, if you work in the sales ledger, you might like to put a stop on some overdue accounts - but the sales personnel would have to agree to implement this as they may consider the potential for future sales more significant than improved cash recovery.

BPP PUBLISHING

Key learning points

- **Planning** involves decisions about **what** to do, **how** to do it, **when** to do it and **who** is to do it. Managers and supervisors are sometimes reluctant to plan.

- **Plans come in various forms**: objectives, strategies, programmes, budgets, policy statements, procedures and regulations.

- **Decision making** is central to both planning and control. Decisions are based both on facts and on judgement. Because problems vary in nature (eg short-term/long-term; easy/complex; quantifiable/qualitative) so too does the task of decision making.

- Decision making is a **sequence**: identify the problem, analyse it, generate alternative courses of action, make the decision, communicate, implement and monitor the decision.

Quick quiz

1 Explain briefly what is meant by each of the following terms.

    (a)   Objective
    (b)   Strategy
    (c)   Programme
    (d)   Budget
    (e)   Policy
    (f)   Procedure
    (g)   Regulation

2 What are the steps in planning for your section?

3 Should plans be rigidly adhered to?

4 What are the disadvantages of procedures?

5 What type of information might be needed for monitoring and control?

6 What are five categories of decision?

7 How can decisions be made about problems which occur regularly?

8 Describe the decision sequence.

Answers to quick quiz

1 These terms are not always used in the same way in by different organisations.

    (a)   Objective is a term that is generally used about planning for the organisation as a whole. In this sense it is a goal towards which all the organisation's activities should be aimed, for example to earn a profit, or provide a certain service. Objectives might also be identified for *individual departments.*

    (b)   *Strategies* follow on from the determination of long-term goals and objectives. Strategies are plans of activity (mainly long-term) and plans for the allocation of resources which will achieve the organisation's objectives.

    (c)   *Programmes* are co-ordinated groups of plans (objectives, policies, procedures, budgets) for the achievement of a particular objective. An example is an expansion programme.

    (d)   The *budget* is a formal statement of expected results set out in *numerical* terms, and summarised in money values (and sometimes in physical quantities). It is a plan for carrying out certain activities within a given period of time, indicating how many resources will be allocated to each department or activity in order to carry out the planned activities. The budget is usually prepared on an organisation-wide basis, so that all the activities of the organisation are co-ordinated within a single plan.

    (e)   *Policies* are general statements which provide guidelines for management decision making. A company's policies might include, for example, to offer 5-year guarantees on all products sold and that employees in the purchasing department should decline gifts from suppliers.

(f) *Procedures* are a logical sequence of required actions for performing a certain task. They exist at all levels of management but they become more numerous, onerous and extensive lower down in an organisation's hierarchy. Prescribed procedures ensure that a task of a certain type will be done in the same way throughout the organisation and reduce the likelihood of inter-departmental friction.

(g) A regulation (or rule) is a specific, definite course of action that must be taken in a given situation. Unlike a procedure, it does not set out the sequence of events. Regulations allow no deviations or exceptions, unlike policies, which are general guidelines allowing the exercise of some discretion by the manager or supervisor.

2 The steps in planning are as follows.

(a) Identify purpose or objective of an activity or your section

(b) Identify key results and key tasks

(c) List performance standards

(d) Set short term objectives

(e) Forecast resource requirements

(f) Organise and schedule tasks

(g) Communicate the plan

(h) Implement and monitor the plan

3 Once formulated plans should be adhered to if controllable circumstances permit, but because the future is uncertain, plans should be changed to meet unforeseen circumstances.

4 People do not use their initiative. They cannot cope with the unexpected. They can waste time.

5 Information for monitoring makes it possible to compare output to standards.

6 (a) Routine planning decisions; typically, budgeting and scheduling.

(b) Short-run problem decisions typically of a non-recurring nature, such as dealing with a staff problem.

(c) Investment or disinvestment decisions. For example, should an item of equipment be purchased?

(d) Longer-range decisions; decisions made once and reviewed infrequently, but which are intended to provide a continuing solution to a continuing or recurring problem.

(e) Control decisions; decisions about what to do when performance is disappointing and below expectation.

7 Problems which recur regularly can be dealt with in a routine and standardised way, perhaps with the help of regulations and procedures. The decision about how to resolve the problem is made once and applied consistently.

8 The sequence is as follows. You might list some of these elements in a different order.

(a) Identify and specify the problem.
(b) Analyse the problem.
(c) Appraise available resources.
(d) List and evaluate possible solutions.
(e) Select the optimum solution.
(f) Draw up an action plan to implement the solution.
(g) Carry out the decision required.
(h) Re-check that planned benefits actually accrue.

Answers to activities

Answer 5.1

A strategy is to exploit the 'art movie' market segment. A programme is the build-up of the distribution system. A policy is home delivery. The £5 charge is an aspect of the budget.

Activity 5.2

(a)   The procedures manual might contain the following sections.

    (i)   Introduction. This section would 'set the scene' by outlining briefly the history of the business, the nature of its products and the location of branches together with relevant telephone numbers. Organisation charts including the names of managers and supervisory staff could also be included in this section.

    (ii)   Summary of accounting procedures. This will list all of the accounting procedures which are to be carried out or supervised by mini-market managers together with due dates for completion of procedures.

        1   There will be the daily routines such as paying in cash receipts which managers will oversee, as well as weekly and monthly procedures.

        2   Details of how cash is to be handled will be provided, including instructions on how often to remove money from tills for safekeeping and on what security measures are to be taken. Procedures covering the recording of stock movements in the mini-markets would also be included.

        3   Notes on policies on return of goods would be included, as well as ordering procedures, including authority limits applying to managers.

    (iii)   Forms. This section will explain the purpose of the various forms and how they are completed. Sample forms - blank or completed, as appropriate - will be provided. For example, for routines covering cash receipts there will be a form completed daily analysing cash receipts and cheque receipts, and splitting these among separate sales categories.

        Forms for weekly wage routines will include time sheets and individual staff records. Weekly summary sheets would show staff attendance records, holidays and other absences, overtime worked and so on.

(b)   The manual should be produced with a layout and presentation which takes into account the following.

    (i)   Professionalism. The manual should have a professional appearance, with a clear, concise and easily followed layout. The presentation of the manual can be given a professional appearance by careful choice of typeface, paper type and binders. A polished appearance will contribute to an impression that the manual has been thoroughly prepared. The inclusion of the company logo on each page may contribute positively to the appearance of the manual.

    (ii)   Updating. If the manual is contained in a loose-leaf binder of sufficient size to allow for possible future expansion of the manual, updating can easily be achieved by exchanging existing pages with updated pages. There should be included within the binder a schedule indicating when updates have been made, so that a user of the manual will be easily able to tell how up-to-date the manual is.

(c)   The advantages for the control of the business of introducing such a manual would be as follows.

    (i)   The manual will be easy for managers to refer to instead of consulting the head office, thus saving administration time at head office.

    (ii)   Errors may be avoided because setting out procedures clearly in a manual will improve manager's overall knowledge of procedures.

    (iii)   The process of documenting the system at the time the manual is compiled may encourage a rethinking of some aspects of the control of the business.

    (iv)   Staff may feel happier and more motivated if their responsibilities are set out clearly in a manual.

    (v)   The manual may provide useful training material for new managers, or may serve as 'retraining' material for existing managers.

    (vi)   The standardisation of procedures in the manual should help to ensure that different individuals do not develop and use their own versions of procedures. If there is no central reference manual, there may be a tendency for people to 'invent' procedures on an ad hoc basis, as the need arises. In an organisation such as this, which is made up of units which should be relatively homogeneous, variations in procedures may simply cause confusion or misunderstandings.

Chapter 6 Co-ordinating and monitoring work

Chapter topic list

1   Allocating tasks and delegating responsibility

2   Communicating requirements

3   Planning work

4   Scheduling activities

5   Managing your time

Learning objectives

On completion of this chapter you will be able to:

	Performance criteria	Range Statement
• *manage your time*	n/a	n/a
• plan work activities in order to optimise the use of resources and ensure completion of work within agreed timescales	10.1.1	1, 2
• clearly communicate work methods and schedules to all individuals in a way which assists their understanding of what is expected of them	10.1.4	1, 2
• work activities are effectively co-ordinated in accordance with work plans	10.1.6	1, 2

The Italicised objective is an area of knowledge and understanding underlying elements of competence for this Unit.

BPP PUBLISHING

1 ALLOCATING TASKS AND DELEGATING RESPONSIBILITY

1.1 Before we can discuss how supervisors and managers go about planning their work we must identify a key issue for work planning and how it relates to organisation structure.

1.2 **Authority, responsibility and delegation**

KEY TERMS

Power is the *ability* to do something, or to get others to do it.

Authority is the *right* to do something, or to get others to do it.

Responsibility is the *liability* of a person to be called to account for the exercise of delegated authority. It is an obligation to do something, or to get others to do it.

Delegation is the process whereby a superior gives a subordinate authority over a defined area which falls within the scope of the superior's own authority. The superior remains responsible and accountable for the results of the tasks and decisions which have been delegated.

(a) A **manager** is usually given **authority** from above, by virtue of holding a position in the **organisation hierarchy**. On the other hand, an **elected team leader**, for example, is given authority from below.

Authority is passed down the organisation structure, by **delegation**.

(b) The delegated authority of a manager over a subordinate in a direct line down the chain of command is sometimes called **line authority**.

(c) Responsibility is also delegated down the organisation.

A person has **responsibility** if he or she has been given a task and has to ensure that it gets done: a responsibility is an obligation.

With responsibility goes **accountability**.

Responsibility without authority

1.3 In many organisations, responsibility and authority are:

	Comments
Not clear	When the organisation is doing something new or in a different way, its existing rules and procedures may be out of date or unable to cope with the new development. Various people may try to 'empire build'. The managers may not have designed the organisation very well.
Shifting	In large organisations there may be real conflict between different departments; or the organisation may, as it adapts to its environment, need to change.

1.4 Authority and responsibility should be comparable. Authority without accountability leads to irresponsible actions. Responsibility without authority is an impossible burden.

DEVOLVED ASSESSMENT ALERT

Lack of clarity as to authority and responsibility could be a problem in an accounting system.

Activity 6.1

You have just joined a small accounts department. The financial controller keeps a very close eye on expenditure and, being prudent, believes that nothing should be spent that is not strictly necessary. She has recently gone on a three week holiday to Venezuela. You have been told that you need to prepare management accounts, and for this you have to obtain information from the payroll department in two weeks time. This is standard procedure. However, there are two problems. One of the other people in your department has gone sick, and a temporary replacement will be needed very shortly. The personnel department say: 'We need a staff requisition from the Financial Controller before we can get in a temp. Sorry, you'll just have to cancel your weekend'. The payroll department is happy to give you the information you need - except directors' salaries, essential for the accounts to be truly accurate.

What is the underlying cause of the problem and what, in future, should you ask the Financial Controller to do to put it right?

Delegation

1.5 Delegation can only occur if the superior initially possesses the authority to delegate; a subordinate cannot be given authority to make decisions unless it would otherwise be the superior's right to make those decisions personally. Delegation is not abdication. A manager might delegate authority and responsibility for all his or her department's functions. The subordinates would then to responsible to the manager **but the manager would still be fully accountable** to his or her own superior for the department's work.

1.6 Managers and supervisors must delegate some authority.

   (a) There are **physical and mental limitations** to the work load of any individual or group in authority.

   (b) Managers and supervisors are free to **concentrate on the aspects of the work** (such as planning), which only they are competent (and paid) to do.

   (c) The **increasing size and complexity** of some organisations calls for specialisation, both managerial and technical.

1.7 However, by delegating authority to assistants, the superior takes on two extra tasks.

   • Monitoring assistants' performance
   • Co-ordinating the efforts of different assistants.

Delegation implies confidence in the subordinate's competence. The greater the competence, the greater the scope for delegation and the lower the need for supervision. Competence depends upon training and experience and it is therefore appropriate for the manager to provide both.

1.8 **The process of delegation**

   Step 1. **Formally** assign tasks to the assistant, who should formally agree to do them.

   Step 2. **Allocate resources and authority** to the assistant to enable him or her to carry out the delegated tasks.

   Step 3. **Specify the expected performance** levels of the assistant, keeping in mind the assistant's level of expertise.

   Step 4. **Maintain contact** with the assistant to review the progress made and to make constructive criticism. **Feedback** is essential for control, and also as part of the learning process.

Remember that **ultimate accountability for the task remains with the supervisor**: if it is not well done it is at least partly the fault of poor delegation, and it is still the supervisor's responsibility to get it re-done.

Problems of delegation

1.9 In practice many managers and supervisors are **reluctant to delegate** and attempt to deal with many routine matters themselves in addition to their more important duties.

(a) **Low confidence and trust** in the abilities of their staff: the suspicion that 'if you want it done well, you have to do it yourself'.

(b) The burden of **accountability for the mistakes of subordinates**, aggravated by (a) above.

(c) A **desire to 'stay in touch'** with the department or team - both in terms of workload and staff - particularly if the manager does not feel at home in a management role, or misses aspects of the more junior job, and the camaraderie.

(d) **Feeling threatened.** An unwillingness to admit that assistants have developed to the extent that they could perform some of the supervisor's duties.

1.10 **Overcoming the reluctance of managers to delegate**

(a) **Train the subordinates** so that they are capable of handling delegated authority in a responsible way. If assistants are of the right 'quality', supervisors will be prepared to trust them more.

(b) Have a system of **open communications**, in which the supervisor and assistants freely interchange ideas and information. If the assistant is given all the information needed to do the job, and if the supervisor is aware of what the assistant is doing the assistant will make better-informed decisions and the supervisor will have greater confidence.

(c) **Ensure that a system of control is established.** Supervisors are reluctant to delegate authority because they retain absolute accountability for the performance of their assistants. If an efficient control system is in operation, the dangers of relinquishing authority and control to assistants are significantly lessened.

When to delegate decision making

1.11 When deciding when to delegate decision making authority, a manager will have to consider certain issues.

- Is the **acceptance** of decisions by staff required for morale or ease of implementation of the decision?

- Is the **quality** of the decision most important, and acceptance less so? Many technical financial decisions may be of this type, and should be retained by the supervisor if he or she alone has the knowledge and experience to make them.

- Is the **expertise or experience** of assistants relevant or **necessary** to the task, and will it enhance the quality of the decision?

- Can **trust** be placed in the competence and reliability of the assistants?

- Does the **decision** require tact and confidentiality, or, on the other hand, maximum exposure and assimilation by employees?

Activity 6.2

You are the manager of an accounts section of your organisation and have stopped to talk to one of the clerks in the office to see what progress he is making. He complains bitterly that he is not learning anything. He gets only routine work to do and it is the same routine. He has not even been given the chance to swap jobs with someone else. You have picked up the same message from others in the office. You discuss the situation with the recently appointed supervisor. She appears to be very busy and harassed. When confronted with your observations she says that she is fed up with the job. She is worked off her feet, comes early, goes late, takes work home and gets criticised behind her back by incompetent clerks.

What has gone wrong?

DEVOLVED ASSESSMENT ALERT

Delegation has two beneficiaries: the manager who gets someone else to do the job, and the subordinate who gets to do more interesting work. Delegation is relevant to motivation.

Empowerment

1.12   Empowerment and delegation are related.

KEY TERM

Empowerment is the current term for making workers (and particularly work teams) responsible for achieving, and even setting work targets, with the freedom to make decisions about how they are to be achieved.

1.13   **Empowerment** goes in hand in hand with three other things.

- **Delayering** or a cut in the number of levels (and managers) in the chain of command, since responsibility previously held by middle managers is, in effect, being given to operational workers. This cuts cost and improves communication.

- **Flexibility,** since giving responsibility to the people closest to the products and customer encourages responsiveness - and cutting out layers of communication, decision-making and reporting speeds up the process.

- **New technology,** since there are more 'knowledge workers'. Such people need less supervision, being better able to identify and control the means to clearly understood ends. Better information systems also remove the mystique and power of managers as possessors of knowledge and information in the organisation.

1.14   **Reasons for empowerment**

'The people lower down the organisation possess the knowledge of what is going wrong with a process but lack the authority to make changes. Those further up the structure have the authority to make changes, but lack the profound knowledge required to identify the right solutions. The only solution is to change the culture of the organisation so that everyone can become involved in the process of improvement and work together to make the changes.' (Max Hand)

The change in organisation structure and culture as a result of empowerment can be shown in the diagram below.

Traditional hierarchical structure: fulfilling management requirements

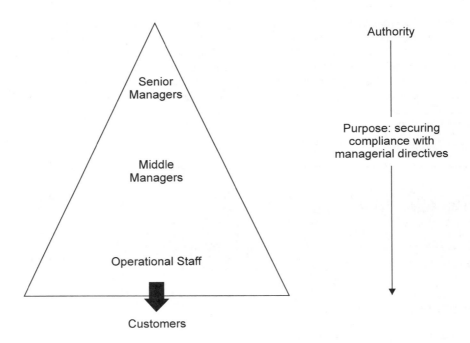

Empowerment structure: supporting workers in serving the customer

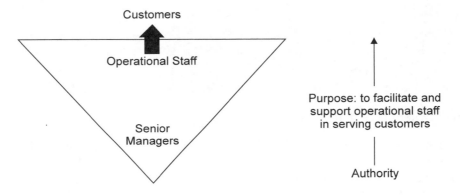

1.15 In practice 'empowerment' has meant different things to different people.

Departmental job descriptions

1.16 Larger businesses are likely to have proper plans for the organisation and for every unit in it, so that objectives of sections and departments contribute properly to organisational objectives and everybody knows what they are supposed to be doing in relation to everybody else.

1.17 No matter how the functional duties are divided in the organisation structure, they must be clear to managers and employees alike. A **departmental job description**, like the individual equivalent, sets out an outline of general aims and duties. This has several desirable effects.

- Individuals recognise the **general aim** of the work of the department and their section of it, and how they relate to it.

- Departmental managers recognise their **sphere of authority**.

- **Specialist work, training and recruitment requirements** can be highlighted in the description of various types of activities.

- **Systems and procedures** can be established, maintained and reviewed on the basis of fulfilling the general aim and specific duties of the section.

- **Duplication of work can be spotted** between and within departments; specialisation, and centralisation of functions are two ways of ensuring that several people are not spending time and money doing the same or similar work in isolation from each other.

Manuals and intranets

1.18 An organisation may have a manual to set out the structure of the organisation and the jobs within it: job descriptions, responsibilities, functions, details of duties and activities, and how all these activities relate to each other. Because the organisation is likely to change, the manual will need to be adaptable - perhaps a loose-leaf system - and regularly reviewed.

1.19 Many firms are putting general data about the organisation and the department within an **intra-net** for all staff to access. This uses internet technology but within the company only.

2   COMMUNICATING REQUIREMENTS

2.1 We have already covered the importance of communication generally, but it is worthwhile revisiting the topic briefly. If you are delegating and allocating tasks, as well as supervising a team, you need to ensure that the communications processes are effective.

How to communicate well

2.2 **Ten commandments of good communication**

(a) **Clarify what you want to say**.

(b) **Be clear why you are communicating**. Communication may be intended to establish and disseminate the goals of the organisation, to develop plans, to monitor and control the performance of subordinates, to obtain essential information or for many other purposes. The purpose of the communication may affect the way in which the message should be conveyed.

(c) **Understand the physical and human context**. For example, should the message be conveyed orally or in writing? Should the message be delivered publicly or in private conversation with an individual? For a written message, is a formal memorandum or a jotted note more appropriate? What is the normal practice of the organisation in conveying particular types of information?

(d) **Get your facts right**.

(e) **Consider the content and the overtones of the message**. The content may be distorted by non-verbal factors, such as tone of voice, facial expressions, the choice of words and phrases in a written communication.

(f) **Communicate something that helps, or is valued by, the receiver**.

(g) **Communication, to be effective, requires follow-up**.

(h) **Communicate messages that are of short-run and long-run importance**. People need to know things in advance.

(i) **Actions must be congruent with communications**. Don't say one thing and so another.

BPP PUBLISHING

(j) **Be a good listener.** Understanding other people's viewpoints is an important element in communicating effectively.

Informal communication channels

2.3 The formal pattern of communication in an organisation is always supplemented by an informal one, driven perhaps by rumours or gossip, which is sometimes referred to as the **grapevine**. Informal communication is speculative and sometimes inaccurate, but it is also 'hotter' and more current

Activity 6.3

After returning from the monthly management meeting, your Financial Director calls a meeting of the senior accounting staff. She is concerned that her colleagues in the other functional areas are not receiving the most efficient service from the accounting departments. The most repeated comment in the management meeting was 'You accountants do not seem able to communicate properly'. To consider this criticism it is agreed to hold a workshop session to re-evaluate the approaches of the various sections. Although the session will be expected to be wide ranging it was recognised that some form of structure for this meeting should be prepared. To assist her in leading this session the Financial Director has now asked you to prepare the appropriate notes, and also to obtain further information from other departments.

(a) Outline the likely points which you anticipate may be raised by the other departments.

(b) Prepare a plan of the possible remedies which may be explored by your department in relation to these points.

3 PLANNING WORK

DEVOLVED ASSESSMENT ALERT

You should give evidence of how you have planned and co-ordinated work activities.

Efficiency

3.1 Whenever people work, they are using up resources, and resources cost money.

- Their own time
- The time of colleagues, bosses and subordinates
- Materials
- Equipment, such as telephones, typewriters and computers
- Other items which cost money - such as electricity
- Cash

3.2 Efficiency depends on two things.

- overall planning and direction
- individual technical expertise, organisational ability and conscientiousness

Work planning

3.3 **Work planning,** as the term implies, means planning how work should be done: establishing work methods and practices to ensure that predetermined objectives are **efficiently** met at all levels. There are several activities which use work planning as a basis.

- Scheduling and allocating of **routine** tasks

- Handling of **high priority** tasks and deadlines

- **Adapting to changes** and unexpected demands; that is, being prepared for emergencies, as far as possible

- **Setting standards** for working, against which performance can be measured

- **Co-ordination** of individual and combined efforts

3.4 The resources at the supervisor's disposal

(a) **Human resources.** A supervisor can deploy staff to do different tasks at different times.

(b) **Material resources.** Some management or supervisory posts give the person responsibility for the use of machinery.

(c) **Financial resources.** Discretion in financial matters varies according to the level in the management hierarchy. Normally the supervisor would be set a budget and be expected to work within it.

3.5 Steps in work planning

(a) **Task sequencing or prioritisation** (ie considering tasks in order of importance for the objective concerned), or at least assessing where the resources are most usefully spent.

(b) **Scheduling or timetabling tasks,** and allocating them to different individuals within appropriate time scales (for example, there will be continuous routine work, and arrangement for priority work with short-term deadlines).

(c) **Establishing checks and controls** to ensure that priority deadlines are being met and routine tasks are achieving their objectives.

(d) **Contingency plans for unscheduled events.** Nothing goes exactly according to plan, and one feature of good planning is to make arrangements for what should be done if a major upset were to occur, for instance if the company's main computer were to break down, or if the major supplier of key raw materials were to become insolvent.

(e) **Co-ordinating the efforts of individuals**

(f) **Reviewing and controlling performance**

3.6 Some jobs are entirely routine, and can be performed one step at a time, but for most people, some kind of planning and judgement will be required.

Assessing where resources are most usefully allocated

3.7 If managers or supervisors are simply given targets, they will be responsible for allocating resources effectively.

(a) **Different routes** may exist to achieve the same objective (eg to increase total profits, sell more, or cut costs).

(b) There may be **competing areas,** where total resources are limited.

3.8 **Pareto analysis.** Pareto, an economist, demonstrated that 80% of the nation's wealth was held by 20% of the population. This 80:20 rules has many other applications. For example, 20% of customers may generate 80% of turnover. This means that the manager will be able to concentrate scarce resources on the crucial 20%; and devise policies and procedures for the remaining 80%.

Priorities

3.9 Some work is **essential** and has to be done fairly **promptly**: other work can wait a bit if necessary. For example, sending out invoices might be an essential daily task, whereas filing office copies of invoices can usually wait a few days. Essential work has a higher priority than other work.

3.10 A piece of work will be **high priority** in the following cases.

- **If it has to be completed by a certain time** (ie a deadline)

- **If other tasks depend on it**

- **If other people depend on it**. An item being given low priority by one individual or department may hold up the activities of others for whom the processing of the item is high priority.

- **If it is important.** There may be a clash of priorities between two urgent tasks, in which case relative consequences should be considered: if an important decision or action rests on a task (eg a report for senior management, or correction of an error in a large customer order) that task should take precedence over, say, the preparation of notes for a meeting, or processing a smaller order.

3.11 **Routine priorities**, or regular peak times such as monthly issue of account statements and yearly tax returns, can be **planned ahead of time**, and other tasks postponed or redistributed around them.

3.12 **Non-routine priorities** occur when **unexpected demands** are made. Thus planning of work should cover routine scheduled peaks and contingency plans for unscheduled peaks and emergencies.

3.13 In practice planning for individuals, sections, departments and organisations may be long-term, medium-term or short-term.

- **Long-range planning** will have to be more general (to allow for change), concerned with objectives and strategy.

- **Medium-term planning** will cover the development of systems and the development of resources to carry out the strategy, for example through training.

- **Short-term planning** will cover the precise details of how resources, including work time, will be used.

Different organisations and functions will have different ideas about what is 'long' or 'short' term.

3.14 A section of a department is unlikely to plan to such long time scales. The end of next year is perhaps the furthest that you, as a supervisor, will have to look ahead. Your **planning periods** may be as follows.

(a) The organisation's **financial year**.

(b) The **calendar year**, if it is not the same as the organisation's financial year. It is common to have a wall planner on which you can record details of your team members' holidays (staff availability), absences through training, the dates of the annual and interim visits from the auditors, seasonal peaks and troughs in workload, and so on.

(c) The next **operating cycle** for your section.

- In a **sales ledger** section, statements sent out at the end of the month may mark the end of one cycle and the beginning of another

- A **payroll department** might have a weekly cycle, ending on a Thursday, say, and a monthly cycle, ending on the 26th of each month

- A **costing section** may be dependent upon production cycles, because information about the costs involved in producing a batch of a product becomes available at the end of the process, every three working days, say

(d) The **next week** and the **next day** are planning periods. We shall say more about this when we discuss personal time management at the end of this chapter.

Deadlines

KEY TERM

A **deadline** is the end of the longest span of time which may be allotted to a task: in other words, the last acceptable date for completion.

3.15 **Setting deadlines** (or having them set for you) may seem easy, but remember that to achieve a deadline, some things will have to be ready an appropriate time beforehand. No employee or group in an organisation is working in isolation. For example, a machine operator on the shop floor cannot start work until he gets the job card telling him what to do and the materials to do it with: this should create a deadline for people in the production planning department to get the job card prepared, and then a deadline for people in the stores department to get the materials into the production room.

Failure to meet deadlines has a 'knock-on' effect on other parts of the organisation, and on other tasks within an individual's duties. If you are late with one task (updating the nominal ledger), you will be late or rushed with the one depending on it (preparing a trial balance).

Work allocation

3.16 Here are some rules of thumb about work allocation.

- **Allocate specialist tasks to specialists**.

- **Some tasks can only be done by one person,** who should not be given tasks which others can do as well. Skills are a scarce resource.

- Some unattractive jobs may have to be done by **rota**.

- **Plan ahead for peak periods** - staff may need to do more than the normal.

- Be **sensitive to people's experience and feelings** about the job they do.

- People's efforts must be co-ordinated.

BPP PUBLISHING

Activity 6.4

Usha has 6 jobs to get completed and she has made a list of them.

	Time
Tidy office	30 mins
Filing	1½ hours
Job A	1 day
Job B	½ day
Job C	2 days
Job D	1 week

What further information do you need to enable you to suggest to Usha what order these jobs should be done in?

4 SCHEDULING ACTIVITIES

4.1 Work planning may be divided into three stages.

- Allocating work to people or machines
- Determining the **order** in which activities are performed
- Determining the **times** for each activity

In practice the term **scheduling** is often used to describe all of these stages, but it may also be used for the time planning aspect in particular.

Who does things?

4.2 The allocation of work to teams or individuals will depend upon a number of factors.

- The precise skills required to do a job

- The other work already allocated to people with the appropriate skills or available to be allocated

- The demand for commonly used facilities which may form **bottlenecks**.

4.3 EXAMPLE

In a firm of accountants the most complex audit tasks will be allocated to the experienced and qualified auditing staff, while checking invoices will be done by trainees. Most jobs may require the use of an accounts preparation package: if there are only five terminals, only five jobs can be in progress at any one time.

What order do you do them in?

4.4 Sequencing provides a list of necessary activities in the **order** in which they must be completed. The priorities will depend on the circumstances and perhaps upon a declared customer service commitment ('we will make you a new pair of glasses in one hour', for example). Here is a list of possible criteria for deciding what order to do tasks in.

Example	Comment
Arrival time (first come, first served)	Serving members of the public in a bank is a typical example.
Least slack time	Find the time when the job is due to be finished and take away the amount of time it will take to finish it. This gives you the slack time. The job with the least slack time is done first.
Most nearly finished	This gets small distractions out of the way.
Shortest job first	Then next shortest, and so on. Once again this gets those niggling little things out of the way.
Longest job first	Then next longest, and so on. This ensures that the worst jobs are not continually put off.

Activity 6.5

Choose a task or event that needs planning. On your own or in a group:

(a)   Make a checklist
(b)   Re-arrange items in order of priority and time sequence
(c)   Estimate the time for each activity and schedule it, working back from a deadline
(d)   Prepare an action sheet
(e)   Draw a chart with columns for time units, and rows for activities
(f)   Decide what items may have to be 'brought forward' later and how.

Scheduling

4.5   **Scheduling** is where priorities and deadlines are planned and controlled. A schedule establishes a timetable for a logical sequence of tasks, leading up to completion date.

- All involved in a task must be given adequate **notice** of work schedules.

- The schedules themselves should allow a **realistic time allocation** for each task.

- Allowance will have to be made for **unexpected events** in the intervening time, and the timetable regularly revised.

4.6   A number of activities may have to be undertaken in sequence, with some depending on, or taking priority over others.

(a)   **Activity scheduling** provides **a list of necessary activities** in the order in which they must be completed. You might use this to plan each day's work, or to set up standard procedures for jobs which you undertake regularly.

(b)   **Time scheduling** adds to this **the time scale for each activity**, and is useful for setting deadlines for tasks. The time for each step is estimated; the total time for the task can then be calculated, allowing for some steps which may be undertaken simultaneously by different people or departments.

Work programmes and other aids to planning

4.7   From activity and time schedules, detailed **work programmes** can be designed for jobs which are carried out over a period of time. Some tasks will have to be started well before the deadline, others may be commenced immediately before, others will be done on the day itself. **Organising a meeting**, for example, may include:

Step 1. Booking accommodation two months before.

Step 2. Retrieving relevant files one week before.

Step 3. Preparing and circulating an agenda 2-3 days before.

Step 4. Checking conference room layout the day before.

Step 5. Taking minutes on the day.

The same applies to stock ordering in advance of production (based on a schedule of known delivery times), preparing correspondence in advance of posting and so on.

4.8 Once time scales are known and final deadlines set, it is possible to produce control documents such as **job cards, route cards** and **action sheets**. Here is an example of an action sheet.

	Activity	*Days before*	*Date*	*Begun*	*Completed*
1	Request file	6	3.9		
2	Draft report	5	4.9		
3	Type report	3	6.9		
4	Approve report	1	8.9		
5	Signature	1	8.9		
6	Internal messenger	same day	9.9		

4.9 Longer-term schedules may be shown conveniently on charts, pegboards or year planners. These can be used to show lengths of time and the relationships between various tasks or timetabled events, as illustrated below.

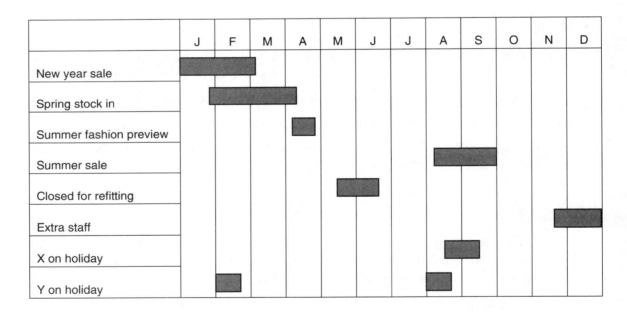

Gantt charts

4.10 Another well-known and widely used form of progressing chart is the Gantt chart. On the Gantt chart a division of space represents both an amount of time and an amount of work to be done in that time. Lines drawn horizontally through the space show the relation of the amount of work actually done in the time to the amount of work scheduled, on a proportional or percentage basis. It shows the relationship between time spent and work done, and what has happened and when. It indicates future action required, so that records charted in this way become dynamic.

4.11 EXAMPLE: A GANTT CHART

The information below about planned work and actual progress is set out in a Gantt chart, to show you what it looks like.

Day	Work Daily schedule	Work Cumulative Schedule	Work done in the day	Cumulative work done	Cumulative position as % of a day in front or % of a day behind
Mon	100	100	75	75	-25%
Tues	125	225	100	175	-40%
Wed	150	375	150	325	-33%
Thu	150	525	180	505	-13%
Fri	150	675	75	580	-63%

The Gantt chart shows the daily schedule, the work actually accomplished each day plus the cumulative schedule and the cumulative work done. The numbers represent hours of time.

(a) Daily schedule and work actually done each day

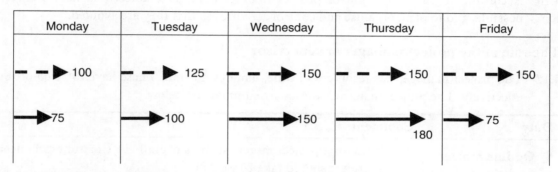

(b) Cumulative schedule and cumulative accomplishment

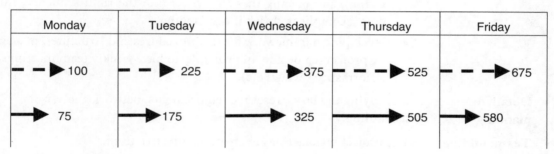

4.12 Another form of scheduling for larger projects is **network analysis**. This is a topic for other Units and it is of limited use for day to day work so we shall not explore it here.

Projects

4.13 The difference between project planning and other parts of planning is that a **project is not a repetitive activity**. That said, it encapsulates on a smaller scale many issues of planning and management, including the details of resource allocation.

4.14 **Characteristics of projects**

- Specific start and end points.
- Well-defined objectives.
- The project endeavour is unique.

- The project is usually limited in terms of funds and time available.
- A project cuts across many organisational and functional boundaries.

4.15 Examples of projects

Project	Comment
Building and construction	Building the Channel Tunnel was a project which ended when the tunnel was opened for normal service. The project involved raising finance, planning the digging, laying tracks and so on.
Manufacturing	The manufacture of an oil rig, involves co-ordinating a large number of separate activities. This will cease when the rig is finished.
Management	Development of an information system: the mounting of a trade exhibition.

4.16 According to Lock, 'the job of **project management** is to foresee as many dangers as possible, and to plan, organise and control activities so that they are avoided.'

The role of the project manager or supervisor

4.17 The project manager has resources of time, money and staff. These have to be co-ordinated effectively. The project manager's duties are summarised below.

Duty	Comment
• **Outline project planning**	• Developing project targets such as overall costs or timescale needed (eg project should take 20 weeks). • Dividing the project into activities (eg analysis, programming, testing), and placing these activities into the right sequence, this is often a complicated task if overlapping. • Developing a framework for the procedures and structures, manage the project (eg decide, in principle, to have weekly team meetings, performance reviews etc).
• **Detailed planning**	Identifying the tasks, resource requirements, network analysis for scheduling.
• **Teambuilding**	The project manager has to create an effective team.
• **Communication**	The project manager must let superiors know what is going on, and ensure that members of the project team are properly briefed.
• **Co-ordinating project activities**	Between the project team and users, and other external parties (eg suppliers of hardware and software).
• **Monitoring and control**	The project manager should estimate the causes for each departure from the standard, and take corrective measures.
• **Problem-resolution**	Even with the best planning, unforeseen problems may arise, and it falls upon the project manager to sort them out, or to delegate the responsibility for so doing to a subordinate.
• **Quality control**	This is a problematic issue, as there is often a short-sighted trade-off between quality and getting the project out on time.

5   MANAGING YOUR TIME

5.1   **Time is a resource** (you are being paid for it) and is something which you have to be able to **manage effectively**. Some people are better at this than others. If you are good at managing time, you will achieve four desirable results.

- Your boss will be happy as you will complete the tasks assigned to you efficiently and effectively

- You will work less overtime, as you will not be wasting time.

- You will avoid stress caused by poor time management.

- You will manage your staff better.

5.2   You cannot make more effective use of your time until you know how you currently spend your time. Do not rely on your memory at the end of the day! Keep a note not only of *how* you spent your time, but also on how effectively you think it was spent. If it was a meeting how valuable was it to you? (or to others?). How much is your work interrupted, by whom and why? Try and establish a true picture of where your time is actually going.

5.3   Produce a breakdown of the way you spend your day or working day.

(a)   The proportion of your time spent:

- In meetings?
- On the phone?
- Travelling? (to and from work/during work)
- Waiting?
- With customers?
- With subordinates?
- With superiors?
- With colleagues?
- Socialising at work?
- Doing routine administration?

(b)   What is the typical breakdown of your time between:

- Work   • Home   • You

(c)   What proportion of your time was spent in ways which were:

- Important to you?
- Important to others?
- Easily delegated to others?

5.4   Once you have completed a few days' you will be able to analyse how efficiently and effectively you spend your time.

5.5   You will also develop four useful abilities.

- To help others undertake a similar analysis

- To identify activities which should be reviewed as they are of little value to you or others

- To identify activities which can be delegated to others

- To identify areas where time is not being used effectively and could be better organised.

BPP PUBLISHING

Time management

5.6 Principles of good time management

- Goals
- Plans
- Lists
- Priorities
- Concentration
- Urgency

Goals

5.7 You might think that your goal at work is to supervise a section of an accounts department and to see that whatever tasks are required get done efficiently. This is fine as an overall description of what you do, but it is not *specific* enough to help you to do it. Nor is there any way of telling whether you have done it or not. As discussed in Chapter 1, to be useful, goals need to be SMART:

Characteristic	Comment
Specific **Attainable** **Realistic**	In work terms you could probably set specific goals by reference to your job description: 'prepare and despatch invoices for all goods sold'; 'issue monthly statements'; 'monitor slow paying customers' and so on.
Measurable **Time-bounded**	If you say 'My goal is to see that invoices are issued and despatched for all goods sold *on the day of sale*' you have a very clear and specific idea of what it is that you and your section have to achieve and whether you are achieving it or not. The same applies to personal goals. 'I'd like a promotion' is just a wish; 'I aim to be promoted to head of the payroll department by the end of next year' gives you something to aim at. How realistic and attainable is it?

Plans

5.8 You must make plans that set out in detail how you intend to achieve your goals: the timescale, the deadlines, the tasks involved, the people to see or write to, the resources required, how one plan fits in with (or conflicts with) another and so on.

5.9 EXAMPLE

Here is a sales ledger section supervisor's plan of how to prepare a list of bad and doubtful debtors for the purposes of the year-end accounts.

BAD AND DOUBTFUL DEBTORS

Action

(a)   Obtain aged debtors listing as at 31 March 1995

(b)   Identify all debts unpaid for over 60 days

(c)   Send out special payment requests to these debtors

(d)   Prepare list of amount of debts identified in (b)

(e)   Investigate all debts over £5,000 by reviewing correspondence files, telephoning the debtor, discussing with sales staff, obtaining third party information if possible

(f)   In the light of (e) prepare list distinguishing bad and doubtful debtors in format requested by auditors

(g)   Discuss with managers whether immediate legal action should be taken to recover any of the debts

(h)   Review position at 30 April in the light of cash received in the month. Amend bad and doubtful debtors lists as appropriate

---

Timescale

The work should be completed over the next three weeks

Deadline

The final list and backing documentation should be ready in time for the auditors' visit commencing on 5 May

---

Lists

5.10   You should work from a list of 'Things to do' all the time. If you don't do this already, try this approach once and you will be hooked. What's more your daily productivity will shoot up.

(a)   **Plan the whole of the coming week in advance**. It is best to do this when you are free from the pressures and distractions of actually being at work, because you are more likely to be able to view the whole picture at these times.

(b)   **Make a list every day before you start work**. Again, it is probably best to do this the night before, so long as you don't forget to take your list into work with you the next day.

(c)   **On the day itself refuse to do anything that is not on your list**. This does not mean that if something more urgent than anything you are currently doing comes up you can ignore it. It means that every new task that arises has to be added to your list.

(d)   **Every time you finish something on your list, cross it off**. This is the really satisfying part of making lists!

(e)   **At the end of the day take all the items that are still on the list and transfer them to your list for the next day.** Don't skip this part and just staple today's unfinished list to tomorrow's unstarted one. The physical act of writing tasks down on paper is an important part of the process. They will not be channelled through your mind if you just look at them.

5.11 **Do not rely on your memory.** You are not just creating a memory-jogger: the idea is that you should be able to see at a glance *all* the things you have to do so that you can get them into perspective.

Priorities

5.12 **Now you can set priorities on your list.** You do this by looking over the list and deciding which tasks are the most important - what is the most valuable use of your time at that very moment. The approach used in Section 3 may help you here.

Concentration: one thing at a time

5.13 Work on **one thing at a time until it is finished.**

5.14 If a task cannot be completely finished in one session, complete everything that it is in your power to complete at that time and use a **follow-up system** to make sure that it is not forgotten in the future. **Correspondence,** in particular, will involve varying periods of delay between question and answer, action and response.

5.15 Make sure that everything that you need is **available before you start work**. If something is not, put it on your **list**.

5.16 Before you start a task clear away everything from your desk that you do not need for that particular task.

(a) Once tidy working becomes a habit, it will take no time at all, because your desk will always be either clear or have on it only the things you are using at that precise moment.

(b) One of the best ways of helping yourself to concentrate and handle things one at a time is to remove less important distractions.

5.17 In accounts work it is not always easy to have a tidy desk. It is not untypical to be working with voluminous A3-sized computer print-out folders, with one for every day of the week. The office furniture in most offices is not really designed for this. This does not, however, alter the basic principle of single handling and tidy working. (And anyway, there may be a solution: would it be possible to print out reports in a smaller font size or on thinner paper to make physical handling easier?)

Urgency: do it now!

5.18 Do not put off large, difficult or unpleasant tasks simply because they are large, difficult or unpleasant. If you put it off, today's routine will be tomorrow's emergency: worse, *today's* **emergency will be even more of an emergency tomorrow**. Do it now!

5.19 Think for a moment about how you behave when you know something is very urgent. If you oversleep, you leap out of bed the moment you wake up. If you suddenly find out that a report has to go out last post today rather than tomorrow afternoon, then you get on with it at once. You should develop the ability to treat everything that you have to do in this way.

How to do it

5.20 **Hints and tips**

(a) **Plan each day**

(b) **Produce a longer-term plan.** A longer term plan can also help you cope with more complicated jobs, by breaking them down into a number of stages. In addition long-term planning helps you anticipate busy periods so that backlogs of routine work are cleared during quieter times.

(c) Always attempt to assess whether or not your time could be used more economically, perhaps by delegation, or re-prioritising.

(d) **The ACIB method of in-tray management.** When a piece of paper comes into your in-tray, you should not simply look at it and put it back! This would mean your handling it more than once. Ideally, you should take one of the following approaches.

Act on the item immediately; *or*

Co-opt someone else to act on it - ie delegate; *or*

Input a time to your diary, when you will deal with it; *or*

Bin it; if you're sure it is worthless.

(e) The **half open door.** Although having an 'open door' is a common policy, do not be available to all comers at all times.

- Be **unavailable.** Use call-diverting facilities on your telephone (and/or ask your secretary, if you have one).

- Set up '**surgery hours**' during which - and *only* during which - your door is open to visitors

- Determining which **people** are urgent or important

- Arranging **regular meetings** with people you have to deal with frequently

- Staying in **control of meetings**, by asking people to come back later or saying that you can spare them X minutes (and no longer)

- **Do not allow people to by-pass the hierarchy.** Most people should deal with your staff first of all

(f) **Stay in control of the telephone.** The telephone can be a major barrier to good time management, by being a source of constant interruption and a means of communication which, through poor technique, is used inefficiently.

(g) **Appointments with yourself.** If you need to spend time alone, making plans, reviewing progress - or indeed making sure that you get 'personal' time at work or at home for rest and relaxation - it is a good idea to treat this as if it were a meeting. Make a time for it in your diary, and stick to it: take it seriously, and do not let other activities encroach on it.

(h) **Work to schedules and use checklists.**

(i) **Organise work in batches,** with relevant files to hand to save time spent in turning from one job to another.

(j) Maintain a **list of 'five-minute' jobs** which can be completed whilst waiting for a meeting or telephone call.

(k) **Take advantage of work patterns,** for instance by telephoning people when they are likely to be available.

(l) **Follow up tasks - see them through.**

BPP PUBLISHING

Activity 6.6

About nine months ago, Andrew Barret was appointed an assistant manager in a large finance department where you are also an assistant manager. Recently he approached you for some guidance because he feels he is not performing as well as he should.

He says that his boss has criticised him because his work is not of sufficiently high quality and his wife criticises him because of the amount of work which he takes home. He is, however, happy with the relationships he has built up with the team who work for him.

You have done some preliminary investigation which reveals that:

(a) Andrew apparently delegates well and there is little scope for the delegation of further aspects of his job;

(b) he has built up his good relationship with his team by encouraging them to bring him their work problems as they arise. He is often willing to devote considerable time to the solutions of these problems;

(c) his job description states only that he is required 'to manage the work and people of his section';

(d) his boss sets him performance standards which concentrate on the qualitative aspects of tasks. In these standards his boss asks Andrew to produce 'excellent' work.

What suggestions would you make to Andrew to help him to improve his time management and his job performance? Give reasons for your suggestions.

Key learning points

- **Delegation** is an important management skill and the principles must be clearly understood. Young managers are often reluctant to accept this.

- **Communication** is essential to get a job done but the process is often faulty. Managers and supervisors should be aware of the possible pitfalls and follow the rules of good communication.

- **Work planning** involves establishing priorities, scheduling tasks and establishing checks and controls to ensure that the work gets done.

- There are a variety of **scheduling methods**, ranging from simple lists to full-scale network analysis.

- **Time management** has six principles: goals, plans, lists, priorities, concentration and urgency.

Quick quiz

1   Briefly describe the matters to be taken into account when considering work allocation.

2   Why must supervisors delegate?

3   List the four stages of the process of delegation.

4   What are the principles of delegation?

5   List five matters that should be considered when deciding whether or not to delegate a piece of work.

6   What are the 'ten commandments' of good communication?

7   What are the basic steps in work planning?

8   When should a piece of work be regarded as 'high priority'?

9   Distinguish between scheduled and unscheduled peaks, giving examples.

10   What are the likely planning periods for a section supervisor in an accounts department?

11   Why is it important to meet deadlines?

12   What is shown on a Gantt chart?

13   Briefly explain some principles of good time management.

Answers to quick quiz

1   The problems of work allocation include the following.

   (i)   Menial tasks such as filing and document copying may not justify the attention of a 'dedicated' employee, but they still need to be done.

   (ii)   If duties need to be redistributed during peak periods, are staff sufficiently flexible to be able to do the required tasks?

   (iii)   Status and staff attitudes must be considered.

   (iv)   Planning must recognise that junior employees may desire and expect challenges and greater responsibility, and may leave if bored and frustrated.

   (v)   Individual abilities and temperaments differ: some staff like routine work, for example, but crack under pressure, and vice versa. Work should be allocated to the best person for the job, but this may not be immediately obvious.

2   Supervisors must delegate some authority because there are physical and mental limitations to the work load of any individual; because the supervisor needs to be free to concentrate on the more important aspects of the work (such as planning), which only he or she is competent (and paid) to do; and because the larger and more complex an organisation is the greater the need for specialisation.

3   The four stages of delegating to an assistant are as follows.

   (i)   The expected performance levels of the assistant should be clearly specified and fully understood and accepted by the assistant.

   (ii)   Tasks should be assigned to the assistant, and the assistant should agree to do them.

   (iii)   Resources should be allocated to the assistant to enable him or her to carry out the delegated tasks at the expected level of performance, and authority should be delegated to enable the assistant to do this job.

   (iv)   The assistant should be made *responsible* for results obtained. However, ultimate *accountability* for the task remains with the supervisor: if it is not well done it is at least partly the fault of poor delegation, and it is still the supervisor's responsibility to get it re-done.

4   Principles of delegation

   (i)   There should be a proper balance: a manager who is not held accountable for any of his authority or power may well exercise his authority in a capricious way; a manager who is held accountable for aspects of performance which he has no power or authority to control is in an impossible position.

   (ii)   The assistant should not have to refer decisions back up to the supervisor for ratification provided that they are within the assistant's scope of delegated authority.

   (iii)   There must be no doubts about the boundaries of authority because where doubts exist, decision making will be weak, confused and possibly contradictory.

   (iv)   If the functions, activities and authority of each department and the ways in which departments are meant to inter-act and co-operate are clear, individuals with authority in each department will more easily be able to contribute to the achievement of the organisation's goals.

5   When considering instances in which he or she should or should not delegate, the supervisor will have to consider the following issues.

   (i)   Whether the *acceptance* of staff is required for morale, relationships, ease of implementation of the decision and so on. They will accept something more readily if they have a large say in how it is done.

   (ii)   Whether the *quality* of the decision is more important than its acceptance. Many technical financial decisions may be of this type, and should be retained by the supervisor if he or she alone has the knowledge and experience to make them.

   (iii)   Whether, on the other hand, the expertise or experience of *assistants* will enhance the quality of the decision. If a manager is required to perform a task which is not within his or her own specialised knowledge or experience, he or she should delegate to the appropriate person.

(iv)   Whether trust can be placed in the competence and reliability of the assistants. The manager should not delegate if there are *genuine* grounds for lack of confidence in the team. In this case, there are other problems to solve first.

(v)   Whether the decision requires tact and confidentiality (for example disciplinary action), or, on the other hand, maximum exposure and assimilation by employees.

6   The 'ten commandments' are as follows.

(i)   Clarify ideas before attempting to communicate.

(ii)   Examine the purpose of communication (which may affect the way in which the message should be conveyed.

(iii)   Understand the physical and human environment when communicating. For example, whether the message is conveyed orally or in writing, or publicly or in private and so on.

(iv)   In planning communication, consult with others to obtain their support as well as the facts.

(v)   Consider the content and the overtones of the message. The content may be distorted by non-verbal factors.

(vi)   Whenever possible, communicate something that helps, or is valued by, the receiver. Seek a favourable reaction.

(vii)   Communication, to be effective, requires follow-up.

(viii)   Communicate messages that are of short-run and long-run importance.

(ix)   Actions must be congruent with communications. Staff will not act in accordance with communications unless they see that their supervisor is doing so himself.

(x)   Be a good listener. Understanding other people's viewpoints is an important element in communicating effectively.

7   Basic steps in work planning include:

(i)   the establishment of priorities;

(ii)   scheduling or timetabling tasks, and allocating them to different individuals within appropriate time scales;

(iii)   establishing checks and controls to ensure that priority deadlines are being met and routine tasks are achieving their objectives;

(iv)   setting up contingency plans for unscheduled events.

8   A piece of work will be 'high priority' in the following circumstances.

(i)   If it has to be completed by a certain time (a 'deadline'). The closer the deadline, the more urgent the work will be.

(ii)   If other tasks depend on it.

(iii)   If other people depend on it.

(iv)   If it is important, considering the relative consequences, for example the correction of an error in a large customer order as opposed to processing a smaller order.

9   A 'peak' is a time when an organisation is at its busiest, for example for retailers at Christmas. A *scheduled* peak is one that can be anticipated with certainty so that, say, extra staff can be employed or work re-scheduled for these times. Unscheduled peaks arise when unexpected events, which cannot be planned for, occur. Examples may include equipment breakdown, staff illness, or environmental factors (suppliers going into insolvency, unanticipated action by competitors).

10   An accounts department section supervisor's planning periods are likely to be as follows.

(i)   The organisation's financial year.

(ii)   The calendar year, if it is not the same as the organisation's financial year.

(iii)   The next 'operating cycle' for the section. For example a costing section may be dependent upon, say, three-day production cycles, because information becomes available for processing at the end of each (three-day) production run.

(iv)   The next week and the next day, for personal and sectional time management purposes.

11   Deadlines are important because failure to meet them has a 'knock-on' effect on other parts of the organisation, and on other tasks within an individual's duties. If you are late with one task (updating the nominal ledger), you will be late or rushed with the one depending on it (preparing a trial balance).

12   A Gantt chart is a form of progress chart. On a Gantt chart a division of space represents both an amount of *time* and an amount of *work* to be done in that time. Lines drawn horizontally through the space show the relation of the amount of work actually *done* in the time to the amount of work *scheduled.* It therefore indicates whether future action is required to catch up with the schedule.

13   (a)   Goals help to focus the mind on what it is that supposed to be achieved. If a person has no idea what it is he is supposed to accomplish, or only a vague idea, all the time in the world will not be long enough to get it done. To be useful, goals need to be *specific* ('do a bank reconciliation', not 'implement controls over the management of pecuniary resources'), and *measurable,* so that the person with the goal can see how far he has got in achieving it.

        (b)   Plans should be made that set out in detail how goals are to be achieved: the timescale, the deadlines, the tasks involved, the people to see or write to, the resources required, how one plan fits in with (or conflicts with) another and so on.

        (c)   A list of 'things to do' should be compiled daily, and worked from and adhered to all the time.

        (d)   The items on the list should be allocated priorities as appropriate and the tasks done in that order.

        (e)   One thing at a time should be worked on until it is finished (or cannot be progressed any further for reasons outside your control).

        (f)   Tasks should be tackled with a sense of urgency.

Answers to activities

Answer 6.1

The underlying problem is that responsibility (for the management of accounts) has been delegated without authority (to hire a temp and to obtain information from the payroll dept).

Answer 6.2

The problem appears to be that the new supervisor is taking too much of the department's work on to herself. While she is overworked, her subordinates are apparently not being stretched and as a result motivation and morale are poor. The supervisor herself is unhappy with the position and there is a danger that declining job satisfaction will lead to inefficiencies and eventually staff resignations.

There could be a number of causes contributing to the problem.

(a)   The supervisor may have been badly selected; she may not have the ability required for a supervisory job.

(b)   Alternatively she may just be unaware of what is involved in a supervisor's role. She may not have realised that much of the task consists of managing subordinates; she is not required to shoulder all the detailed technical work herself.

(c)   There may be personality problems involved. The supervisor regards her clerks as incompetent and this attitude may arise simply from an inability to get on with them socially. (Another possibility is that her staff actually are incompetent.)

(d)   The supervisor does much of the department's work herself. This may be because she does not understand the kind of tasks which can be delegated and the way in which delegation of authority can improve the motivation and job satisfaction of subordinates.

As manager you have already gone some way towards identifying the actual causes of the problem. You have spoken to some of the subordinates concerned and also to the supervisor. You could supplement this by a review of personnel records to discover how her career has progressed and what training she has received (if any) in the duties of a supervisor. You may then be in a position to determine which of the possible causes of the problems are operating in this case.

Answer 6.3

(a)   The following points might be raised by members of other departments.

    (i)   'Accounting reports are often produced too late for us to use for decision-making. What is the point in telling us what has gone wrong when it is too late for us to put it right?'

    (ii)   'We often get a lot of accounting information which is of no use to us. We cannot be expected to spend a lot of time sorting through lengthy reports to find what is relevant to our department.'

    (iii)   'The information which concerns my work is all sent to my senior manager, who then passes it on to me. It is really of no use to my senior manager, so why send it to him?'

    (iv)   'I get daily computer reports on labour variances, which I simply put in the bin. What I need is weekly and monthly summaries.'

    (v)   'Accounting information is often compiled without any explanation or commentary.'

    (vi)   'I do not understand a lot of the terms used in reports which I receive. For example, I do not know what "DCF return" means, and it has never been explained to me.'

    (vii)   'The accounts department sends out information late in July and August. They say that it is because of staff holidays.'

    (viii) 'The accountants seem to put their own interpretation on data, even when they do not have the authority to do so.'

    (ix)   'It is very difficult to make anything of cost information, because the cost categories keep changing.'

(b)   A number of areas may be identified in which the accounting departments may consider taking action in response to the points raised by other departments. First of all, it is useful to identify the qualities of good accounting information, which may be summarised as follows. Accounting information should be:

    (i)   relevant to its recipients;

    (ii)   understandable by the recipients;

    (iii)   reliably accurate;

    (iv)   complete for its particular purpose;

    (v)   objectively presented;

    (vi)   comparable with related information (eg relating to other periods or sections, as appropriate);

    (vii)   on time.

The possible points raised by other departments identified in (a) above can each be associated with one or more of the above qualities of good information. The following areas may be addressed to improve the quality of accounting information.

    (i)   *Staff training*. Training of accounting staff providing information, whether oral or written, could be extended to include communication skills training specifically.

    (ii)   *Morale of accounting staff*. If accounting staff feel that they are always on the receiving end of criticism, morale may have been adversely affected, and staff may lack the motivation to try to make improvements. This is really a matter to be considered by accounts department management.

    (iii)   *Briefing of recipients*. Recipients of accounting information should be fully briefed on the interpretation and use of the information. Briefing may be in written form - eg manuals, explanatory notes - or through seminars and meetings.

    (iv)   *Presentation*. Presentation of information may be an area for improvement, ideally following research of the views of information users. Presentation may be improved by technical innovations, such as the use of colour in reports.

    (v)   *Quality control*. Information should be subject to checking and review by appropriately qualified staff before being released. However, it should be borne in mind that it may be better to be 'about right' and on time than precisely right too late.

    (vi)   *Timeliness of reporting*. As implied in the above point about quality control, information becomes of less value the later it is delivered. The timeliness of reporting may be investigated by monitoring the publication dates of reports over a test period.

(vii)   *User feedback.* It may be useful to provide on an on-going basis channels of communication by means of which information users can feed back comments on their needs to information providers.

Answer 6.4

Here are some suggestions.

(a)   What are the deadlines for jobs A to D?

(b)   Are any of them late already?

(c)   Do any of them depend on the office being tidy or filing being done? This should be done before the job(s) in question if so.

(d)   Does Usha need help or training before any of the jobs can be tackled?

(e)   Is she waiting for somebody else to finish their work before she can start work on certain jobs?

(f)   Is there a queue for resources that Usha will need, such as computer time or the assistance of more junior staff?

(g)   What are the consequences of jobs not being finished? They could include lost income, disgruntled customers and holding up other people's work.

Answer 6.6

Andrew's informal advisor might make the following suggestions.

(a)   Andrew obviously has too much work - since he has to take so much home - despite his ability and willingness to delegate effectively. Something has to go. The first step for Andrew would be to keep a detailed time diary, which might highlight areas on which he is spending sizeable portions of time, or the frequency of interruptions during the day for various reasons. Superfluous activity and drains on Andrew's time might then be identified.

(b)   Andrew devotes 'considerable time' to the solution of his team's work problems and deals with them 'as they arise'. Although he is justifiably satisfied that his relationship with his team is good, and although it seems he has achieved that through his 'ever-open door' policy, it is one aspect of his job that should be looked at. It may be possible for him to appoint (and perhaps coach if necessary) a member of the team to be supervisor, so that at least the routine work problems can be dealt with by someone else. Alternatively, he could schedule 'surgery hours': only problems of an urgent nature would be brought to him 'as they arise'. He could still maintain good relationships by making sure that he talks to his team where opportunities do arise to do so and so on.

(c)   Andrew's own work is making sizeable inroads on his family life. This may be a question of poor time management or inefficient performance by Andrew, in which case he needs guidance on the following.

(i)   *Job management.* Andrew must assess his job and his own capabilities to perform it. Ideally, this would be done as part of a formal appraisal by Andrew's boss.

(ii)   *Time management.* Andrew should be encouraged to identify objectives and the key tasks that are most relevant to achieving them, and to weed out desirable but unnecessary drains on his time. He should be advised to prioritise and schedule his tasks, and to stick to a schedule as far as possible.

(d)   Another reason for Andrew spending too long on his work may, however, be that too much is expected from him. The fact that he is seeking informal guidance because he 'feels he is not performing as well as he should' indicates that he has not sat down formally with his boss to appraise his performance and participate in formulating his targets and standards.

The most important suggestion and the most fraught with potential difficulties, is that Andrew should request an interview with his boss. He should stress the following.

(i)   The volume of work is large. (If Andrew can show his boss the measures he has taken to improve his time management - as suggested above - he will be in a stronger position.) It may be that the boss is delegating too much work to Andrew, or that he demands 'excellence' because he doesn't realise the volume is so great.

(ii)   The performance standards of 'excellence' are unrealistic in this context. They seem to have been set by the boss without Andrew's participation, and they are qualitative rather than

BPP PUBLISHING

quantitative: 'excellence' has obviously conjured up a target of perfection in Andrew's conscientious mind. What is required is a set of specific, quantifiable and realistic objectives, as a basis for Andrew's efforts and as a standard against which his performance can be more objectively measured.

Part B
Identifying opportunities to improve the effectiveness of an accounting system

Chapter 7 Control

Chapter topic list

1 Control in the organisation

2 Types of control

3 Improving control in your section

4 Internal controls and internal checks

5 Internal audit and internal control

Learning objectives

On completion of this chapter you will be able to:

	Performance criteria	Range Statement
• identify problems or queries concerning work activity	10.1.7	1
• ensure quality standards are being met	10.1.5	1
• make recommendations supported by a clear rationale	10.2.4	1
• identify weaknesses and potential improvements	10.2.1	1

BPP PUBLISHING

1 CONTROL IN THE ORGANISATION

KEY TERMS

The action, 'to **control**', means to check or to regulate, or to give directions, so as to ensure that action is taken to achieve a goal or target, or to conform to expectations.

The thing, '**a control**', describes a device or technique for putting control into practice. This is what we are principally concerned here.

1.1 **Control** is a management function which ensures that plans are followed and objectives are achieved. We looked briefly at control in Chapter 5. In this section, we are going to describe **formalised systems** of control, although the principles also apply to more informal and 'one-off' control measures - for example, a supervisor telling off a staff member who is not performing as he should.

Managers and supervisors as controllers

1.2 The management function of **control** comprises the measurement of results and correction of activities. This is to ensure two things.

- The goals of the organisation, or planning targets, are achieved
- To point out departures from plans to rectify them

In short, control is making sure that the right things get done.

1.3 **Plans and standards**

Plans state what should be done. Standards and targets specify a desired level of performance. Here are some examples.

- **Manufacturing standards** such as units of raw material per unit produced

- **Cost standards.** These convert physical standards into a money measurement by the application of standard prices. For example, the standard labour cost of making product X might be 4 hours at £5 per hour = £20

- **Capital standards.** These establish some form of standard for capital invested (eg the ratio of current assets to current liabilities) or a desired share price

- **Revenue targets.** These measure expected performance in terms of revenue earned (such as turnover per square metre of shelf space in a supermarket)

- **Deadlines for programme completion.** Performance might be measured in terms of actual completion dates for parts of a project compared against a budgeted programme duration

- The **achievement of stated goals** (eg meeting profit objective)

- **Intangible standards.** Intangible standards might relate to employee motivation, quality of service, customer goodwill, corporate image, product image etc. It is possible to measure some of these by attitude surveys, market research and so on

Stages in the control cycle

1.4 Control as we have seen is dependent upon the issue, receipt and processing of **information**. The basic control process or control cycle in management has six steps.

Step 1. **Making** a plan: deciding what to do and identifying the desired results. Without plans there can be no control.

Step 2. **Recording** the plan formally or informally, in writing or by other means, statistically or descriptively. The plan should incorporate standards of efficiency or targets of performance.

Step 3. **Carrying out** the plan, or having it carried out by subordinates recording what happens and measuring actual results achieved.

Step 4. **Obtaining** actual results and comparing them with the plan. This is sometimes referred to as **feedback**.

Step 5. **Evaluating** the comparison, and deciding whether further action is necessary the ensure the plan is achieved.

Step 6. Where **corrective action** is necessary, this should be implemented.

The control system

1.5

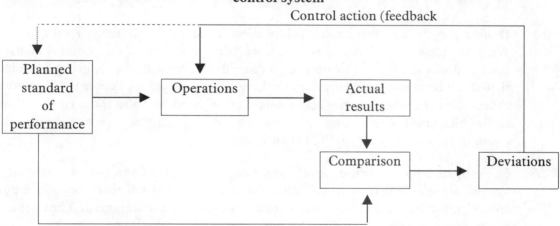

Closed loop feedback control system

Under this system the results of operations are compared with the standard of performance set in the plan. Deviations from plan are measured and form a basis for control action which aims to bring operations back into line with the plan. It may be necessary to change the plan if it proves over- or under-ambitious.

'Feedback' is a term which has been borrowed from engineering and simply means control action, in this context.

The control loop is called a **closed** loop because **no external input from the environment is required**. Control is in terms of what was planned and what has been achieved.

KEY TERM

Feedback occurs when the results (outputs) of a system are used to control it, by adjusting the input or behaviour of the system.

Businesses use feedback information to control their performance.

1.6 Feedback is sometimes described in two ways.

(a) **Negative feedback** indicates that results or activities must be brought back on course, as they are deviating from the plan.

(b) **Positive feedback** results in control action continuing the current course. You would normally assume that positive feedback means that results are going according to plan and that no corrective action is necessary: but it is best to be sure that the control system itself is not picking up the wrong information.

1.7 It may be the case, especially with uncontrollable factors, that tinkering with inputs and processes may not be enough. The plan itself may have to change and so a comparison of actual results against the existing plan might be invalid.

KEY TERMS

- **Single loop feedback** results in the system's behaviour being altered to meet the plan.

- **Double loop feedback** can result in changes to the plan itself.

1.8 **Double loop feedback** is control information transmitted to a higher level in the system. Whereas single loop feedback is concerned with 'task control' (the control loop), higher level feedback is concerned with overall control. The term 'double loop' feedback indicates that the information is reported to indicate both divergences between the observed and expected results where control action might be required, and also the need for adjustments to the plan itself. Controlling operations is usually a routine task but altering the plan usually requires reference to a higher authority.

1.9 In an **open loop system**, control is exercised regardless of the output produced by the system. Since information from **within** the organisation is **not** used for control purposes, control must be exercised by **input from the external environment**. The output of the system is not coupled to the input for measurement.

1.10 A business organisation uses feedback for control, and therefore has a closed loop control system. However, external and environmental influences are not ignored. Organisations thus use a combination of closed and **open loop** control.

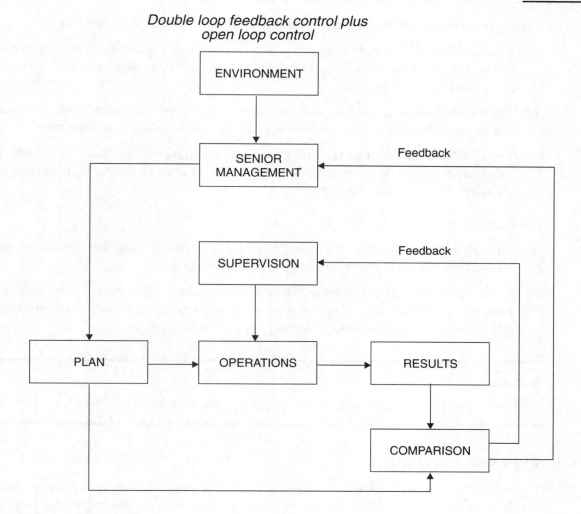

Double loop feedback control plus
open loop control

1.11 EXAMPLE

We now relate the control system to a practical example, such as **monthly budgetary control variance reports.**

(a) Standard costs and a master budget are prepared for the year. Management organises the resources of the business (inputs) so as to achieve the budget targets.

(b) At the end of each month, actual results (output, sales, costs, revenues etc) are reported back to management. The reports are the measured output of the control system, and the process of sending them to the managers responsible provides the feedback loop.

(c) Managers compare actual results against the plan and where necessary, take corrective action to adjust the workings of the system, probably by amending the inputs to the system.

1.12 Both negative and positive feedback information may result from two factors.

(a) **Controllable factors**, such as high labour turnover resulting from bad management. This should lead to control action.

(b) **Uncontrollable factors**, such as changes in the weather affecting production (eg of agricultural crops), a sudden rise in raw material prices. By definition, no control action is possible. It may be necessary for higher management to amend the organisations plans.

1.13 A **budgetary control system** may incorporate double loop feedback and open loop control.

   (a) **Unmeasured output** might include the morale and motivation of staff, the number of labour hours wasted as idle time or the volume of complaints received about a particular product or service.

   (b) The **master budget** might have to be changed if it is realised that actual sales volumes will be radically different from those budgeted (eg as a result of a new competitor).

   (c) There will be **environmental influences** (eg government legislation about safety standards) affecting both inputs to the system and also how the budget is established or amended. This is **open loop control**.

1.14 **Feedforward control**

   (a) **Control delay.** A timelag may occur between the actual results and the corrective action. However these results might have been anticipated.

   (b) **Feedforward control** uses **anticipated** or forecast results, and compares them with the plan. **Corrective action** is thus taken **in advance**, before it is too late to do anything effective. Control is exercised before the results, rather than after.

Activity 7.1

What factors might you have to consider when designing a control system?

---

2 TYPES OF CONTROL

2.1 The control models outlined in Section 1 above are ideal for controlling performance which can be measured easily. However, many control issues are not so **easily** reduced to quantitative data, even though control theory can still be applied.

2.2 EXAMPLE

In **service industries** that the cost of attracting a new customer far exceeds the cost of keeping existing customers satisfied: repeat business, rather than new business, is the origin of success. The factors that lead to repeat business are often intangible, such as **staff courtesy**. How do you control these factors?

   (a) Regular staff appraisal is an example, as is a simple reprimand for rudeness, but that only occurs **after** the event.

   (b) You can possibly apply a feedforward control system. Although you cannot **predict** when a member of staff is going to be rude, you can **train** staff in stress management, so they can control their own behaviour.

A wider concept of control is therefore needed to include staff controlling their own performance, to some extent.

2.3 There are three main **design choices** in the structure of a management control system.

   • The degree of **centralisation or decentralisation** of decision-making.

   • The degree of **formality or informality** in control (in other words, the operation of rules and procedures as opposed to managerial discretion).

   • The **degree of personal supervision** that managers exercise over subordinates.

Control strategies

2.4 These design choices can be implemented in four **control strategies**.

(a) **Personal centralised control**

- Centralised decision-making
- Personal leadership; direct supervision
- Often a feature of small owner-managed companies

(b) **Bureaucratic control**

- Based on rules and procedures, budgets and budgetary control

- Features as much programmed decision-taking as possible. The amount of individual discretion is limited. For example, customers over thirty days late in payment are **always** sent a letter

- Control is based on the principles of scientific management (see Chapter 5) - specialisation of work, simplification of work methods, and standardisation of procedures

(c) **Output control**

Systems of **responsibility accounting** are operated so that authority over operations and responsibility for output are delegated to operational managers. In other words **control is exercised over results.**

(d) **Cultural control**

Management promote a culture under which all employees develop a strong personal identification with the goals of the organisation and take responsibility for their own performance. This is sometimes suggested as the only way in which very large, global organisations can be controlled.

Activity 7.2

Sally Keene works for a large department store, as a manager.

(a) At the beginning of each year she is given a yearly plan, subdivided into twelve months. This is based on the previous year's performance and some allowance is made for anticipated economic conditions. Every three months she sends her views as to the next quarter to senior management, who give her a new plan in the light of changing conditions.

(b) She monitors sales revenue per square foot, and sales per employee. Employees who do not meet the necessary sales targets are at first counselled and then if performance does not improve they are dismissed. Sally is not unreasonable. She sets what she believes are realistic targets.

(c) She believes there is a good team spirit in the sales force, however, and that employees, whose commission is partly based on the sales revenue earned by the store as a **whole**, discourage slackers in their ranks.

What kind of control, control system or control information can you identify in the three cases above?

Control over employee behaviour

2.5 Two types of control strategies are related to employees.

- **Behaviour control** deals with the behaviour of individual employees. In other words, control is exercised over the **procedures,** to ensure they are correctly executed.

- **Output control** is where management attention is focused on **results,** more than the way these results were achieved.

2.6 EXAMPLE

An example of behaviour control is that exercised by audit managers over their juniors. Audit procedures have to be carried out **in the right way** for the information to be of any use. This is because audit procedures are investigative: and to ensure that the investigations are done in the **right** way, so that the information is reliable for the audit manager or partner to come to an opinion, control must be exercised over how the work is done. The 'output' of the audit (whether or not to qualify the accounts) comes at the end: junior staff are not assessed as to whether they reach favourable opinions or not.

3 IMPROVING CONTROL IN YOUR SECTION

Good control systems

3.1 **Features of a good control system** (six As).

- **Acceptable** to the organisation's members. Achieving the organisation's goals depends on the efforts of the members. The control system's methods must therefore be acceptable to them.

- **Appropriate.** Controls should be tailored to the capabilities and personalities of individual managers.

- **Accessible.** Controls should not be too sophisticated, using techniques of measurement and analysis which only a statistical or accounting expert might understand.

- **Action oriented.** A control system must prompt management into taking corrective action when required.

- **Adaptable.** Controls should continue to be workable even when events show that original plans are un-achievable (and should therefore be changed) perhaps due to unforeseen circumstances which arise. In other words, controls must be flexible and adaptable to new circumstances.

- **Affordable.** Controls should be economical and worth their cost in terms of the benefits obtained. Control will probably be economical if it is tailored to the critical control points of the organisation's work, the size of the organisation and areas where performance has a significant impact.

Improving your section's control system

DEVOLVED ASSESSMENT ALERT

This may be one of the key areas where you can suggest *improvements* in your accounting section - particularly the *control information* available to it and produced by it.

3.2 Here are some suggestions for improving control information.

3.3 **Qualities of good information**

- **Accuracy.** Inaccurate control information will either misdirect the people that need the information and make them overlook matters requiring control action, or else it will make them take incorrect and inappropriate control decisions.

- **Timeliness,** so as to avoid control delay and encourage prompt control action. Information for control should therefore ideally be reported at the earliest opportunity.

- **Clarity,** so that the person receiving a control report will understand what the report is telling him.

- **Comprehensiveness**. Unless there is a complete picture of events, the inadequate and insufficient information might be used to make an inappropriate control decision.

- **Cost effectiveness**. However, resources should not be wasted on collecting information which is of little use.

3.4 Relevant information

(a) **Information should have a purpose,** and it should **be relevant to its purpose**. For example, if you are the supervisor of department A, you should receive control information about the performance of department A only.

(b) There should be a **hierarchy of control reports,** so that each manager in the organisation is made responsible for the activities over which he has authority. The information required by a divisional manager will differ enormously from the information for a supervisor and this will differ again from the information needed by junior staff.

3.5 **Objective information**. Subjective measurements (for instance on the morale of staff, or the goodwill of customers) might be disbelieved by the manager or supervisor receiving the report, so that he will take no control action, or at best, make only half-hearted efforts at control.

3.6 **Draw attention to critical success factors**. These are points about performance that require special attention because they are judged **critical to the success of operations**.

DEVOLVED ASSESSMENT ALERT

Control is very relevant to the issue of fraud, discussed in Chapters 11 and 12. You might identify two types of failures in how control systems work.

(a)   The control system and control procedures are badly designed.
(b)   The control system is largely over-ridden or ignored.

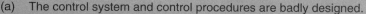

Activity 7.3

U Ltd carries out its business in an industry where it is customary to settle invoices after 30 days. It is one of the objectives of the company to minimise outstanding debtors. To achieve this, the credit control department has been set a target that 'no more than 25% of accounts receivable should be outstanding for more than 30 days'. Each individual credit clerk has the same target. The credit clerks' pay is performance-related.

Andrew, one of the credit clerks, has worked very enthusiastically persuading customers that prompt payment will enable U Ltd to provide an even better service. As a result, many of the accounts for which he is responsible have paid promptly.

Just before the end of this accounting period, the accounts in Andrew's section of the sales ledger were outstanding in the sum of £100,000, of which £25,000 exceeded the 30-day limit. He then received notification of further cheques of £20,000 from customers paying within the normal payment period. This meant that only £80,000 was outstanding, making the percentage overdue £25,000/£80,000 = 31.25%, ie well outside the target.

To avoid missing his own target and embarrassing the department, Andrew decided not to record the cheques for £20,000 for a few days, until the next accounting period. No one would know because the mail was so irregular, and the cash book and banking systems functioned independently of the credit control department. He would then have a good start towards his target for the next period.

(a)   Discuss the basis on which the targets are set for the credit control department, with particular reference to Andrew's behaviour.

(b) how else could the performance of the credit control department be measured?

4 INTERNAL CONTROLS AND INTERNAL CHECKS

Internal control systems and internal controls

> **KEY TERM**
>
> An **internal control system** is 'the whole system of controls, financial and otherwise, established by the management in order to carry on the business of the enterprise in an orderly and efficient manner, ensure adherence to management policies, safeguard the assets and secure as far as possible the completeness and accuracy of the records. The individual components of an internal control system are known as controls or internal controls'. (Auditing guideline: *Internal controls*).

4.1 This definition of **internal control** should draw your attention to several matters which you should keep clear in your mind.

   (a) **Internal control** refers to **control by management** - that is, controls applied from within the organisation itself.

   (b) A system of internal control **extends beyond matters that relate to accounting** and the work of the finance and accounting department of an organisation. It embraces all types of controls implemented by management - such as controls over late attendance by employees and control over operator efficiency levels.

Types of internal control

4.2 **Types of internal controls**

   (a) **Administrative controls.** These consist of the plan of organisation and all methods and procedures that are concerned mainly with operational efficiency and adherence to management policies. These controls will emphasise statistical analysis, time and motion study, performance reports, quality control, employee training programmes and so on.

   (b) **Accounting controls**. These consist of all **methods** and **procedures** that are concerned with the safeguarding of assets and the reliability of financial records. Such controls will include systems of authorisation and approval, separation of duties concerned with asset custody, physical controls over assets and internal auditing.

> **DEVOLVED ASSESSMENT ALERT**
>
> Much of your report may concern accounting controls, but administrative controls are just as important.

4.3 A list of the range of internal controls which may exist in an organisation is given in the appendix to the Auditing Guideline *Internal controls*.

KEY TERM

There are eight types of control listed. One way of remembering them is to use the mnemonic **SPAM SOAP**.

Segregation of duties

Physical

Authorisation and approval

Management

Supervision

Organisation

Arithmetical and accounting

Personnel

Segregation of duties

4.4 Clear **job descriptions** should segregate **execution** from **control** tasks. One of the prime means of control is the separation of those responsibilities or duties which would, if combined, **enable one individual to record and process a complete transaction**.

Segregation of duties reduces the risk of intentional manipulation or error and increases the element of checking. Some functions should be separated whenever possible.

- Authorisation
- Execution
- Custody
- Recording
- Systems development and daily operations.

4.5 EXAMPLE

A classic example of segregation of duties, which both internal and external auditors look for, concerns the receipt, **recording and banking of cash**. It is not a good idea for the person who **opens the post** to be the person responsible for **recording that the cash has arrived**. It is even poorer practice for that person to be responsible for **taking the cash to the bank**. If these duties are not segregated, there is always the *chance* that the person will simply pocket the cash, and nobody would be any the wiser. More about this when we cover fraud.

Physical controls

4.6 **Procedures and security measures** are needed to ensure that access to **assets** is limited to authorised personnel. Such controls include locks, safes, entry codes and so on.

Authorisation and approval

4.7 The Guideline states that 'all transactions should require authorisation or approval by an appropriate responsible person. The limits for these authorisations should be specified.'

4.8 EXAMPLE

A company might make a regulation that the head of a particular department may authorise revenue expenditure up to £500, but that for anything more expensive he must seek the approval of a director. Such authorisation limits will vary from company to company: £500 could be quite a large amount for a small company, but seem insignificant to a big one.

Management controls

4.9 Management controls are exercised by management outside the day-to-day routine of the system.

- Overall supervisory controls
- Review of management accounts and comparison with budgets
- Internal audit function
- Special review procedures

Supervisory controls

4.10 'Any system of internal control should include the **supervision** by responsible officials of day-to-day transactions and the recording thereof.'

Organisation as a control

4.11 Enterprises should have a plan of their organisation, defining and allocating responsibilities and identifying lines of reporting for all aspects of the enterprise's operations, including the controls. The delegation of authority and responsibility should be clearly specified.

4.12 EXAMPLE

An employee in a company may work for two managers, say a brand manager (who is responsible for the marketing and profitability of one particular product) and a production manager who supervises the production of all products. As you know, a company which is organised in this overlapping fashion is said to have a matrix organisation. The point here is that all the employee's actions must be supervised by one or other of the two managers.

Arithmetical and accounting controls

4.13 These controls within the recording function which check that the transactions to be recorded and processed have **been authorised**, that they are all **included** and that they are **correctly recorded** and **accurately processed**.

- Checking the arithmetical accuracy of the records
- The maintenance and checking of totals
- Reconciliations
- Control accounts
- Trial balances
- Accounting for documents

4.14 **Accounting** controls (and many administrative controls) depend on the accounting system of the organisation, and the information and reports produced by the system.

Personnel controls

4.15 **Personnel controls** are 'procedures to ensure that personnel have capabilities commensurate with their responsibilities', since 'the proper functioning of any system depends on the competence and integrity of those operating it. The qualifications, selection and training as well as the innate personal characteristics of the personnel involved are important features to be considered in setting up any control system.'

4.16 EXAMPLE

A company accountant should be suitably qualified. Nowadays, 'qualified' tends to mean someone who possesses a professional qualification of some sort, but it is important to remember that others are still able to do a job because of work experience - they are 'qualified' through that experience.

The internal control system

4.17 A company will select internal controls from the SPAM SOAP list above and incorporate them into its organisation. Which controls it selects depends on the particular circumstances of the company, but the range of internal controls it ends up with is called the company's **internal control system**.

4.18 An organisation may not possess all of the SPAM SOAP internal controls - or indeed may not be able to implement all of them. For example, a very small organisation may have insufficient staff to be able to organise a desirable level of segregation of duties.

4.19 **If controls are absent, managers should be aware of the risk**. It is then the responsibility of management to decide whether the risk is acceptable, or whether the missing control should be instituted.

Internal checks

4.20 Internal controls should not be confused with *internal checks*, which have a more restricted definition.

> **KEY TERM**
>
> **Internal checks** are defined as: 'the checks on the day-to-day transactions which operate continuously as part of the routine system whereby **the work of one person is proved independently or is complementary to the work of another**, the object being the prevention or early detection of errors and fraud; it includes matters such as the delegation and allocation of authority and the division of work, the method of recording transactions and the use of independently ascertained totals against which a large number of individual items can be proved.'

Internal checks are an important feature of the day-to-day control of financial transactions and the accounting system. **Arithmetical** internal checks include pre-lists, post-lists and control totals.

BPP
PUBLISHING

KEY TERMS

A **pre-list** is a list that is drawn up before any processing takes place.
A **post-list** is a list that is drawn up during or after processing.

A **control total** is a total of any sort used for control purposes by comparing it with another total that ought to be the same.

A pre-list total is a control total, so that for example, when cash is received by post and a pre-list prepared and the receipts are recorded individually in the cash book, and a total of amounts entered in the cash book is obtained by adding up the individual entries, the control total obtained from the cash book can be compared with, and should agree with, the pre-list control total. Control totals, as you should already be aware, are frequently used within computer processing.

4.21 **Aims of internal checks**

- **Segregate tasks**, so that the responsibility for particular actions, or for defaults or omissions, can be traced to an individual person.

- **Create and preserve** the records that act as confirmation of physical facts and accounting entries.

- **Break down routine procedures** into separate steps or stages, so as to facilitate an even flow of work and avoid bottlenecks.

- **Reduce the possibility of fraud and error**. The aim should be to **prevent** fraud and error rather than to be able to **detect** it after it has happened. Efficient internal checks make extensive fraud virtually impossible, except by means of collusion between two or more people (and even then, the fraud will come to light eventually if there is job rotation and staff are periodically moved from one task to another).

4.22 **Internal checks**, importantly, imply a **division of work**, so that the work of one person is either **proved independently** or else is complementary to the work of another person

Activity 7.4

The Geton Company specialises in providing cleaning services for offices, hospitals etc. It is currently undertaking an expansion programme, much of which is achieved by supplying services previously carried out by employees of the organisation. In many cases these same employees are then recruited by Geton to work on the contracts using the improved procedures developed through its specialisation in this type of work.

For each large contract, or a number of small contracts in the same location, a supervisor is appointed to oversee the activities of the employees and to provide basic control data for hours worked, materials issued, use of equipment and so on. Invoices are prepared centrally as are wages. These are paid weekly in arrears via BACS. Each supervisor has a van in which the materials are kept and replenished from a central store. Equipment is normally kept at the purchasing organisation.

As a senior accounts assistant with Geton you have been asked to oversee the clerical activities associated with the work of the supervisor.

(a) Outline and explain the basic data you would expect to be completed by the supervisor:

(b) Explain what *checks* you would apply to confirm the correctness of the data provided.

Characteristics of a good internal control system

4.23 (a) **A clearly defined organisation structure**

- **Different operations must be separated** into appropriate divisions and sub-divisions.

- Officers must **be appointed to assume responsibility** for each division.

- **Clear lines of responsibility** must exist between each division and sub-division and the board.

- There must be overall **co-ordination of the company's activities** (through corporate planning).

(b) **Adequate internal checks**

- **Separation of duties** for **authorising** a transaction, **custody** of the assets obtained by means of the transaction and **recording** the transaction.

- **'Proof measures'** such as control totals, pre-lists and bank reconciliations should be used.

(c) **Acknowledgement** of work done: persons who carry out a particular job should acknowledge their work by means of signatures, initials, rubber stamps and so on.

(d) Protective devices for **physical security**.

(e) **Formal documents should acknowledge the transfer of responsibility for goods.** When goods are received, a goods received note should be used to acknowledge receipt by the storekeeper.

(f) **Pre-review:** the authorisation of a transaction (for example a cash payment, or the purchase of an asset) should not be given by the person responsible without first checking that all the proper procedures have been carried out.

(g) A clearly defined **system for authorising transactions** within specified spending limits.

(h) **Post-review:** completed transactions should be reviewed after they have happened; for example, monthly statements of account from suppliers should be checked against the purchase ledger accounts of those suppliers.

(i) There should be **authorisation, custody** and **re-ordering** procedures.

- Funds and property of the company should be kept under **proper custody**. Access to assets (either direct or by documentation) should be **limited to authorised personnel**.

- Expenditure should only be incurred after authorisation and all expenditures are properly accounted for.

- All revenue must be properly accounted for and received in due course.

(j) **Personnel** should have the capabilities and qualifications necessary to carry out their responsibilities properly.

(k) An **internal audit** department should be able to verify that the control system is working and to review the system to ensure that it is still appropriate for current circumstances.

BPP PUBLISHING

Limitations on the effectiveness of internal controls

4.24 Not only must a control system include sufficient controls, but also these **controls must be applied properly and honestly**. 'No internal control system, however elaborate, can by itself guarantee efficient administration and the completeness and accuracy of the records, nor can it be proof against fraudulent collusion, especially on the part of those holding positions of authority or trust.'

- Internal controls depending on **segregation of duties can be avoided by the collusion** of two or more people responsible for those duties.

- **Authorisation controls can be abused** by the person empowered to authorise the activities.

- **Management can often override the controls they have set up themselves.**

Activity 7.5

Jones and Jones Limited is a firm of electrical contractors. The Directors, George and his sister Alice, are responsible for estimating, tendering and contracting for jobs and for the supervision of the workforce. The firm does not have an accounts department; responsibility for the accounts is shared among its office staff as follows.

John keeps records of all purchases and expenses. He also makes out cheques for the directors' signatures and records them in the cash book.

Joyce maintains records of jobs done. She sends out invoices and statements, looks after the sales ledger, records receipts in the cash book and prepares a monthly balance which she does not reconcile with the bank.

Betty calculates the wages, draws an appropriate amount of money from the bank, makes them up and distributes them among the firm's employees. She is also responsible for petty cash for which she periodically draws £100 from the bank.

You are required to produce a report to the directors in which you advise them on what you see as weaknesses in the internal control of the firm's accounts and recommend ways of securing effective control of the accounts.

5 INTERNAL AUDIT AND INTERNAL CONTROL

5.1 Internal audit

KEY TERM

Internal audit has been defined as:

'An independent appraisal activity established within an organisation as a service to it. It is a control which functions by examining and evaluating the adequacy and effectiveness of other controls.

'Originally concerned with the financial records, the investigative techniques developed are now applied to the analysis of the effectiveness of all parts of an entity's operations and management

5.2 The work of internal audit is distinct from the external audit which is carried out for the benefit of shareholders only and examines published accounts. Internal audit is part of the internal control system.

The features of internal audit

5.3 From these definitions the two main features of internal audit emerge.

(a) **Independence:** although an internal audit department is part of an organisation, it should be independent of the line management whose sphere of authority it may audit.

(b) **Appraisal:** internal audit is concerned with the appraisal of work done by other people in the organisation, and internal auditors should not carry out any of that work themselves. The appraisal of operations provides a service to management.

Types of audit

5.4 Internal audit is a management control, as it is a tool used to ensure that other internal controls are working satisfactorily. An internal audit department may be asked by management to look into any aspect of the organisation.

5.5 Five different types of audit can be distinguished.

- Operational audit
- Systems audit
- Transactions audit
- Social audit
- Management investigations

The first three types are considered further in the following paragraphs.

5.6 **Operational audits** can be concerned with **any sphere** of a company's activities. Their prime objective is the monitoring of management's performance at every level, to ensure optimal functioning according to pre-determined criteria. They concentrate on the outputs of the system, and the efficiency of the organisation. They are also known as '**management**', '**efficiency**' or '**value for money**' audits

5.7 A **systems audit** is based on a testing and evaluation of the **internal controls** within an organisation so that those controls may be relied on to ensure that resources are being managed effectively and information provided accurately. Two types of tests are used.

- **Compliance tests** seek evidence that the internal controls are being applied as prescribed.

- **Substantive tests** substantiate the entries in the figures in accounts. They are used to discover **errors and omissions**.

5.8 The auditor will be interested in a variety of processing errors when performing compliance tests.

- At the wrong time
- Incompleteness
- Omission
- Error (for example, advance payments from customers being credited to sales)
- Fraud

5.9 The key importance of the two types of test is that **if the compliance tests reveal that internal controls are working satisfactorily, then the amount of substantive testing can be reduced**, and the internal auditor can concentrate the audit effort on those areas where controls do not exist or are not working satisfactorily.

5.10 EXAMPLE

Suppose a department within a company processes travel claims which are eventually paid and recorded on the general ledger.

(a) When conducting **compliance tests**, the internal auditor is **looking at the controls** in the travel claim section to see if they are working properly. This is not the same as looking at the travel claims themselves. For example, one of the internal controls might be that a clerk checks the addition on the travel claim and initials a box to say that he has done so. If he fails to perform this arithmetic check, then there has been a control failure - regardless of whether the travel claim had, in fact, been added up correctly or incorrectly.

(b) When conducting **substantive tests**, the internal auditor is examining figures which he has extracted directly from the company's financial records. For this sort of test, the auditor is concerned only with establishing whether or not the figure in the ledger is correct. He or she is not concerned as to how it got there.

5.11 **A transactions or probity audit** aims to detect fraud and uses only substantive tests.

Accountability

5.12 Ideally, the internal auditor should be directly responsible to the highest executive level in the organisation, preferably to the audit committee of the Board of Directors. There are three main reasons for this requirement.

- The auditor needs access to all parts of the organisation.

- The auditor should be set free to comment on the performance of management.

- The auditor's report may need to be actioned at the highest level to ensure its effective implementation.

In practice, however, the internal auditor is often responsible to the head of the finance function.

Independence

5.13 Given an acceptable line of responsibility and clear terms of authority, it is vital that the internal auditor **is and is seen to be independent**. Independence for the internal auditor is established by three things.

- The responsibility structure;
- The auditor's mandatory authority;
- The auditor's own approach.

5.14 Internal audit requires a highly professional approach which is objective, detached and honest. Independence is a fundamental concept of auditing and this applies just as much to the internal auditor as to the external auditor. The internal auditor should not install new procedures or systems, neither should he engage in any activity which he would normally appraise, as this might compromise his independence.

Activity 7.6

The Midas Mail Order Company operates a central warehouse from which all merchandise is distributed by post or carrier to the company's 10,000 customers. An outline description of the sales and cash collection system is set out below.

Sales and cash collection system

Stage	*Department/staff responsible*	*Documentation*
(1) Customer orders merchandise (Orders by phone or through the postal system)	Sales dept Sales assistants	Multiple copy order form (with date, quantities, price marked on them) Copies 1-3 sent to warehouse. Copy 4 sent to accounts dept. Copy 5 retained in sales dept
(2) Merchandise requested from stock rooms by despatch clerks	Storekeepers	Copies 1-3 handed to storekeepers. Forms marked as merchandise taken from stock. (Note. If merchandise is out of stock the storekeepers retain copies 1-3 until stockroom is re-stocked). Copies 1-2 handed to despatch clerks. Copy 3 retained by store-keepers.
(3) Merchandise despatched	Despatch bay Despatch clerks	Copy 2 marked when goods despatched and sent to accounts department
(4) Customers invoiced	Accounts dept: sales ledger clerks	2-copy invoice prepared from invoiced details on copy 2 of order form received from despatch bay Copy 1 of invoice sent to customer. Copy 2 retained by accounts dept and posted to sales ledger
(5) Cash received (as cheques, bank giro credit, or cash)	Accounts dept: cashier	2-copy cash receipt list Copy 1 of cash receipt list retained by cashier Copy 2 passed to sales ledger clerk

(a) State four objectives of an internal control system.

(b) For the Midas Mail Order Company list any four major controls which you would expect to find in the operation of the accounting system described above and explain the objective of each of these controls.

(c) For each of the four controls identified above, describe briefly two tests which you would expect an internal auditor to carry out to determine whether the control was operating satisfactorily.

Key learning points

- There are various types of control in an organisation.

- The main **internal controls** that an organisation may adopt are those covered by the SPAM SOAP mnemonic.

- **Internal checks** are part of the internal controls in an accounting system: they are designed to check that everything that should be recorded is recorded, that any errors come to light and that assets and liabilities genuinely exist and are recorded at the correct amount.

- Internal audit is itself an internal control whose function is to assess the adequacy of other internal controls. The main types of audit are systems audits, transactions audits and value for money audits.

Quick quiz

1   List the steps in control.

2   What is feedback?

3   List four strategies for control.

4   List features of a good control system.

5   What is an internal control system?

6   Distinguish between administrative controls and accounting controls.

7   What is the well-known mnemonic for the eight types of internal control listed in the Auditing Guideline *Internal Controls*, and what does it stand for?

8   The person who authorises a transaction should ideally be separate from the person who executes it. Give an example of this and state what other functions should be kept separate

9   What is the purpose of arithmetical and accounting controls? Give some examples.

10   What is an internal check?

11   Briefly describe five characteristics of a good internal control system.

12   Are internal controls foolproof? If not, why not?

13   What is internal audit?

14   Distinguish between internal audit, internal control and internal check.

Answers to quick quiz

1   Make a plan. Record the plan. Carry out the plan. Compare results with plan. Evaluate comparison. Take corrective action.

2   Outputs of a system which are used to control it.

3   Personal, bureaucratic, output, cultural control.

4   Acceptable, appropriate, accessible, action-oriented, adaptable, affordable.

5   An *internal control system* is 'the whole system of controls, financial and otherwise, established by the management in order to carry on the business of the enterprise in an orderly and efficient manner, ensure adherence to management policies, safeguard the assets and secure as far as possible the completeness and accuracy of the records. The individual components of an internal control system are known as controls or internal controls'. (Auditing Guideline: *Internal controls*). The overall *system* of internal control consists of a number of individual controls known as internal controls.

6   *Administrative* controls consist of the plan of organisation and methods and procedures that are concerned with operational efficiency and adherence to management policies. Examples are time and motion study, performance reports, quality control, and employee training programmes. *Accounting* controls consist of methods and procedures that are concerned with, and relate directly to, safeguarding of assets and the reliability of financial records. Examples are systems of authorisation

and approval, separation of duties concerned with asset custody, physical controls over assets and internal auditing.

7 The eight types of control listed in the Auditing Guideline can be remembered using the mnemonic SPAM SOAP.

(i)   **S**egregation of duties

(ii)   **P**hysical controls

(iii)   **A**uthorisation and approval controls

(iv)   **M**anagement controls, such as internal audit or review of management accounts

(v)   **S**upervision

(vi)   **O**rganisation (that is, the formal structure of authority and responsibility)

(vii) **A**rithmetical and accounting controls

(viii) **P**ersonnel controls

8 An example would be the authorisation for the payment of a supplier's invoice and the drawing up and signing of the cheque. Other functions that should be kept separate are the custody of assets (for example cheque books), and the recording of transactions (writing up the payment in the cash book and purchase ledger). The Auditing Guideline also gives the example, in the case of a computer-based accounting system, of systems development and daily operations.

9 Accounting and arithmetical controls check that the transactions to be recorded and processed have been a*uthorised,* that they are all *included* and that they are *correctly* recorded and *accurately* processed. Examples are:

(i)   checking the arithmetical accuracy of the records;
(ii)   the maintenance and checking of totals;
(iii)   reconciliations;
(iv)   control accounts;
(v)   trial balances;
(vi)   accounting for documents.

10 Internal checks are: 'the checks on the day-to-day transactions which operate continuously as part of the routine system whereby *the work of one person is proved independently or is complementary to the work of another,* the object being the prevention or early detection of errors and fraud'. Control totals and pre-lists are examples of them.

11 The characteristics of good internal control in the accounting system are as follows. (You are only asked for five.)

(i)   A clearly defined organisation structure

(ii)   Adequate internal checks

(iii)   Acknowledgement of work done

(iv)   Protective devices for physical security

(v)   The use of formal documents to acknowledge the transfer of responsibility for goods

(vi)   Pre-review of transactions

(vii) A clearly defined system for authorising transactions within specified spending limits.

(viii) Post-review: completed transactions should be reviewed after they have happened

(ix)   Authorisation, custody and re-ordering procedures over the funds, property and expenditure of the organisation.

(x)   Personnel should be adequately trained, and there should be appropriate remuneration, welfare, promotion and appointment schemes (adequate 'hygiene' and 'motivation', in Herzberg's terms). There should also be adequate supervision by responsible officials and management

(xi)   An internal audit department should be able to verify that the control system is working and to review the system to ensure that it is still appropriate for (changing) current circumstances.

12   Internal controls have to be applied properly and honestly in order to work.

13   Internal audit is a form of control which has been defined as 'An independent appraisal activity established within an organisation ... which functions by examining and evaluating the adequacy and effectiveness of other controls'. It can be applied to the analysis of the effectiveness of all parts of an organisation's operations and management.

14   Internal *controls* embrace *all* controls (both financial and non-financial) established by management to ensure efficiency and adherence to management policies, properly safeguarded assets and complete and accurate records. Internal *checks* are specific types of internal controls in an accounting system, and are procedures designed to ensure complete and correct recording of transactions and other accounting information, and the discovery of errors or irregularities in processing accounting information. Internal *audit* is a part of the internal control system acting as a 'watchdog' over the other internal controls.

Answers to activities

Answer 7.1

Here are some ideas.

(a)   How should output be measured, and in what ways should it be reported?

(b)   What is the importance of environmental factors?

(c)   What inputs should be regarded as controllable, and which of these would be worth attempting to control (the cost of one part of a control system might exceed the value of the benefits arising from its implementation).

(d)   Who is responsible for exercising control, and how?

Answer 7.2

(a)   This shows the operation of double loop feedback and some open loop input. The plan has to be altered. There is also some feedforward control in the form of Sally's views on the next quarter.

(b)   This was a closed single loop system. Counselling is control action to improve the individual's performance. Dismissal is control action too, if the employee is replaced by someone who performs better, thus raising the performance of the department as a whole.

(c)   This is an example of cultural control, perhaps.

Answer to 7.3

(a)   (i)   The target is badly designed, as **it leads to behaviour directly opposed to the company's objectives**. Just before the end of the accounting period, Andrew's outstanding debtors were £100,000 of which 25% exceeded thirty days. By posting the £20,000 Andrew's total outstanding receivables would be £80,000; whilst the amount outstanding over 30 days remains the same (£25,000) in percentage terms it has risen from 25% to 31.25%, and Andrew's pay will suffer. This is a very important aspect of management control of people. Human beings will put their efforts into what benefits themselves. This means that the control system must try to measure what is good for the organisation very precisely. If the aims of the organisation, the targets set and the objectives of the workpeople are identical, there is **goal congruence** - if not, **dysfunctional decision making** like Andrew's will result.

      (ii)   The 25% figure on accounts outstanding seems questionable. U's customer base probably includes *small, medium* and *large firms* who may have lodged small, medium and large orders respectively. Should there be 25% of *key account* (large orders) outstanding at any one time, U Ltd is likely to experience *severe* cash flow problems.

      (iii)   The debtors do not seem to be analysed any further (eg into 30 days, 60 days, 90 days overdue etc). Once the 25% target has been met, there is no incentive to collect the remainder.

(iv)   Wider company objectives have not been incorporated into Andrew's work. The *purpose* of the target does not seem to have been explained to him. If it had, he may not have delayed banking the cheque; but it is still wrong that performance measures should reward 'bad' behaviour.

(v)   Other aspects of Andrew's performance could be rewarded.

(b)   Credit control is often measured in terms of debtor days which looks at the magnitude of outstanding debt in the light of turnover achieved. Simply measuring debtors would be misleading as the value would be bound to change if turnover went up or down. Debtor days would also be affected by any change in credit policy and this would have to be taken into account when assessing performance.

Answer 7.4

(a)   *Basic data to be completed by the supervisor*

(1)   *Materials usage.* This will be determined by records of the use of van materials by job, materials drawn from central store to replenish the van and so forth. To assess usage the quantity and type of materials in stock at the beginning and the end of the week may need to be recorded, unless a running total is kept. Although the supervisor keeps the van topped up, it is not certain whether there is a minimum level kept in the van.

(2)   *Van expenses.* It is a relatively simple matter to record the miles run on company business, just by checking the clock. The supervisor will need to keep dockets and receipts of amounts paid for petrol and oil, to enable reimbursement. Alternatively, a company charge card might be used.

(3)   *Hours worked.* For each employee, the employee's name, grade if appropriate, hours at basic rate, and hours at overtime rates, type or category of work (if the company analyses its time in this way)   .

(b)   *Checks to ensure data accuracy*

Geton can take a variety of approaches. They could require a great deal of documentation to ensure that errors do not arise. They could have a roaming inspection department to check on compliance with recording procedures. Other controls include the following.

(i)   *Materials usage*

(1)   Comparison between different jobs for reasonableness
(2)   Van stock counts
(3)   Reconciliation of van stock counts with recorded usage
(4)   Materials usage could be part of the budget

(ii)   *Van expenses*

(1)   The company will not pay for private mileage so the mileage recorded must be reasonable. The meter on the van can be checked. The supervisor might be required to log journeys and to produce all garage receipts, including those for cleaning the van.

(2)   A mileage budget will be established to check for the reasonableness of any claims. Again, mileage on a job can be compared with other similar jobs.

(iii)   *Work done*

(1)   A budget can be set for each job. Actual hours worked can be compared to it: the difference may be perfectly reasonable but the supervisor will have to explain any significant variance. On occasions, a member of the inspection team can carry out further checks.

(2)   The job to be done should be specified and the job specification might arise out of the contract itself. One of the supervisor's jobs will be to ensure that the work is done as required. In addition, an inspection team may visit the site now and then to ensure that standards are adhered to. Clients can also be sent questionnaires asking them about their satisfaction with the service.

Answer 7.5 _____

Date: *30 June 19X5*

To: *George and Alice Jones, Directors, Jones and Jones Limited*

From: **Accounting Technician**

Subject: *Internal control*

You have asked me to advise on weaknesses in the internal control of your firm's accounts and to recommend ways in which effective control may be secured. My report has been based upon discussing the established work practices with the staff of Jones and Jones Limited and observing these work practices in operation. I have also reviewed the company's books.

Findings

Three members of your office staff, John, Joyce and Betty, are responsible for maintaining the accounting records. Unfortunately little attention has been paid to internal control, with the result that there are virtually no internal checking procedures and any discrepancy which arose (either deliberately or accidentally) would almost certainly escape detection.

(a)   John keeps the record of all purchases and expenses but also makes out cheques for the directors to sign and records these payments in the cash book. He is thus in a prime position either to pay fictitious expenses (as a way of lining his own pocket) or to pay twice against the same invoice (through an error) without either transaction being queried.

(b)   Joyce is responsible for recording all work done but also for receiving payment and for credit control. If she fails to invoice a customer, or to record a cash receipt, this would not be picked up.

(c)   Betty could steal money from the firm simply by drawing more than she needs from the firm's bank account and altering the wage records to hide what she had done. She could also overpay members of staff without this being detected.

The fact that no fraud appears to have taken place so far is attributable entirely to the honesty of your staff who are being given every opportunity to steal from your firm, should they wish. The errors I discovered in the accounts were all small ones, but they had not been spotted previously and could have been very much larger. In short, your internal control system requires a radical overhaul if it is to be effective.

Recommendations

The changes outlined below are designed to ensure that the tasks of preparing and handling initial documents (such as sales invoices and suppliers' invoices), preparing records and handling cash are reallocated, as far as possible, between different employees and to introduce a proper internal checking procedure. However, I recognise that prior consultation with your office staff will be necessary if these improvements are to be implemented successfully.

(a)   *Expenses and purchases*

John can continue to be responsible for maintaining trade creditor records. However, Joyce should check all suppliers' invoices against purchase orders before they are given to John for recording. The responsibility for preparing cheques should fall to Betty, who would draw cheques against suppliers' invoices passed to her by John. As directors, you should ensure that invoice(s) and cheque match before you sign each cheque.

(b)   *Debtor balances*

Joyce should retain her present function of maintaining the sales ledger. However, the responsibility for initiating sales invoices should pass to John and the responsibility for receiving cash should pass to Betty. This is not ideal, though it is probably the best arrangement which can be achieved given the very small numbers of staff.

(c)   *Cash payments and receipts*

Betty should be responsible for maintaining the cash book, recording both amounts paid and received. She would also be required to handle cheques received from debtors. The cash book must be reconciled with the bank statements. Preferably, this would be done by someone other than Betty. Joyce would be the most appropriate candidate for this task.

For petty cash payments, an imprest system would be appropriate. John or Joyce could pay claims as they were submitted, recording them in a petty cash book. This would be submitted to Betty when reimbursement was required.

(d)   *Wages*

Wages represent a substantial expense item for the business. The procedures for calculating, checking and paying wages should be as secure as possible. Betty could calculate the wages due using the employee time records. Her figures could be checked by John, who would then record them in the wages book. It might be worthwhile to consider paying all employees by cheque, which would avoid some of the security problems associated with paying wages in cash. Wages cheques made out to individual employees could be submitted to yourselves for signature, along with the wages book. Alternatively, a single wages cheque could be presented. After signature by yourselves, this would be taken to the bank by Joyce and Betty, who would make up the wages ready for paying out by you.

(e)   *General supervision*

To ensure that these arrangements are working properly, you yourselves should inspect the accounting records on a regular basis to ensure that the operations of the business are being recorded in a timely and accurate manner.

Answer 7.6

(a)   Four objectives of an internal control system are as follows.

   (i)   To enable management to carry on the business of the enterprise in an orderly and efficient manner.

   (ii)   To satisfy management that their policies are being adhered to.

   (iii) To ensure that the assets of the company are safeguarded.

   (iv)   To ensure, as far as possible, that the enterprise maintains complete and accurate records.

(b)   Four major controls which should be applied in the operation of the accounting system described, and an explanation of their objectives, are detailed below.

   (i)   *Control over customers' creditworthiness.* Before any order is accepted for further processing, established procedures should be followed in order to check the creditworthiness of that customer. For new customers procedures should exist for obtaining appropriate references before any credit is extended. For all existing customers there should be established credit limits and before an order is processed the sales assistants should check to see that the value of the current order will not cause the debtor's balance to rise above their agreed credit limit.

          The objective of such procedures is to try to avoid the company supplying goods to debtors who are unlikely to be able to pay for them. In this way the losses suffered by the company as a result of bad debts should be minimal.

   (ii)   *Control over the recording of sales and debtors.* The most significant document in the system is the multiple order form. These forms should be sequentially pre-numbered and controls should exist over the supplies of unused forms and also to ensure that all order forms completed can be traced through the various stages of processing and agreed to the other documents raised and the various entries made in the accounting records.

          The main objective here will be to check the completeness of the company's recording procedures in relation to the income which it has earned and the assets which it holds in the form of debtors.

   (iii) *Control over the issue of stocks and the despatch of goods.* Control procedures here should be such that goods are not issued from stores until a valid order form has been received and the fact of that issue is recorded both on the order form (copies 1-3) and in the stock records maintained by the store-keepers.

          The objectives here are to see that no goods are released from stock without appropriate authority and that a record of stock movements is maintained.

   (iv)   Control over the invoicing of customers. The main control requirement here will be to use sequentially pre-numbered invoices with checks being carried out to control the completeness of the sequence. Checks should also be conducted to ensure that all invoices are matched with the appropriate order form (Copy 2) to confirm that invoices have been raised in respect of all completed orders.

          The major concern here will be to ensure that no goods are despatched to customers without an invoice subsequently being raised.

(v)   (*Tutorial note.* The question merely required four controls to be considered, but for the sake of completeness, each of the five main stages in processing as indicated by the question are considered here.)

Control over monies received. There should be controls to ensure that there is an adequate segregation of duties between those members of staff responsible for the updating of the sales records in respect of monies received and those dealing with the receipt, recording and banking of monies. There should also be a regular independent review of aged debtor balances together with an overall reconciliation of the debtors' ledger control account with the total of outstanding debts on individual customer accounts.

The objectives here are to ensure that proper controls exist with regard to the complete and accurate recording of monies received, safe custody of the asset cash and the effectiveness of credit control procedures.

(c)   Appropriate tests in relation to each of the controls identified in (b) above would be as follows.

(i)   *Controls over customers' creditworthiness*

(1)   For a sample of new accounts opened during the period check to see that suitable references were obtained before the company supplied any goods on credit terms and that the credit limit set was properly authorised and of a reasonable amount.

(2)   For a sample of customers' orders check to see that at the time they were accepted, their invoice value would not have been such as to cause the balance on that customers' account to go above their agreed credit limit.

(ii)   *Controls over the recording of sales and debtors*

(1)   On a sample basis check the completeness of the sequence of order forms and also that unused stocks of order forms are securely stored.

(2)   For a sample of order forms raised during the period ensure that they can be traced through the system such that there is either evidence that the order was cancelled or that a valid invoice was subsequently raised.

(iii)   *Control over the issue of stocks and the despatch of goods*

(1)   For a sample of entries in the stock records check to ensure that a valid order form exists for all issues recorded as having been made.

(2)   Attend the stockrooms to observe the procedures and check that goods are not issued unless a valid order form has been received and that the appropriate entries are made in the stock records and on the order form at the time of issue.

(iv)   *Control over the invoicing of customers*

(1)   On a sample basis check the completeness of the sequence of invoices raised and also that the unused stocks of invoice forms are securely stored.

(2)   For a sample of invoices raised during the period ensure that they have been properly matched with the appropriate order form (copy 2).

Chapter 8   Monitoring and improving the system

Chapter topic list

1   Looking at the system

2   Efficiency

3   Analysing work

4   Improving work

5   Cost

Learning objectives

On completion of this chapter you will be able to:

	Performance criteria	Range Statement
• plan work activities in order to optimise the use of resources and ensure completion within agreed timescales	10.1.1	1
• monitor work activities closely so that quality standards are met	10.1.5	1
• identify weaknesses and potential for improvements to the accounting system and consider their impact on the operation	10.2.1	1
• review methods of operating in respect of their cost-effectiveness, reliability and speed	10.2.2	1

BPP
PUBLISHING

1 LOOKING AT THE SYSTEM

1.1 The previous chapter covered internal controls in isolation. Your project will want to take a broader look at the system than just the control aspects.

1.2 A useful technique is to apply **SWOT analysis** to your section. SWOT stands for:

- Strengths
- Weaknesses
- Opportunities
- Threats

1.3 An accounting system might be **strong or weak** in areas such as:

- Design of controls
- Implementation of controls
- Computer systems
- Ability of staff
- Resources available
- Reputation with internal customers

1.4 **Opportunities** and **threats** can come from outside.

- Increasing workload might lead to pressure to 'cut corners'.
- New computer technology can speed up processing and operations.

1.5 Another overall framework is to look at the **quality** of the system.

> **KEY TERM**
>
> **Quality** is 'fitness for use': how good is a product/service at satisfying the customer's needs.

- Quality is something that requires *care* on the part of the provider.
- Quality is largely subjective - it is in the eye of the *beholder*, the customer.

1.6 The **management** of quality is an aspect of control and involves advance planning.

Step 1. Establish standards of quality for a product or service.

Step 2. Establish procedures and methods to ensure that these required standards of quality are met.

Step 3. Monitor actual quality.

Step 4. Take control action when actual quality falls below standard.

1.7 EXAMPLE

The postal service might establish a standard that 90% of first class letters will be delivered on the day after they are posted, and 99% will be delivered within two days of posting. Procedures would have to be established for ensuring that these standards could be met (attending to such matters as frequency of collections, automated letter sorting, frequency of deliveries and number of staff employed). Actual performance could be monitored, perhaps by taking samples from time to time of letters that are posted and delivered. If the quality standard is not being achieved, the management of the postal service should take control action (employ more staff or advertise the use of postcodes again).

1.8 Principles of quality

(a) Preventing mistakes is less costly in the long run. The aim should therefore be to **get things right first time**. 'Every mistake, every delay and misunderstanding, directly costs a company money through wasted time and effort, including time taken in pacifying customers.'

(b) **Continuous improvement**. It is always possible to improve and so the aim should be to 'get it more right next time'. A 'continuous improvement cycle' can achieve this.

> *Step 1.* **Describe**
> Having identified an area for improvement it must be determined exactly what the problem is, when it started, who is affected by it, and what its effects are in terms of cost, dissatisfied customers and so on.

> *Step 2.* **Analyse**
> This has two sub-steps.
>
> (i) Identify potential causes of the problem.
> (ii) Collect data to verify which is the root cause.

> *Step 3.* **Correct**. This means identifying the best solution to the root cause, implementing it, and measuring its effects to make sure that it has produced the expected improvement.

> *Step 4.* **Prevent**. Only permanent solutions lead to continuous improvement. This step identifies what needs to be done to prevent recurrence of the problem, perhaps by redesigning other parts of the process to complement the new, improved method of dealing with the original problem.

1.9 Internal customers

(a) Any unit of the organisation whose task contributes to the task **of other units can be** regarded as a **supplier of services**. The **receiving units are thus customers of that unit**.

(b) The concept of **customer choice** operates within the organisation. If an internal service unit fails to provide the right service at the right time and cost, it cannot expect customer loyalty: it is in **competition** with other internal and external providers of the service.

(c) The service unit's objective thus becomes the efficient **identification and satisfaction of customer needs** - as much within the organisation as outside it. This has the effect of integrating the objectives of service and customer units throughout the organisation.

1.10 Internal customers of the accounting function

- Line management, who need accounting information to help them do their jobs

- Senior management and shareholders, who need information to assess how well jobs are being done

- Employees, who also need information to do their jobs, and who are almost equivalent to external customers for some accounting services like payroll.

Activity 8.1

Eleanor Ferguson is the head of a management accounts department in her organisation. Her department supplies accounting data and other management information to other departments, as well as to customers.

Eleanor was perturbed to receive a memorandum from George Henderson, a manager in a department which uses the services of Eleanor's department regularly.

The following is an extract from George's memorandum:

'..... It seems to me that the changes which you are making take no account of our information needs as users.

'Whilst I can appreciate that these changes will assist you by containing your costs I would have expected, as a major and regular user of your services, to have been consulted prior to their implementation, since their introduction has had the predictable effect of limiting my ability both to cut my own costs and to enhance the service to my customers.

'I'm told that it would now be too disruptive and costly for you to meet my requirement for this year, and that rewriting your computer programme in time for next year may prove difficult.

'Furthermore, I do not take kindly to being told by letter by your staff that I should 'get my priorities right' and understand that the interests of the organisation and of the organisation's customers must come before those of my department. I do, after all, use your services in connection with managing one of the organisation's most high-profile and important customers.'

Eleanor's low-key investigation has established that George's memorandum is substantively correct.

Required

(a)   Discuss the issues which George's memorandum raises for Eleanor.
(b)   How would you advise her to deal with these issues?

2   EFFICIENCY

> **KEY TERMS**
>
> - **Effectiveness** means achieving the desired objective.
>
> - **Economy** means operating at minimum cost.
>
> - There will normally be a trade-off between effectiveness and economy. **Efficiency** means being effective at minimum cost or controlling costs without losing operational effectiveness. **Efficiency** is therefore a **combination of effectiveness and economy.**

2.1   One means of raising the efficiency of an operating unit is to study what is being done at present and re-organise the work where it is beneficial to do so: in short by work study.

Work study

> **KEY TERMS**
>
> There are two main aspects of work study.
>
> - **Method study**: the systematic recording and critical examination of existing and proposed ways of doing work as a means of developing and applying easier and more effective methods, and reducing costs.
>
> - **Work measurement**: the application of techniques designed to establish the time for a qualified worker to carry out a specified job at a specified level of performance.

Method study is therefore concerned with how work should be done, and work measurement with how long it should take.

2.2   Work study is of value for five reasons.

- Tangible results are produced quickly.

- No large capital outlay is required.

- It is, in its basic form, simple and readily grasped in outline, by all.

- The facts it produces can be used to increase efficiency throughout the organisation.

- There is no work to which it cannot be applied; in office work it is called Organisation and Methods study (O&M).

Organisation and method

2.3 **Objectives of organisation and method study**

(a) Determine the way in which work should be organised and what methods should be adopted for jobs.

(b) Review and improve existing methods, so that effort, time, materials and machinery will be used to greater advantage.

2.4 The study is sometimes carried out by **specialists**, but in some organisations, **supervisors** might do it themselves to analyse the work done in their section.

2.5 O & M attempts to increase the efficiency of an organisation by improving procedures, methods and systems, communication and controls, and organisation structure. The principal aim of O & M may therefore be described as the **elimination of waste**. This includes waste of time, human effort and skills, equipment and supplies, space, and money. Eliminating waste will increase productivity, reduce administrative costs and improve staff morale and satisfaction.

2.6 Types of problems which an O & M investigation is likely to be concerned

(a) **Getting a job done more efficiently** and so more cheaply

(b) **'Rationalising' work** - questioning whether work needs to be done at all, or whether it can at least be done *more simply* and with less effort; alternatively trying to establish whether better use can be made of existing idle time, by spreading employees' work loads more evenly over their working time

2.7 The aim of O & M is not to *add* **new systems** to old ones, but to **simplify systems** and their relation to each other, to cope with new demands. If an aspect of a system or organisation structure is unnecessary, or even necessary but over-complicated, it is **wasteful of resources**.

2.8 The approach to a full-scale O & M study is as follows.

Step 1. Establish an area for investigation

Step 2. Establish terms of reference (say, the general system components to be investigated, the symptoms of the problem to be tackled, the resources available for the investigation and any limitations on investigative activity)

Step 3. Investigate the existing methods by observation, asking questions, studying procedure manuals and other written records

Step 4. Record the existing methods, by narrative, or using charts and diagrams (organisation charts, procedure flowcharts)

Step 5. Analyse the existing methods, identify weaknesses and strengths, develop alternative methods and discuss these with the operations staff and management affected

BPP PUBLISHING

Step 6.   Document an alternative method, and recommend it for implementation

Step 7.   If accepted, the new method should be installed, reviewed and improved as necessary

2.9   You are not a trained O&M specialist, but you may be able to apply some of these ideas in your work.

DEVOLVED ASSESSMENT ALERT

New methods might involve changes in planning and control systems, a new organisation structure, changing the numbers and location of equipment (such as telephones and computer terminals, and the size and number of filing cabinets); recommending computerisation of some activities; or changing methods of working or documents used. In all such plans, the supervisor in the relevant sections will be involved - at least in the implementation of the recommendations. In your project, you might have to make recommendations.

3   ANALYSING WORK

Collecting data

3.1   The full investigation starts with **research of the existing system**.

3.2   **Sources of data**

- Existing records, including organisation charts and manuals, job descriptions and specifications, procedure manuals

- Observation of procedures, forms and control systems in action

- Discussion with managers, supervisors and employees

- Questionnaires

3.3   **Data will then be recorded** to show:

- **What** is done in the course of an operation - what steps are accomplished?

- **Why** it is done - does each step contribute to the efficiency and effectiveness of the operation?

- **How** it is done - what work methods, procedures and equipment are used?

- **Where** it is done - how much movement is involved?

- **Who** does it - what department/individual? who is responsible?

- **When** it is done - what is an operation's place in a sequence? what timescales are involved?

3.4   The recording of data may take various forms.

- It may start with a **procedure narrative**. This is a narrative statement of the steps involved in a procedure, detailing the name, duties and actions of each person.

- **Charts** are also commonly used in O & M, as they can show at a glance what is going on in a system and where faults are occurring.

Narrative notes

3.5 Narrative notes have the advantage of being simple to record but are awkward to change. The purpose of the notes is to describe and explain the system, at the same time making any comments or criticisms which will help to demonstrate an intelligent understanding of the system.

- What functions are performed and by whom?
- What documents are used?
- Where do the documents originate and what is their destination?
- What sequence are retained documents filed in?
- What books are kept and where?

Charts

3.6 **Documented flowcharts** show the movement of forms between staff and departments. A vertical column is drawn for each department or staff member involved in the process.

(a) **Procedure flow charts** are simplified document flow charts. A point or rectangle representing a document is inserted in the column for each one it passes through: horizontal lines join the points to represent movement. For example, in ordering stores:

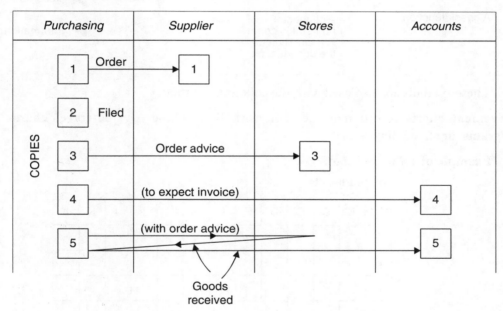

(b)   The full set of document flow chart symbols is given below:

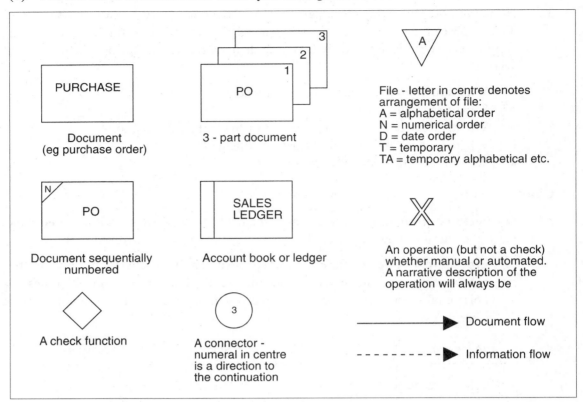

These symbols are also used with the columnar method.

3.7   **Movement charts** record movement or work flow. These may be **travel charts, flow diagrams, or string diagrams.**

(a)   **Example of a Travel Chart**

To departments:

		A	B	C	D	E	F	G	H	I	J	K	L
From departments:	A		//			////							
	B												
	C						###						
	D												
	E			///									
	F							////					
	G									### /		### /	
	H												
	I												
	J				///								
	K									/			
	L					//		////					

A number of columns represent possible destinations and rows represent possible starting points. As each journey is made, it is recorded in the appropriate row and under the appropriate column.

(b) **Flow diagrams** display the workplace and locations of the various activities, drawn to scale. The five standard process chart symbols are used and the diagrams refer to personnel, equipment and materials. They are, in effect, flow process charts of the workplace which are drawn to scale.

(c) **String diagrams** also use a plan of the workplace, drawn to scale, and the routes of movement are shown by a fine string which is stretched between pins at the terminal points. The advantage of this method is that repeated journeys over common routes can be shown without risk of obliteration or confusion and distances can be easily measured by removing the string and measuring it. This type of diagram will display faults in a layout which cause bottlenecks, back or cross-tracking or other movement difficulties.

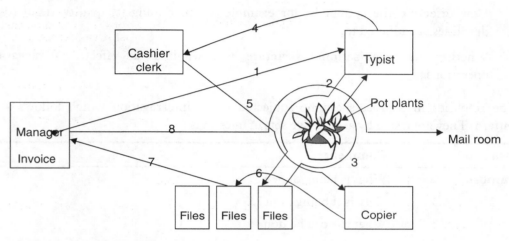

3.8 Other types of flow chart in regular use

- **Operational flowcharts**, commonly used for data processing operations.

- **Information flowcharts**, which are similar to document flowcharts but chart only significant information flows, ignoring unimportant documents and copies.

3.9 Advantages of using flowcharts

- After a little experience they can be **prepared quickly**. It is often found that an investigator can draw a draft chart as the interviewee describes the system.

- As the information is presented in a **standard form**, they are fairly easy to follow and to review.

- They generally ensure that the **system is recorded in its entirety**, as all document flows have to be traced from beginning to end and any 'loose ends' will be apparent from a cursory examination.

- They **eliminate the need for extensive narrative** and can be of considerable help in highlighting any strengths and weaknesses in the system.

3.10 Disadvantages

- **They are only really suitable for describing standard systems.** Procedures for dealing with unusual transactions will normally have to be recorded using narrative notes.

BPP PUBLISHING

- They are **useful for recording the flow of documents,** but once the records or the assets to which they relate have become static they can no longer be used for describing the controls (for instance over valuable equipment).

- **Major amendment is difficult** without redrawing (unless the charting system is computerised).

- Time can be wasted by charting areas that are of no significance (a criticism of *document* not *information* flowcharts).

Examination and development

3.11 Once collected, data will be analysed in order to reach conclusions.

- How **efficiently** the system creates, moves and stores documents and utilises available personnel and resources of time, space, equipment, materials and services.

- How **effective** the system is, for example whether budgets, quality standards and deadlines are adhered to.

- Whether **the organisational structure** as a whole is an effective framework for operations.

3.12 The activities in a process can be subjected to an interrogation which follows a fixed pattern. They are tested by asking five sets of questions.

Issue	Comment
Purpose	What is being done?
	Why is it being done?
	What *else* can be done?
	What *should* be done?
Place	Where is it being done?
	Why there?
	Where *else* could it be done?
	Where *should* it be done?
Sequence	When is it done?
	Why then?
	When *else* could it be done?
	When *should* it be done?
Person	Who does it?
	Why that person?
	Who *else* might do it?
	Who *should* do it?
Means	How is it done?
	Why that way?
	How *else* could it be done?
	How *should* it be done?

3.13 These questions are asked **in the above order**. If the 'purpose' is not worthwhile, for example, all other questions are pointless. If the means were questioned first, a great deal of effort could be spent in analysing and improving a method which is later found to serve no useful purpose. Be aware that some apparently purposeless activities take place for their value as **internal controls**.

Typical recommendations

3.14 Once faults have been examined, recommendations can be drawn up, suggesting revisions to organisational structure or procedures. These might involve the achievement of one or all of the aims of O & M mentioned above.

- Reorganise **office layout**, to smooth the path of workflow or increase productivity through worker morale

- **Re-allocate duties** (centralising a function, distributing work loads)

- **Computerise** routine procedures

- **Redesign or eliminate forms** (for example using carbonised document sets and the like to cut down on rewriting and movement)

- **Establish procedures** (with manuals and schedules as appropriate) or revising them

- **Improve control mechanisms** to cut down errors in or abuse of the system

- **Reduce staff** (on the basis of natural wastage if possible)

- **Change IT configuration** or requirement

Implementing recommendations

3.15 Once the study itself has been made, its recommendations have to be dealt with.

3.16 **They must be considered by and sold to the staff concerned.**

(a) Outline plans, and later detailed schedules of how changes will affect the department should be looked over and discussed, and perhaps given a 'dummy run' demonstration.

(b) Staff should be allowed to air their worries, criticisms and opinions: they will, after all, be called upon to work with the new procedures. It should be recognised, however, that staff will be resistant to change, especially if existing practices are long established.

3.17 **Recommendations must be planned, scheduled, authorised and implemented.**

(a) Procedure manuals might be written as a guide to action, a role which could also be filled by procedure and process flow charts.

(b) Test runs of the new system, in parallel with the existing arrangements, should ensure that objectives of the change will in fact be met, and will give staff time to adjust; staff will have to be trained in the use of new methods and equipment.

3.18 **Recommendations should also be followed up and maintained.**

(a) O & M staff will help deal with any 'bugs' that appear in the new system, or any difficulties encountered by staff.

(b) Once the system is operating smoothly, results should be measured for comparison against former methods, and might thereafter be 'audited' regularly to ensure continuing effectiveness and efficiency.

BPP PUBLISHING

Forms and input screens

3.19 **Principles of form design**

(a) Forms should be **easy to** *read* **and to** *use.*

- Wording of instructions and requirements should be clear and concise.

- Adequate space should be provided for entries.

- Layout should enable information and identification to be easily found.

- Title of the form (Invoice, Delivery Note) and name of the organisation should be prominent; different sections should be separated, marked and in logical order.

(b) **Size.** Forms should not be too small and cramped (for use, and attractiveness), but size should take into account mailing and filing requirements.

(c) **Paper and print** quality should be considered in relation to the handling the form is likely to receive.

(d) The **number of operations** involved in filling forms should be reduced as far as possible: document sets with selective carbon backing or the equivalent could be used instead of writing details in quadruplicate or photocopying. In this way, a single design and input of data can be adapted for many purposes.

(e) **Colour coding of copies** may be convenient in any set of forms, and if copies of a master form act variously (for example as order, confirmation, goods received, invoice and so on) they should be clearly identified.

3.20 Forms in use should be reviewed to ensure five things.

- Their contents are still needed.
- They are still used in practice.
- All their elements are still relevant.
- They are not duplicating the work of other forms.
- No changes in practice need to be added.

3.21 If it becomes necessary to change forms, or design new forms for revised systems, a simple procedure should be followed.

- Inform staff
- Withdraw old forms from circulation
- Issue all new forms from a central store
- Keep a register of form designs now in use

3.22 Similar considerations apply to the design **of computer input screens and computer output.**

(a) The design will partly be determined by the system but some applications allow reasonable flexibility of layout.

(b) The design of computer output may be something you can experiment with, particularly as many applications offer shading, different fonts and a variety of formats.

DEVOLVED ASSESSMENT ALERT

Redesigning forms can make your staff's job easier, if all relevant information is collected on one sheet. This is an issue your project can consider.

Activity 8.2

The Smith and Otis Company manufactures small items of brass giftware. Over recent years there has been a continuing expansion in sales, both home and overseas, with the consequent increase in the activities in all departments. This has led to ever increasing demands for information such as sales reports, manufacturing costs, departmental expenses and wages analyses. Because of the pace of the expansion and the continuing pressure on staff, all the reports have been drawn up in haste with no attempt at even standardising the sizes of forms.

The company has now entered a period of consolidation and there is a full establishment of staff. The Managing Director has asked the Chief Accountant to look at all the various aspects of reporting within the organisation. She has also suggested to the Chief Accountant that you, as the first accounting technician appointed by the company, should be involved in the initial investigations into this problem.

You have been asked to investigate the Cost Office and the Work Study Department in the first instance. It has been established already that the cost office prepares 38 reports, which with the differing levels of circulation are received by 120 recipients. The corresponding figures for the Work Study Department are 10 reports and 23 recipients. (Recipients who have more than one report from a department have been recorded for each report they receive.)

(a)   Outline the steps you would take in this initial investigation.

(b)   Prepare the draft of an informal report you would make to the chief accountant commenting on the problem after you have completed your initial investigation. You may make up (or draw from experience) any further information you wish.

4   IMPROVING WORK

4.1   **Work measurement** is one of the techniques used in O&M. It is used to set **standards** for the quality and quantity of work produced. A full work measurement exercise is a job for a specialist, but some of the ideas involved in work measurement are useful to anybody supervising office work.

4.2   Not all types of work can be easily measured in terms of 'output' (jobs completed). **Clerical work measurement** is difficult in this respect.

(a)   **Routine or repetitive** jobs in production, or in the office, and most jobs involving machine operation and output will be easier to set standards for and measure. For example how many orders are processed per hour, how many ledger entries made or pages typed, how many envelopes franked, copies made, documents filed.

(b)   Meetings, telephone calls, planning, research, non-routine or non-repetitive and 'thinking' tasks will be harder to evaluate: what is their value to the organisation relative to the time they take? Measuring the overall time taken in these activities (which will have to be the way they are evaluated) may be hard, because the office rarely allows pure and uninterrupted execution of a piece of work (the phone goes, unscheduled tasks or visitors arrive, decisions have to be made).

(c)   Even routine tasks will vary greatly as to time taken and resources used. A particularly difficult draft to type up, for example, or a telephone call from a particularly demanding customer may not be readily quantified.

4.3   **Standard times** are most accurately set by observation of the activity and the application of an assessment of its difficulty (a **rating**). This is a specialist task. However, other, simpler methods may be used by the supervisor to produce time estimates which are good enough for making improvements.

4.4 **Estimates**

(a) **Estimates** may be **made by employees**. They will be familiar with their own tasks and how long they take, but they might not be entirely objective, giving a shorter standard time to 'look good' or a longer one because they know they will have to live up to it later.

(b) **Supervisors** might also give estimates, if they are sufficiently experienced, closely involved and aware of exactly how subordinates' time is spent.

4.5 **Time and diary sheets** are a more precise way of keeping track of the allocation and duration of tasks, provided that they are conscientiously maintained and truthful. Sheets are filled in on a daily or weekly basis and summarised for each individual or group to show amounts of time actually spent on various activities. This is particularly useful for activities which cannot be measured in output terms, only in 'time spent' such as answering phones, dealing with visitors, or running errands.

4.6 When estimating how long work should take, take into account factors that may not have appeared in the figures. **Allowances** will have to be made for the following.

Allowance	Comment
Rest and relaxation	No-one can work at 100% speed without a break: energy and concentration will flag (and so will effectiveness) if a rest period is not allowed. VDU operators, for example, are advised by European standards to have a 10 minute break in every hour.
Refreshment	Tea or coffee breaks and lunch breaks are similarly essential to employee satisfaction and continuing effectiveness.
Fluctuating performance	Trainees, temporary staff and new employees will probably work more slowly and less efficiently than established staff who know the routines and environment. Each employee's performance will also fluctuate according to time of day, pressure of work and physical and emotional state.
Contingencies	Standard times usually incorporate an allowance for contingencies such as machine breakdowns.

4.7 When comparing performance with target, also consider:

(a) **The variable nature of work**. Even routine and measurable tasks like typing (where lines per hour is the simplest measurement) may be held up by a variety of problems.

- Difficult work, such as tabulations and calculations
- Standard of written drafts or dictation making it difficult to recognise words
- Intervening tasks (having to consult files) and interruptions

(b) **The variable nature of work flow**. There is no point reprimanding an employee for low productivity (compared to standard) if (s)he was not given a 'standard' amount of work to do, in other words a full day's steady work load.

Activity analysis

4.8 **Activity analysis** calculates the **proportion of time** spent by a member of staff on each of his or her various tasks. Here is an example

---

ACTIVITY ANALYSIS

Job title: Office junior

Department: Office Services

Activity	Hours per week
Filing	8
Typing	16
Inward mail	2
Outward mail	4
Switchboard/reception	5
	35

4.9 By **combining individual analyses** in tabulated form, an overall picture of division of **work in the department can be obtained**. This may reveal anomalies such as a shorthand typist spending a large proportion of time on less demanding tasks like copy-typing, or a general drain on office staff from a particular task such as duplicating, in which case alternative methods (or delegation of the function to outside services) might be considered.

How can quality be maintained and improved?

4.10 Standards for quality control will depend on the circumstances of each activity and the organisation or section in which it takes place.

(a) People are bound to make mistakes, but some errors will be more costly than others.

    (i) **Time**. An error may mean re-doing a job (say re-typing a contract) or other delays (waiting for a reply to a letter which was wrongly addressed, dealing with customer complaints).

    (ii) **Money**. Loss of time will mean a drop in productivity, which will increase overhead costs for each 'unit' produced. The organisation may also lose money through calculation or copying errors on invoices or statements or the cost of running a large complaints department.

    (iii) **Image**. No customer or supplier will be impressed by ill-presented correspondence, inaccurate transaction details to chase up, mis-spelt names, faulty products, late deliveries, or 'mix-ups' of any sort, no matter how apologetic the company is.

(b) However, achieving 100% accuracy is also time-consuming and costly. An employee may have to spend too much time on **ensuring** complete accuracy and even more time will be spent on **checking** that he has done so.

DEVOLVED ASSESSMENT ALERT

These factors must be 'juggled' to ensure that the cost of accuracy and checking does not exceed the benefit or importance of having errors avoided or corrected. It *might* be permissible and cost-effective in some situations to allow or tolerate a level of error or inaccuracy. However, such situations are rare in accounting work: how would you like it if your salary were rounded down to the nearest pound every month?

BPP
PUBLISHING

4.11   **Methods of checking**

- **100% checking** - this is time-consuming and expensive, so it would only be used for important work.

- **partial checking** - only important parts of a task are checked, or parts which are prone to error (checking for common mistakes) or are otherwise under suspicion.

- **random sampling** - frequent checks of random pieces of work, which should turn up areas prone to error or inaccuracy.

4.12   Where errors are discovered, there may be a **root cause** which will continue to produce errors if not identified and dealt with.

- The worker himself if he is badly organised or trained, inexperienced, tired or just inattentive.

- The fault might be traced back to **managers and supervisors**: ill-planned recruitment, unreasonable expectations, lack of clear instruction, bad morale or badly designed systems and forms.

- **Office environment** also affects performance. Temperature, lighting, noise, humidity, easy availability of facilities like filing space and photocopying and the appropriateness of furniture and décor can all influence both attitudes and achievement.

5   COST

5.1   **Work should be carried out to the standard required to meet the section's objectives but at the lowest cost commensurate with this aim.**

Control	Comment
Expenditures	When staff have the authority to spend money (for example on supplies) they should avoid unnecessary spending.
Resources and productivity	Costs can get out of hand because of poor productivity or because othe carelessly or wastefully - for example, time is wasted because of disorga handling, heating is left running unnecessarily, vehicles are used so in carrier would be cheaper.

5.2   In the first analysis, cost control for a supervisor means that staff are properly supervised, and all work procedures are carried out as they should be. Good supervision should ensure that costs are kept under control as a matter of course, and that the section contributes more to the organisation's revenues than it incurs in costs.

Budgetary control and standard costs

5.3   Cost control activities are closely associated with budgeting. Supervisors may be involved in a variety of tasks.

- Preparing the budget (sometimes)

- Reviewing the regular budgetary control report, showing budgeted performance levels and costs, actual performance levels and costs, and the differences between them (variances)

- Investigating the cause of any significant variances, and taking action to rectify any problems that are identified

- Explaining any control actions

5.4 **Costs of the accounts department**

- **Wages of permanent staff;** this is the biggest cost, especially when overtime is taken into account.

- **Wages of temporary staff**

- **Costs of equipment and software**

- **Stationery**

- **Overheads** such as heating, lighting and rent: there may be a 'management charge' for cost allocation purposes.

5.5 As a supervisor, you are rarely free to spend as you wish, and the accounts department budget will normally be determined at the beginning of the year. You should thus try to schedule work to avoid unnecessary overtime or weekend working and to avoid the unnecessary use of temporary staff.

Cost reduction

5.6 Cost reduction is the task of reducing the current or planned level of costs. For example, if a procedure currently has a cost of £10 per unit, cost control might be concerned with ensuring that actual costs do not exceed £10, whereas a cost reduction programme might be concerned with reducing the cost to £9 per unit.

5.7 Cost reduction programmes are planned campaigns to cut expenditure; they should preferably be continuous, long-term campaigns, so that short-term cost reductions are not soon reversed and forgotten.

5.8 **Difficulties with cost reduction programmes**

(a) **Resistance by employees** to the pressure to reduce costs, sometimes because the nature and purpose of the campaign have not been properly explained to them, and they feel threatened by the change; sometimes because they genuinely *are* threatened.

(b) They may be **limited to a small area of the business** (eg to one department) with the result that costs are reduced in one cost centre only to reappear as an extra cost in another cost centre.

(c) Cost reduction campaigns are often a **rushed, desperate measure** instead of a carefully organised, well-thought-out exercise.

5.9 **Help of supervisors in cost reductions**

(a) Many of the best ideas for particular cost reductions might come from a supervisor and his or her staff

(b) Any cost-reducing measures must be put into effect by the supervisors.

Guidelines

5.10 (a) **Beware of compromising quality.** A reduction in quality may be justifiable in order to save cost. For instance, internal reports might be produced on cheap paper and stapled rather than bound; this would hardly affect their usefulness. However, there is no point in reducing processing costs by, say, 10% if the resulting documents are riddled with errors.

(b) **Identify any constraints** on opportunities for cost reduction. For example, if the organisation decides that there must be no redundancies as a result of cost reductions,

BPP PUBLISHING

and every employee must be guaranteed security for his or her job, this constraint must be recognised, otherwise you might end up recommending job cuts as the best approach to reducing costs.

(c) **Concentrate on areas of high expenditure** as they are more likely to produce savings potential.

(d) **Committed costs are fixed** in the short term, which means that they are immune from immediate cost reduction measures.

5.11 **Areas to consider for cost reductions**

- **Reducing personnel** levels

- **Deferring expenditure** on new equipment and continuing to use existing equipment. This cuts the planned costs of interest and depreciation

- Using **cheaper supplies** or buying in bulk to obtain discounts

- **Stricter rules about how resources are used** or money spent (at a very simple level, for example, making sure that lights are switched off, or heating equipment not kept on longer than necessary)

- **Changing operations to make them cheaper** (for example, paying employees by BACS rather than by cheques or in cash)

- **Training staff** so that they work more efficiently

- **Rationalisation measures**. Where organisations grow, especially by means of mergers and takeovers, there is a tendency for work to be duplicated in different parts of the organisation. The elimination of unnecessary duplication and the concentration of resources is a form of rationalisation

5.12 **Savings in direct labour costs** will inevitably be a focus of attention for a cost reduction programme. The ideal solution for management might be to achieve the same output levels with a smaller workforce, but there may be problems.

- Reductions in labour costs might involve more capital expenditure on labour-saving machinery;

- The costs of redundancy payments to sacked employees might be high.

- 'Surviving' staff members' morale may be adversely affected.

5.13 In any proposal for improvement or change, you must estimate the resources you need and cost them as best you can.

Key learning points

- **Quality** focuses on the **needs of customers**. For the accounting function many of these are internal customers.

- One means of raising the efficiency of an accounts section is by **work study** - analysing how things are done and how they can be done better, and finding ways of measuring work.

- **Method study** (or O & M) aims to eliminate waste of time, effort, skills, equipment, supplies, space and money.

- **Data may be collected** in the form of notes, flow process charts, procedure flow charts, document flow charts and so on. It must then be analysed to see where improvements can be made.

- **Forms** are used extensively in accounts departments. They should be carefully designed, regularly reviewed and carefully controlled.

- **Measurement of clerical work** procedures is **not always easy**. A supervisor can apply some of the ideas of O & M by estimating target times for simple operations and analysing staff activity.

- **Quality control** methods include 100% checking, partial checking and random sampling.

- **Accounting departments** should operate **cost-effectively** just like any other part of the business. The supervisor is likely to be involved in cost control and may sometimes be required to implement cost reduction measures.

Quick quiz

1   Explain how quality can be managed.

2   What are the implications of the internal customer concept, and who are the accounting function's internal customers?

3   What are the two main aspects of the study of work?

4   What types of problems is an Organisation and Method (O & M) study likely to be concerned with?

5   Why is it a good idea to eliminate waste?

6   What sources of data will be used in an (O & M) study?

7   What will this data show?

8   What is recorded on a procedure flow chart?

9   What are the five sets of questions that should be asked when analysing data about work?

10   What are the principles of form design?

11   How hard or easy is it to measure office work?

12   What is the drawback of time sheets?

13   Suggest three methods of checking work.

14   How might a budgetary control system affect a section supervisor?

15   What are the major difficulties with cost reduction programmes?

16   If you were told to reduce costs in your section what areas of spending would you concentrate on?

Answers to quick quiz

1   The management of quality involves:

(a)   establishing standards of quality for a product or service;

(b)   establishing procedures and methods which ought to ensure that these required standards of quality are met in a suitably high proportion of cases;

(c)   monitoring actual quality;

(d)   taking control action when actual quality falls below standard.

2   The internal customer concept implies the following.

(a)   Any unit of the organisation whose task contributes to the task of other units can be regarded as a supplier of services. The receiving units are thus *customers* of that unit.

(b)   The concept of *customer choice* operates within the organisation as well as outside. If an internal service unit fails to provide the right service at the right time and cost, it cannot expect customer loyalty: it is in *competition* with other internal and external providers of the service.

(c)   The service unit's objective thus becomes the efficient and effective *identification* and *satisfaction of customer needs* - whether within the organisation or outside it.

The internal customers of the accounting function include *line management*, who need accounting information to help them do their jobs (they may prefer to generate their own information if they get poor service from accounts); *senior management* and *shareholders*, who need information to assess how well jobs are being done; and *employees*, who also need information to do their jobs, and who are almost equivalent to external customers for some accounting services like payroll (which could be contracted out).

3   The two main aspects of work study are *method study,* which is concerned with how work should be done, and *work measurement*, which is concerned with how long it should take.

4   A typical O & M investigation is likely to be concerned with:

(a)   getting a job done more efficiently

(b)   questioning whether work needs to be done at all, or whether it can at least be done more simply and with less effort

(c)   trying to establish whether better use can be made of existing idle time, by spreading employees' work loads more evenly over their working time.

5   Eliminating waste (particularly wasted effort) increases productivity, reduces administrative costs and improves staff morale and satisfaction. It brings about these benefits by, for example, cutting out unnecessary operations and streamlining remaining ones, using staff and equipment to the full, and using office space effectively.

6   Data for an (O & M) study may be drawn from:

(a)   organisation charts and manuals, job descriptions and specifications, procedure manuals;

(b)   observation of procedures, forms and control systems in action;

(c)   discussions with managers, supervisors and employees;

(d)   questionnaires.

7   The data will show *what* is done, *why* it is done, *how* it is done, *where* it is done, *who* does it, and *when* it is done.

8   *Procedure flow charts* show the movement of forms between staff and departments. A vertical column is drawn for each department or staff member involved in the process, and a point or rectangle representing a document is inserted in the column for each one it passes through: horizontal lines join the points to represent movement.

9   Data about a process or method can be analysed by asking five sets of questions. These fall into a clear pattern.

Purpose	*Place*	*Sequence*	*Person*	*Means*
What is being done?	Where is it being done?	When is it done?	Who does it?	How is it done?
Why is it being done?	Why there?	Why then?	Why that person?	Why that way?
What else can be done?	Where else could it be done?	When else could it be done?	Who else might do it?	How else could it be done?
What should be done?	Where should it be done?	When should it be done?	Who should do it?	How should it be done?

10   The principles of form design are as follows.

(a)   Forms should be easy to *read* and to *use,* with clear and concise wording, adequate space for entries, and user-friendly layout (both for the person completing the form and the person who deals with it).

(b) Forms should not be too small and cramped (for use, and attractiveness), but size should take into account mailing and filing requirements.

(c) Paper and print quality should be considered in relation to the handling the form is likely to receive: for example the machines or writing implements that will be used, whether the form needs to last, or whether it will be read by somebody important.

(d) The number of operations involved in filling forms should be reduced as far as possible: document sets with selective carbon backing or the equivalent could be used instead of writing details in quadruplicate or photocopying. In this way, a single design and input of data can be adapted for many purposes.

(e) Colour coding of copies may be convenient in any set, and if copies of a master form act variously (for example as order, confirmation, goods received, invoice and so on) they should be clearly identified.

11 Routine or repetitive jobs in the office are fairly easy to set standards for and measure (how many orders are processed per hour, how many pages typed, and so on). Much office work falls into this category.

Non-routine or 'thinking' tasks will be harder to measure, because the office rarely allows uninterrupted execution of a piece of work. It is not easy to determine an accurate time that someone spends planning and reviewing work, or managing or handling people Even routine tasks may vary greatly as to time taken and resources used.

12 Time sheets rely on the individuals completing them to do so conscientiously and truthfully.

13 Methods of work checking include:

(a) 100% checking, which is time-consuming and expensive, and so should only be used for important work;

(b) partial checking, where only important parts of a task are checked, or parts which are prone to error or otherwise under suspicion;

(c) random sampling - frequent checks of random pieces of work, which should turn up areas prone to error or inaccuracy.

14 A supervisor should ideally be involved in the preparation of the budget for his section, although he might instead be given budget targets and standard performance levels that have been set by someone else. A regular budgetary control report will be given to the supervisor, showing budgeted performance levels and costs, actual performance levels and costs, and the differences between them (variances). The supervisor will be required to investigate the cause of any significant variances, and to take action to rectify any problems that are identified, and that are within his ability to control. The supervisor might be required to explain to his superior any control actions he has taken, because his superior will be responsible for the costs incurred by all the sections below him.

15 The major difficulties with cost reduction programmes are as follows.

(a) Resistance by employees to the pressure to reduce costs, sometimes because the programme has not been properly explained to them and they feel threatened by the change, or sometimes because they genuinely *are* threatened.

(b) The programme may be limited to a small area of the business with the result that costs are reduced in one cost centre only to reappear as an extra cost in another cost centre.

(c) Cost reduction campaigns are often introduced as a rushed, desperate measure instead of a carefully organised, well-thought-out exercise.

16 To make the best use of time, the investigation should concentrate on the areas most likely to produce savings: high-cost areas rather than low-cost areas, and areas of discretionary expenditure rather than costs that are already committed and cannot be avoided, at least in the short term. Some obvious areas to consider for cost reductions are: reducing manpower levels; deferring expenditure on new equipment and continuing to use existing equipment; using cheaper supplies or buying in bulk to obtain discounts; and 'rationalisation' measures to eliminate unnecessary duplication.

Answers to activities

Answer 8.1

(a) *The issues for Eleanor raised by the memorandum.*

    (i)   Interdepartmental communication seems to be poor, as evidenced by George's memo. Clearly, he had not been consulted. Furthermore, what communication that does exist between the departments has been contaminated by the noise arising from George's off-hand treatment by one of Eleanor's staff. This has given the issue unpleasant personal overtones.

        If George is as important a user as he says he is, then Eleanor should, as a matter of routine, have consulted him about any changes.

    (ii)   Lack of systems thinking. Clearly, staff in both departments have a difficulty in seeing exactly how their activities relate to the wider whole or even to the immediate users of their services. Eleanor's staff perhaps were unaware of the role of George's department, but they also seem unaware of the importance of their own.

    (iii)   Lack of internal 'marketing orientation'. Eleanor's staff talk about giving value to customers, but they do not appear to relate to their **internal customer**, who is George.

    (iv)   High level conflict between systems. It would appear that the instructions given to Eleanor to contain her costs were developed without any real thought as to the implication of the cutbacks for operations. This indicates that perhaps there is poor co-ordination at higher level, with budgets set simply on departmental lines, leading to conflicts between budgeting and marketing systems.

    (v)   Is George more angry about being unable to cut his own costs, or being unable to enhance the service? It may be that he is under budgetary pressures too, and hopes that Eleanor will take the blame for his failure to cut costs in other ways.

    Other problems relate to the way in which the specific issue was handled.

    (i)   Eleanor's staff did not reply in an appropriate way to George. She needs to discover why the personal relationships between the staff member and George deteriorated to the extent that they resulted in such a brusque letter.

    (ii)   Eleanor should have known about the potential problem in advance. Her staff should have told her. Perhaps she has delegated too much of her job, and allowed subordinates too much unmonitored autonomy. Eleanor herself had not considered the wider implications of the changes she had authorised.

    (iii)   She needs to encourage an internal customer approach amongst her staff.

(b) *What Eleanor should do*

    We know that George has a genuine case, as Eleanor has already conducted an investigation.

    (i)   George should be contacted immediately.

    (ii)   Eleanor should apologise to George for the rather cavalier way in which he has been treated.

    (iii)   She should endeavour to rectify the situation, winning extra resources from senior management if necessary, with the active co-operation of George. However, if resources of time, personnel and money are limited then she might have to reorder the priorities of her department, and perhaps defer some less critical projects. This might mean that other departments will have to be inconvenienced.

    (iv)   Some of her staff should be sent on customer care programmes - directed of course, to improving their relationships with internal customers.

    (v)   She must remember to include George's needs in her plans for next year.

Answer 8.2

(a) Firstly, ensure that all of the departments concerned have been informed of the investigation, and of its purpose. The most appropriate way of doing this would probably be for a memorandum to be sent to departmental supervisors from the chief accountant. The memorandum would explain that the investigation had been requested by the managing director.

The memorandum would explain that the investigation is to examine the reports and forms used within the organisation. The next stage would be to build up information on all of the reports and forms used in each department. This information would be gathered by visiting and interviewing supervisors and other departmental staff.

Samples of each form and report would be collected, and details compiled (from the department generating the form or report) of:

(i) the purpose of forms;
(ii) recipients of forms;
(iii) sources of data;
(iv) methods of processing the forms;
(v) time taken to prepare;
(vi) frequency of preparation;
(vii) processing of forms.

It may transpire that because of particular problems or considerations highlighted by departmental staff visited, additional information should be added to the list of information to be compiled.

The departments to whom the reports and forms are circulated could then be approached, and the following questions asked.

(i) What is your view of the purpose of this form?
(ii) How much of the information which it contains do you use, and how do you use it?
(iii) Do you receive the information at the frequency required?
(iv) Is the information supplied in the correct format?
(v) Does the form duplicate information which you also receive from elsewhere?
(vi) What is your overall opinion of the value of the form?

Having completed the process of gathering information, it will be appropriate:

(i) to make an initial assessment of the extent of any problems revealed;
(ii) to formulate some recommendations about how to copy out a full investigation; and
(iii) to draft an informal report to the Chief Accountant based on the above.

(b) **MEMORANDUM**

To: The Chief Accountant
From: A B C Technician
Subject: Reporting within the organisation
Date: 4 February 19XX

I have now completed my initial investigations of reporting within the organisation along the lines discussed by Ms Green and yourself. My investigation involved a survey of forms and reports produced by the costing office and the work study department. A schedule of the forms and reports issued by these two departments is attached, together with samples of each form, at Appendix A.

I received full co-operation from the staff members concerned in carrying out my investigation. My initial findings can be summarised under the following headings.

(i) *Use and frequency of information in forms and reports*

Recipients of forms were asked how the information of the form or report was used by them. The results of canvassing are summarised in the table below.

BPP PUBLISHING

	Cost office	Work study dept
Documents circulated	38	10
Number of recipients	120	23
Recipients' comments		
Useful	15	7
Some use	60	10
Very limited use	30	3
No information used	15	3
Total	120	23
Reports too frequent	25	2
Report frequency satisfactory	71	14
Reports not frequent enough	24	7
Total	120	23

(ii)   *Format of the forms*

Some of the forms which are prepared manually take some time to complete because of the need to enter codes manually on sheets.

More explanatory information setting out how forms should be completed could usefully be included on the face of the forms. Many members of staff found some of the forms difficult to complete without consulting other staff or referring to manuals.

(iii)   *Presentation*

There is currently no standardisation of layout in the forms, nor are standard sizes of paper used for forms. Various different types of code are used to identify particular forms. Some forms which are identified by different codes include very similar information. In particular, forms 01 and G3 produced by the cost office are so similar that no recipients understood why two forms were generated rather than just one. Colour coding of forms may be a useful means of differentiating types of form.

Recommendations

The findings highlight the need for a rethink of the design, presentation and circulation of forms and reports within the organisation. I suggest that the following points merit further consideration.

(i)   The development of a consistent policy throughout the organisation covering forms and reports. A policy of consistency in layout and in the size of forms and reports will greatly 'streamline' the processes of preparing, copying and filing of the documents.

(ii)   Extension of the survey to all departments. The pilot survey carried out has indicated the general need for revision of the current forms and reports. The pilot survey provides sufficient information to formulate proposals for revision of the forms and reports in the two departments examined. However, considerably more time would be necessary to extend the survey to all departments.

(iii)   Evaluation of savings arising from the exercise. This evaluation will, I believe, demonstrate the value of extending the survey to all departments.

(iv)   A formal means of control over all forms and reports in the organisation. This will ensure that the standardisation of forms and reports used is maintained in the future.

Chapter 9   Problems and contingencies

Chapter topic list

1   Contingency plans

2   Computer security

3   Personnel issues

Learning objectives

On completion of this chapter you will be able to:

	Performance criteria	Range Statement
• ensure that contingency plans to meet possible emergencies are prepared with management and if necessary implemented within agreed timescales	10.1.3	1, 2
• ensure that work activities are effectively co-ordinated with work plans and contingencies	10.1.6	1, 2
• ensure that problems or queries are referred to the appropriate person	10.1.7	1, 2

BPP PUBLISHING

1 CONTINGENCY PLANS

1.1 A contingency plan sets out what needs to be done to restore normality after something has gone wrong. The plan has some essential features.

- **Standby procedures** so that some operations can be performed while normal services are disrupted

- **Recovery procedures** once the cause of the problem has been addressed

- The **personnel management policies** to ensure that (a) and (b) above are implemented properly

What can go wrong?

1.2 Here are some suggestions of things that can go wrong. These are of varying degrees of importance.

(a) **Computer problems**
- Fire, floods or explosions destroying data files and equipment
- A computer virus completely destroying a data or program file
- For new systems or parts of systems, software bugs not discovered at the design or parallel running stages
- Accidental damage to telecommunications links (for example if builders sever a cable)

(b) **Procedural difficulties**
- Data input errors, such as posting invoices or crediting cash receipts to the wrong accounts, posting the wrong amounts, making single entries, and so on
- Processing errors, for example closing down the ledgers and running the month-end program before all the month's data has been input or using incorrect opening balances
- Other accounting errors, due to uncertainty about how to treat certain items, or about how the system is supposed to work

(c) **Staff problems**
- Insufficient staff, due to sickness, strikes and so on
- The departure or temporary absence of key personnel
- Disciplinary problems
- Conflict between individuals or between supervisor and those supervised

(d) **Sudden changes in operating conditions**
- The failure or takeover of a **competitor**, causing a sudden increase in demand and therefore transactions

- The bankruptcy of a major **supplier**
- A takeover by a **new senior management** with different reporting requirements
- A **new tax** affecting all transactions

Contingency plans and controls

1.3 After reading the chapter on internal controls you may be thinking that some of the above problems should not arise in the first place if proper controls are in place. To justify setting up a control, **the risk of the problem arising must be great enough to outweigh the cost,** in terms of time and resources, of operating the control. If it is not, the organisation will run the risk, but it must remain aware that there *is* a risk, and have a plan ready to deal with the problem in the unlikely event that it does arise.

How do you prepare a contingency plan?

1.4 **Identify risks.** You cannot prepare a contingency plan without first being aware that the contingency exists. **Risk identification** should be a continuous process, so that new risks and changes affecting existing risks may be identified quickly and dealt with appropriately, before they can cause unacceptable losses.

(a) **Keep abreast of all the events affecting the work of the accounts department** at present and in the future and anticipating problems that could occur. It helps, though, if there are good two-way communications between your section and everybody else that it deals with in the organisation and if you take a keen interest in new developments in your organisation and in its business environment.

(b) **Speak to people** who have been in the organisation longer than you have, and have encountered problems in the past.

(c) **Speak to your staff**, who may be aware of problems starting to become crises long before you are.

(d) **Speak to others outside your organisation** who may have encountered problems that could equally well be faced by your section. Sharing experiences in class will be fruitful, as will chatting to friends in similar jobs.

(e) **Encounter the problem itself and dealing with it**. This is almost certainly the commonest way in practice. It means that a contingency plan should have been in place, but wasn't! In the light of this **experience** a contingency plan is formed after the event to ensure that mistakes that were made in dealing with it the first time do not happen again.

1.5 **Decide action.** Once the problem has been identified the next step is to decide what to do. A distinction is sometimes made between the **emergency plan** and the **recovery plan**.

(a) The **emergency plan** should be designed to ensure that action at the time of the event is swift and decisive. Everyone should know where to go, what to do, when to do it and when to stop.

(b) The **recovery plan** comes into play once the initial crisis is dealt with and is intended to make sure that the business gets back on its feet as soon as possible.

BPP PUBLISHING

1.6 **Prepare contingency plans.**

(a) **Define responsibilities.** Somebody should be designated to take control in a crisis. This individual can then delegate specific tasks or responsibilities to other designated personnel.

(b) **Priorities** must be **established in advance.** Section heads may have a distorted view of the organisation's overall needs or be self-interested so priorities need to be **agreed with more senior management.**

(c) **Up-to-date information.** How, for example, do you turn *off* the sprinklers once a fire is extinguished? If you don't know you will have a flood as well! All the information that will need to be available during and after the event should be gathered in advance. This will include names and addresses of staff, details of equipment maintenance firms and so on.

(d) **Communication with staff.** The problems of disaster can be made worse by poor communications between members of staff.

(e) **Public relations.** If the disaster has a public impact, the recovery team may come under pressure from the public or from the media. If your organisation has a PR department all enquiries should be referred to them. The best way for you to deal with the media is to tell them nothing at all.

(f) **Heath and safety.** Many contingencies involve threats to health and safety and these may continue during the recovery phase. Do not compromise on dealing with risks to health and safety.

(g) **Practice.** Unless the plan has been tested there is no guarantee that it will work.

Absence cover

1.7 **EXAMPLE**

Here a firm has become aware that most of its staff will be affected if a series of threatened public transport strikes goes ahead. When this first appears in the news an outline plan is drawn up showing how different sections of the business will be affected (only two sections are shown below).

Action	Example	Consequence	
		Sales section	*Payroll section*
Identify contingency	Disruption to public Transport	All staff have difficulty getting to work	All staff have difficulty getting to work
Draw up emergency plan	Operate whatever level of service is necessary to minimise the (financial) loss to the business	Take orders: this requires a skeleton staff of 3 persons to man the telephones	No service need be provided: salaries paid monthly by BACS; no weekly paid staff
Draw up recovery plan	Restore operations to normal	Process backlog of orders	Clear backlog due to lost time

1.8 Once it is confirmed that the strikes are going ahead the plans are fleshed out.

Emergency plan

Aim

To operate as normally as possible depending upon the number of staff available. The priority is to ensure that sufficient staff are available to take a typical day's orders: the minimum staffing requirement is the section supervisor or assistant supervisor plus two others with appropriate experience.

Action

(a) The section supervisor should make whatever arrangements are necessary to ensure that she can be on site at 9 am. If a taxi or hotel accommodation are needed the company will pay for this.

(b) Any staff who are likely to have difficulties in getting to work on time should call in with an estimate of when, if at all, they expect to arrive. Staff who do not call in will be assumed to be taking a day's holiday. Staff who notify the company that they are unable to get to work will be paid, but they should clearly understand that their full co-operation will be expected in implementing recovery procedures.

(c) The section supervisor will be responsible for making whatever arrangements are necessary to ensure that the sales telephones are manned. This may mean securing the assistance of staff from other sections, or failing this, authorising or arranging for transport for staff members at the company's expense. The appended list *[not shown in this text]* gives addresses and telephone numbers of all staff with appropriate skills and the approximate distance of their homes from head office.

(d) *Customer care.* Staff should understand that some customers may become angry or frustrated if there are delays in getting through and should make apologies as appropriate. Customers placing orders should be told that there may be a slight delay in processing their order because the disruption to public transport means that only a skeleton staff is operating. Customers should be asked whether they wish their order to be treated as urgent, once normal services are resumed. A note of all urgent orders should be passed to the section supervisor or assistant supervisor.

Appendix

This would contain information such as names and addresses of staff, taxi firms and hotels, and a brief guide to relevant sales section procedures (in case inexperienced or 'rusty' staff have to be used).

Recovery plan

Aim

To maintain a normal level of service and also to clear the processing backlog caused by the disruption as quickly as possible.

Action

The three options in order of preference are as follows.

(a) Temporarily transfer appropriately skilled staff from other sections to help clear the backlog

(b) Overtime working: approximately 21 hours should be required if no order processing is done on the day of the disruption

(c) Employ temporary staff

Note. Given equal pressures on other sections, option (b) is the most likely to be implemented. Staff should clearly understand that it is in their own best interests as well as the company's that the backlog is cleared as soon as possible.

BPP PUBLISHING

Crisis management

1.9 EXAMPLE

A few days after sending out the July statements to her company's customers, Claudia, the head of the sales ledger section began to receive phone calls querying the amounts shown. Over the succeeding days a flood of complaints was received and it was clear that the problem was a serious one, affecting a large proportion of the company's many debtors.

(a) Claudia's investigations revealed that each of the customers affected had had at least one false invoice added to their account. This appeared to be the work of one of the invoicing assistants who had resigned the previous week after being passed over for promotion. After further investigation it transpired that all documentary evidence that would have enabled the company to identify the extent of the problem quickly (original orders, the false invoices themselves, etc) had disappeared. The invoicing assistant responsible had not left a forwarding address or contact number and had long since moved away from the address shown in the company's records. He was thought to be abroad on holiday.

(b) To deal with the emergency Claudia took the following emergency and recovery action.

   (i) All complaints were put straight through to her.

   (ii) She wrote to all of the company's debtors asking them to ignore the July statements.

   (iii) The extent of the problem was isolated by establishing that the statements issued at the end of June had been correct.

   (iv) All cash received from debtors since the beginning of August was posted to a carefully documented suspense account (rather than allowing attempts to be made to match it against open items shown on debtors' accounts)

   (v) Two employees were appointed to carry out the task of matching up despatches during July (as shown in warehouse records) to invoices, to determine which were genuine and which were not. (The arrangement of relevant information in the systems used by the company was such that this was an extremely laborious and painstaking operation.)

   (vi) Recovery procedures were implemented. Once the spurious invoices had all been identified they were cleared off the system, the cash received was credited to accounts and new statements were issued, with further apologies and assurances. Customers who had actually paid the false invoices were sent cash refunds and letters of apology.

1.10 We have not described this case in full detail, but there are clearly lessons to be learnt from it. It would be unlikely that a contingency plan would exist for this problem. However, some general principles could be established for dealing with emergencies of this type.

- Customer care is vitally important and supervisors should take personal charge of problems affecting more than, say, 3 customers simultaneously as this would indicate a system fault.

- Customers should receive a clear and reasonably open notification of the nature of the problem.

- The PR department should be informed (not mentioned here).

- Problems of this type should be reported to higher management up to a suitable level - probably director, or in a large organisation, the general manager of the site.

1.11 A contingency plan would not be likely because the case illustrates a general lack of control. You may like to make your own list before continuing: these are just suggestions.

- The guilty invoicing assistant's bitterness towards the organisation was not recognised at all until after the event.

- The perpetrator managed to override a number of controls. These would need to be strengthened if possible.

- There was no way of identifying which invoicing assistant was responsible for posting which invoices. An enhancement to the system is required in the longer term, and in the meantime more careful records should be kept regarding the allocation of work.

- Links between sales order processing information and the despatch system need to be strengthened.

- Employee records were not being kept up to date.

- No monitoring procedures seem to have been operating on the section's work.

1.12 We have now established the basic principles of dealing with contingencies. In the remainder of this chapter we are going to concentrate on two areas in particular - computer problems and people problems.

Activity 9.1

Samdip is the supervisor of a small section of 10 staff, including himself. In July, which is the section's busiest time of the year, one of his staff is on honeymoon for three weeks, two are injured in a car accident and are not expected to be back at work for the foreseeable future and one is believed to have won the National Lottery, since she was only seen fleetingly on Monday morning stuffing her personal belongings into a Harrods carrier bag before jumping into a Ferrari and driving away.

Identify the problems for Samdip's section and discuss possible ways of dealing with them.

---

2 COMPUTER SECURITY

2.1 One of the worst things that could happen in a computerised accounts section is the loss of all the up-to-date data on a **current file** or the loss of a program.

(a) Files can be physically **lost** (for example the librarian might misplace a file, or a file may be stolen).

(b) A file can become **corrupted** when it is written and so include false data. A file might also be **physically damaged** and become unreadable.

An important set of procedural controls is therefore to enable a data or program file to be recreated if the original is lost or corrupted. To recreate a master file, it is possible to go back to earlier generations of the master file and transactions files, do the data processing all over again and create a new version of the up-to-date master file.

Back-up and stand-by facilities

2.2 Many organisations ensure that a **minimum of two copies** is always held in addition to the original data. The reason for holding two back-up copies is simple. If the original data is lost, the back-up becomes the only version in existence and is no longer a back-up. It is now the master.

2.3 The **grandfather-father-son** technique is used on systems where the main data storage is on replaceable magnetic media such as tape. Data on the 'grandfather' tape is updated with transactions and the update stored on the 'father' tape. When further transactions are processed, the 'father' tape is used and output stored on the 'son' tape. When the next batch of transactions is processed, the output is stored on the 'grandfather' tape, which thus becomes the new 'son' tape and the other two generations move up one stage. There are thus 3 generations available at anytime, plus all the transactions relating to them.

2.4 A different approach will be used with PCs and smaller network servers using hard disks. One technique is to make backups daily using a set of weekly media, one for each working day in the week. These are thus re-used once each week. A further set of backups may then be made of each month-end with the media being reused annually. Finally, a backup is taken at year end and kept permanently. Once again, it is necessary to store the transaction inputs if it is to be possible to re-create data.

2.5 **Back-up media**

(a) Backing up a hard disk on to floppy disks can be tedious, because a hard disk holds much more data than a floppy disk. However, ZIP-drives can speed things up.

(b) Backing up a **hard disk on to a tape** is quicker and more convenient, although the user has to go to the expense of buying a tape streamer unit. **File server data** can be backed up every day in this way.

(c) CD-ROM. Many computer systems have a CD-ROM drive. CD-ROMs can store a huge amount of data in a small space.

(d) In networked systems, copies can be backed up on to the hard disk drive as well as on to the **file server**.

2.6 Back-up copies should be stored in a different place from the original file and preferably in a fire-proof safe.

2.7 The backing-up of data is a critical requirement for systems security. However, data on a back-up file will not itself be entirely secure unless some additional measures are used. If there is a **hardware fault** which causes data loss or corruption the fault must be diagnosed and corrected before the correct data is put at risk in the system.

2.8 The back-up data should also be **isolated from the operations staff** so that it is not too readily available. Back-up data which is easily available could be used before system errors have been fully corrected and may then become corrupted too. An organisational policy which dictates the systems tests necessary prior to the loading of back-up data is vital for ensuring that the back-up data is itself protected against system and human faults.

Stand-by hardware facilities

2.9 **Hardware duplication** will permit a system to function in case of breakdown. The provision of **back-up computers** tends to be quite costly, particularly where these systems have no other function.

(a) Many organisations will use many PCs and so protection against system faults can be provided by **shifting operations** to one of the working PCs still functioning.

(b) Where an organisation has only a single system to rely on, this ready recourse to a backup facility is unavailable. In these instances one response would be to negotiate a **maintenance contract** which provides for backup facilities.

2.10 **Available standby hardware facilities**

(a) **Computer bureaux** can agree to make their own systems available in the event of an emergency. Such an arrangement has to be specified in advance, as there might be other demands on a bureau's resources.

(b) Co-operating with **other organisations** in the locality, through a mutual aid agreement, may be a way of pooling resources. However, these other organisations themselves might not, in the event, be able to spare the computer time.

(c) **Contingency centres** (specially set up computer rooms only used for the purpose) are rare and expensive, and the disaster-stricken organisation may pay large amounts in hardware rental. Also, the organisation's staff would have to be familiar with the hardware so equipped. As with a bureau, membership of such a scheme limits system developments in house to those compatible with the backup facility.

Other security measures to guard against contingencies

2.11 With the vast quantities of computers and computer material around the risks of data corruption have increased.

Unauthorised access: passwords and user profiles

2.12 Email, intranets and the internet means that computer systems are increasingly connected over telecommunications lines. These are rarely completely secure, and an expert **hacker** can easily enter the system.

> **KEY TERM**
>
> A **password** is a unique code a person uses to enter the system. A **user profile** in a networked system only allows certain people access to particular files, but does not involve a password.

2.13 Hackers may programme their own computers to try many combinations of characters in the hope of finding a password by a process of elimination. Keeping track of these attempts can alert managers to repeated efforts to break into the system; in these cases the culprits might be caught, particularly if there is an apparent pattern to their efforts.

2.14 (a) **User profiles** can prevent people accessing the **system at all** without a password.

(b) User profiles allow a person access to a system, but with **restrictions** to the files that can be used.

- Computer files marked 'restricted access' might only be accessed by a few people with appropriate profiles. This is very important for database or network systems.

- Data and software will be classified according to the **sensitivity and confidentiality** of data.

(c) Records can be kept of access to files, so that a 'trail' can be left of unauthorised attempts at entry.

2.15 **Passwords** ought to be effective in keeping out unauthorised users, but they are by no means foolproof. By experimenting with possible passwords, an unauthorised person can gain access to a programme or file by guessing the correct password. This is not as difficult as it may seem when too many computer users specify 'obvious' passwords for their files or programmes. Someone who is authorised to access a data or programme file may tell an unauthorised person what the password is, perhaps through carelessness.

2.16 For a password system to be effective, passwords should be:
- Changed regularly
- Confidential
- Difficult to guess
- Hidden

Viruses

2.17 A virus is a computer program that infects a computer system and replicates itself within it, much in the same way as a human being catches a cold. Some viruses can destroy data and files; other just display messages. The best way to deal with viruses is to **avoid infection** in the first place.

2.18 **Identifying a virus**

- It may be possible to identify it before it does any damage.
- The second option is to identify it when it is activated.

2.19 It is difficult for the typical user to identify the presence of a virus.

(a) **Anti-virus software** such as Dr Solomon's is capable of detecting and eradicating a vast number of viruses before they do any damage. Upgrades are released regularly to deal with new viruses. The software will run whenever a computer is turned on and will continue to monitor in the background until it is turned off again.

(b) Organisations must guard against the introduction of unauthorised software to their systems. Many viruses have been spread on **pirated versions** of popular computer games or possibly the Internet.

(c) **Check any disk received from the outside is virus-free** before the data on the disk is downloaded.

(d) Any flaws in a widely used program should be rectified as soon as they come to light.

(e) Do not open email attachments.

Network security

2.20 When data are transmitted over a network or a telecommunications line (especially the Internet) there are numerous security dangers.

(a) Corruptions such as viruses on a single computer **can spread through the network** to all of the organisation's computers.

(b) Unless care is exercised it is **easy to overwrite somebody else's data**.

(c) **Disaffected employees** have much greater potential to do deliberate damage to valuable corporate data or systems because the network could give them access to parts of the system that they are not really authorised to use.

(d) If the organisation is linked to an external network, persons outside the company (**hackers**) may be able to get into the company's internal network, either to steal data or to damage the system. Intranets can have **firewalls** (which disable part of the telecoms technology) to prevent unwelcome intrusions into company systems, but a determined hacker may well be able to bypass even these.

(e) Employees may download **inaccurate information** or imperfect or virus-ridden software from an external network. For example 'beta' (free trial) versions of forthcoming new editions of many major packages are often available on the Internet, but the whole point about a beta version is that it is not fully tested and may contain bugs that could disrupt an entire system.

(f) Information transmitted from one part of an organisation to another may be **intercepted**. Data can by 'encrypted' (scrambled) in an attempt to make it unintelligible to eavesdroppers, but there is not yet any entirely satisfactory method of doing this.

(g) The **communications link** itself may break down or distort data.

Data transmission

2.21 One of the big problems in transmitting data down a public or private telephone wire is the possibility of distortion or loss of the message. There needs to be some way for a computer to:

(a) Detect whether there are **errors in data transmission** (eg loss of data, or data arriving out of sequence, ie in an order different from the sequence in which it was transmitted)

(b) Take steps **to recover the lost data**, even if this is simply to notify the computer or terminal operator to telephone the sender of the message that the whole data package will have to be re-transmitted. However, a more 'sophisticated' system can identify the corrupted or lost data more specifically, and request re-transmission of only the lost or distorted parts.

(c) Both of these functions are provided by the TCP/IP communication protocols which are now widely used on networks.

3   PERSONNEL ISSUES

The meaning of discipline

3.1 Lack of discipline is certain to impair the efficiency of a section and maintaining discipline among employees is an integral part of the **directing** function of management.

> ### KEY TERM
>
> **Discipline** promotes good order and behaviour in an organisation by enforcing acceptable standards of conduct. It can be maintained by sanctions, encouraged by example or created by individuals' own sense of what is fitting and proper.

3.2 Unhappily, there are always some employees in every organisation who will fail to observe the established rules even after having been informed of them. Firm action is required to maintain responsible employee behaviour. One test of a good line manager or supervisor is how he deals with disciplinary situations.

3.3 **Common disciplinary problems.**

- Absenteeism
- Excessive lateness in arriving at work
- Defective and/or inadequate work performance

- Poor attitudes which influence the work of others or which reflect on the public image of the firm

- Breaking rules regarding rest periods and other time schedules such as leaving work to go home early

- Improper personal appearance

- Breaking safety rules

- Alcoholic intoxication

- Sexual harassment

3.4 Disciplinary incidents are usually unpleasant for all concerned but the supervisor must learn to **deal with them rather than try to avoid them**. Disciplinary action requires that the supervisor should utilise some of the authority inherent in his supervisory position, even though he or she might prefer to 'pass the buck' to someone in higher management.

Taking disciplinary action

3.5 Any disciplinary action must be undertaken with sensitivity and sound judgement on the supervisor's part. The purpose of discipline in organisations is not punishment or retribution. Disciplinary action must have as its goal the improvement of the future behaviour of the employee and other members of the organisation.

3.6 Normally, a good supervisor will not have too many occasions to take disciplinary action. Taking disciplinary action will involve an interview with the 'offender' and the supervisor should try to prepare himself properly for it.

- Investigate first and stay calm.
- Discipline in private

Progressive discipline

3.7 ACAS guidelines suggest a series of progressive responses to repeated indiscipline. The following is a list of suggested steps of progressive disciplinary action.

Step 1. **The informal talk.** If the infraction is of a relatively minor nature and if the employee is one whose record has no previous marks of disciplinary action, an informal, friendly talk will clear up the situation in many cases. It may be appropriate to make a note of the discussion for inclusion in the person's personnel file.

Step 2. The **oral warning or reprimand** will be appropriate for second offence. The supervisor emphasises the undesirability of the subordinate's repeated violation, and that ultimately it could lead to serious disciplinary action. Despite the warning being oral, it should be noted in writing in the personnel file.

Step 3. **Written or official warning.** A written warning should detail the offence and the possible consequences. It may be a final warning, indicating that a subsequent offence will result in a severe sanction such as suspension or dismissal. Written warnings are particularly necessary in unionised workplaces, so that the document can serve as evidence in case of grievance procedures.

Step 4. **Disciplinary layoffs, or suspension.** This course of action would be next in order if the employee has committed repeated offences and previous steps were of no avail. Disciplinary lay-offs usually extend over several days or weeks. Some employees may not be very impressed with oral or written warnings, but they will find a disciplinary layoff without pay a rude awakening.

Step 5.   **Demotion**. Another disciplinary measure (the value of which has been seriously questioned) is demoting an employee to a lower-paying job. This course of action is likely to bring about dissatisfaction and discouragement, since losing pay and status over an extended period of time is a form of constant punishment. This dissatisfaction of the demoted employee may easily spread to co-workers. Most enterprises avoid downgrading as a disciplinary measure.

Step 6.   **Dismissal**. Dismissal is the most drastic form of disciplinary action. It should be reserved only for the most serious offences. The personnel department should advise before this step is taken.

Step 4 and step 5 may well be a breach of the contract of employment unless they are specifically provided for.

3.8   Normally, a supervisor's role would be limited to an informal talk. Invoking any further disciplinary procedures is a serious matter, and more senior management would be involved.

The employee's rights

3.9   ACAS procedures require that the employee should have the opportunity to state his or her case, accompanied by a fellow employee or union representative, and have a right of appeal.

Counselling

3.10   Earlier in this chapter we described an imaginary situation in which a disgruntled employee did severe damage to an organisation's debtors system. This was not a case for disciplinary action (after the event, it was *too late*), but the problem might have been avoided if the employee's unhappiness had been recognised earlier. 'Counselling can be defined as a purposeful relationship in which one person helps another to help himself. It is a way of relating and responding to another person so that that person is helped to explore his thoughts, feelings and behaviour with the aim of reaching a clearer understanding. The clearer understanding may be of himself or of a problem, or of the one in relation to the other.'

(Rees, *The Skills of Management*)

3.11   The IPM statement makes it clear that effective counselling is not merely a matter of pastoral care for individuals, but is very much in the organisation's interests.

(a)   Appropriate use of counselling tools can prevent under-performance, reduce labour turnover and absenteeism and increase commitment from employees. Unhappy employees are far more likely to seek employment elsewhere.

(b)   Effective counselling demonstrates an organisation's commitment to and concern for its employees and so is liable to improve loyalty and enthusiasm among the workforce.

(c)   The development of employees is of value to the organisation, and counselling can give employees the confidence and encouragement necessary to take responsibility for self and career development.

(d)   Workplace counselling recognises that the organisation may be contributing to the employees' problems and therefore it provides an opportunity to reassess organisational policy and practice.

3.12   Effective counselling requires training and practice.

Activity 9.2

You are concerned about the attitude and performance of Ian Dalgleish, a member of your section. Since your appointment as supervisor of the section a few months ago, you have been able to come to terms with the rest of the team. Performance was mediocre when you arrived but you have obtained improvements by discussing and agreeing new ideas, by establishing clear short term goals for all your staff, and by giving them frequent feedback. It has not worked with Ian. His work is sloppy and untidy. He misses deadlines. He sometimes comes in late and goes early. He seems to resent you and to take perverse pleasure in thwarting your intentions. You know he has considerable potential. He is honorary treasurer of two local societies both of which are full of praise for him. He runs a football team very successfully and is popular with his colleagues.

(a) What are the issues raised by this scenario? State any potential problems that you have *ruled out*, in making your analysis.

(b) What are the possible *reasons* for Ian's problems?

(c) Before taking any further action, how would you go about gathering further information?

(d) What action could you take to solve the problem?

Key learning points

- A wide variety of problems can arise in an accounts section and they will be dealt with more effectively if they are anticipated and planned for. Contingency planning entails identifying the risks and drawing up an emergency plan and a recovery plan.

- One of the biggest dangers is the loss or corruption of computer data. Back-up procedures are vital.

- The most common problems are likely to be problems with people. Disciplinary action aims to improve the future behaviour of an employee, not to punish. The supervisor should attempt to minimise resentment by giving advance warning, acting quickly, being consistent and applying the hot stove rule.

- Counselling aims to help employees to help themselves.

Quick quiz

1 What is a contingency plan?

2 List problems that might arise in an accounts department.

3 What is the link between contingency plans and controls?

4 How can risks be identified?

5 What is the difference between an emergency plan and a recovery plan?

6 What provisions may be included in a contingency plan?

7 In what way may a disaster be beneficial to an organisation and its staff?

8 How can a master file be recreated?

9 If a back-up copy of data is taken, is the data then secure? (Several points should be made in your answer.)

10 What problems arise in making provisions for the breakdown of computer hardware? (Again, there are several points you can make.)

11 What are passwords used for?

12 What is the purpose of disciplinary action?

13 What should be done before disciplinary action is taken?

14 Briefly, what are the steps to follow in a system of progressive discipline?

15   What is counselling?

Answers to quick quiz

1   A contingency plan sets out what needs to be done to restore normality after something has gone wrong. It provides for: standby procedures so that some operations can be performed while normal services are disrupted; recovery procedures once the cause of the problem has been addressed; and appropriate personnel management policies to allow standby and recovery procedures to be implemented properly.

2   Here are some examples

    (a)   Computer problems
    (b)   Procedural difficulties
    (c)   Staff problems
    (d)   Sudden changes in operating conditions
    (e)   Fraud

3   To justify setting up a control to avoid a problem, the risk of the problem arising must be great enough to outweigh the cost, in terms of time and resources, of operating the control. If it is not, the organisation will run the risk, but it must remain aware that there *is* a risk, and have a contingency plan ready to deal with the problem in the unlikely event that it does arise.

4   Means of identifying risks

    (a)   Keeping abreast of all relevant events at present and in the future and anticipating problems that could occur. This is very difficult in practice.

    (b)   Speaking to experienced people in the organisation who may have encountered problems in the past.

    (c)   Speaking to staff, whose more direct involvement in operations may mean that they have early warning of problems.

    (d)   Speaking to people outside the organisation who may have encountered problems that could equally well affect your section. Some consultants advise on risks for a living, and insurance companies also specialise in this area.

    (e)   Encountering the problem itself and dealing with it.

5   The emergency plan is intended to ensure that action *at the time of* the event is swift and decisive. The recovery plan comes into play once the initial crisis is dealt with. It is intended to make sure that the business gets back on its feet as soon as possible.

6   A contingency plan will include provisions for each of the following.

    (a)   *Definition of responsibilities*: someone should take control and delegate specific tasks or responsibilities to other designated personnel.

    (b)   *Priorities.* Some tasks are more important than others and these must be established and agreed with senior management in advance.

    (c)   *Information.* All the information that will need to be available during and after the event should be gathered in advance, kept up to date and circulated to anyone who might need it.

    (d)   *Communication with staff.* Everyone should be made aware of the problems that are possible and how they can be controlled.

    (e)   *Public relations.* Refer to his PR department. Say nothing to the media.

    (f)   *Practice.* If a full scale test is not possible, simulations should be as realistic as possible and should be taken seriously by all involved. The results of any testing should be monitored so that amendments can be made to the plan as necessary.

7   A disaster may be beneficial if it is used as a *learning* experience, and action is taken to ensure that the same mistakes are not made twice. All too often this is not the case, however.

8   To recreate a master file it is necessary to keep copies of earlier 'generations' of the master file and transactions files. Lost or unrecorded data processing has to be done again from the original input sources, and so these too must be kept.

9   The data is more secure than if no copy is taken, but there are still potential problems.

(a)   The data is not really secure if it is the *only* other copy: if the original data is lost the single back-up becomes the only version in existence.

(b)   It is not secure if it is stored on the same site as the original, or somewhere else where it is liable to get damaged.

(c)   If there is a hardware fault which causes data loss or corruption the fault must be diagnosed and corrected before the correct data is put at risk in the system. The usefulness of data on back-up would be entirely negated if it were fed mindlessly into a faulty system.

(d)   The back-up data may also be at risk if it is too readily available to operations staff. Back-up data which is easily available could be used before system errors have been fully corrected and may then become corrupted too.

For all of these reasons it is better to keep *two* back-up copies.

10   The provision of back-up hardware tends to be quite costly, particularly where these systems have no other function. Arrangements with computer bureaux have to be specified in advance, as there might be other demands on a bureau's resources.

Pooling resources with other organisations may be a way of obtaining stand-by facilities, but these other organisations themselves might not, in the event, be able to spare the computer time. If the damage was caused by a local power surge or a terrorist attack, for example, all of the organisations might be equally badly affected.

Contingency centres (specially set up computer rooms only used for the purpose) are rare and expensive, and in any case the organisation's staff would have to be familiar with the hardware so equipped.

In addition, membership of any such scheme limits system developments in house to those compatible with the backup facility.

11   Passwords are used to deny access to the system entirely and to restrict access to particular files.

12   Disciplinary action should have as its goal the improvement of the future behaviour of the employee and other members of the organisation. The purpose, obviously, is the avoidance of similar occurrences in the future. It is not vindictiveness and retribution against individuals.

13   The supervisor should guard against undue haste or unwarranted actions, caused by bias or anger. Before doing anything, a supervisor should investigate what happened and why. Consideration should be given to the employee's past record and all other pertinent information about the situation before any disciplinary action is taken.

14   Possible steps in a system of progressive discipline are as follows.

(a)   The informal talk
(b)   Oral warning or reprimand
(c)   Written or official warning
(d)   Disciplinary layoffs, or suspension
(e)   Demotion
(f)   Discharge

15   'Counselling is a way of relating and responding to another person so that that person is helped to explore his thoughts, feelings and behaviour with the aim of reaching a clearer understanding of himself or of a problem, or of the one in relation to the other.' In short it is a way of helping people to help themselves.

Answers to activities

Answer 9.1

Problems

The personnel in Samdip's department have been reduced from 10 to 6 at the busiest time of the year. Although the absence due to honeymoon should have been known about and planned for long in advance the other events are quite unexpected. The section is clearly going to have problems in getting its work done.

Solutions

A variety of measures are possible.

(a)   *Clarify the situation*. Find out exactly how long the injured staff will be away. Make sure that the lottery winner has resigned and take immediate steps to recruit a permanent replacement.

(b)   *Samdip* will probably have to get more involved in the day-to-day work of the section.

(c)   It may be possible to *borrow* suitable staff from other parts of the organisation.

(d)   *Recruit temporary staff*. This may be possible if the knowledge required to do the work of the section is not particularly specialised. However it is an expensive option.

(e)   *Work overtime*. The section is down to almost half of its normal numbers so the amount of overtime involved would be considerable - perhaps unacceptable.

(f)   *Renegotiate deadlines*. Whether this is possible depends on the type of work involved.

(g)   *Establish clear priorities*. Possibly there are tasks which are good practice but not essential to get the job done: these could be neglected to free up time for essential tasks.

(h)   Taking a longer term perspective, Samdip should *monitor* the way in which the section copes with the crisis carefully, since this will provide valuable evidence either:

   (i)   to justify the current 10 person manning level of the section; or

   (ii)   to identify ways in which the size of the section could be permanently reduced.

Answer 9.2

(a)   *Problems*

The problem is Ian Dalgleish's failure to use his obvious talents in making a real contribution to the departmental goals and objectives of the organisation. The problem is complicated by an attempt to challenge your leadership of the section. For example many of his failures (timekeeping) are public failures which can be observed by other members of the department.

We can assume that the problem is not related to :

   (i)   your failure to use standards or provide feedback on performance (so presumably Ian knows your views about the kinds of failures in his performance);

   (ii)   Ian's lack of ability or talent (as the question indicates this both directly and indirectly eg 'you know he has considerable potential', and praise for his work as a treasurer);

   (iii) a lack of training, since his treasurer's activities would indicate a sound grasp of accounting activities.

(b)   *Reasons*

Ian has demonstrated leadership qualities (eg successful running of the football team), and you have only recently been appointed supervisor. These facts may indicate that Ian's attitudes are influenced by the following considerations.

   (i)   He wanted or it was widely assumed (by the section) that he would be promoted to supervisor. Therefore he is personally frustrated and publicly embarrassed by your appointment and his behaviour is an attempt to compensate for his frustration.

   (ii)   His outside activities give him more challenge and responsibility and therefore provide more satisfaction of his need to achieve. Therefore 'accounting work' does not command a high priority on his enthusiasm and efforts.

It is also possible that he does not respond to your chosen style of leadership, or even that he has personal problems which are affecting his work performance and attitudes.

(c)   *Further Information*

Fact-finding might include:

   (i)   a discussion with the previous supervisor as to Ian's work before you came, his ambitions and objectives, and attitude towards your predecessor's leadership;

   (ii)   an examination of Ian's personnel file to discover his background, appraisal ratings and any factors which may be influencing his behaviour such as problems at home, family bereavement;

   (iii) informal discussions with other members of the group, although care must be taken to ensure that this does not appear as gossiping behind Ian's back;

   (iv)   an interview with Ian himself, to invite him to be open about his attitudes, feelings and interpretation of the current situation.

BPP PUBLISHING

(d)   *Courses of action*

A full counselling interview should be held with Ian, to discover the causes of the problem. This may be taken by you, or possibly by the personnel manager, if Ian finds it difficult to talk to you (as the root of his problem)   .

Depending on the outcome - and if the causes outlined in (b) above are the problem - other actions may include the following.

(i)   Consider the areas of your authority you can delegate to Ian. This will depend on the extent to which you can win back his trust and build a co-operative relationship.

(ii)   Attempt to provide more challenging work and also try to accommodate his pressures by providing facilities to help his treasurer's work: calculators, paper, photocopier etc. Demonstrate your admiration for his outside work in front of his colleagues.

(iii)   Explain the benefits to Ian of a participative style of management, and point out that managers of the future would be expected to display their skills with people just as much as the ability to complete tasks.

(iv)   Give him advice and sympathy, and possibly time off to let him sort out his personal problems.

(v)   Follow-up later. If Ian's performance and attitude have not improved, he may need to be transferred to another section with another leader or greater promotion prospects.

Chapter 10 Appraisal and training

Chapter topic list

1   Appraisal and performance management

2   The process of appraisal

3   Follow-up

4   Development and the role of training

5   Identifying training needs

6   Methods of development and training

7   Learning

8   The supervisor's role

Learning objectives

On completion of this chapter you will be able to:

	Performance criteria	Range Statement
• ensure that the competence of individuals undertaking work is reviewed and the necessary training is provided	10.1.2	1
• resolve problems or queries regarding work activities	10.1.7	1

BPP PUBLISHING

1 APPRAISAL AND PERFORMANCE MANAGEMENT

1.1 This chapter deals with appraisal and training together because they are both essential parts of a system of staff development and performance management.

Performance management: set objectives for the future

> **KEY TERM**
>
> **Performance management** is an approach which aims 'to get better results from the organisations, teams and individuals by measuring and managing performance within agreed frameworks of objectives and competence requirements, assessing and improving performance'. Performance management is part of the control system of the organisation.

Appraisal: review past performance to establish the current position.

> **KEY TERM**
>
> Whilst performance management as a whole is forward looking, the process of **appraisal** is designed to review performance over the past period, with a view to identifying any deficiencies and improving it in the future.

1.2 **Objectives of appraisals**

- Establishing what **the individual has to do** in a job in order that the objectives for the section or department are realised

- Establishing the **key or main results** which the individual will be expected to achieve in the course of his or her work over a period of time

- **Comparing the individual's level of performance against a standard**, to provide a basis for remuneration above the basic pay rate

- Identifying the individual's **training and development needs** in the light of actual **performance**

- Identifying **potential candidates for promotion**

- Identifying **areas for improvement**

- Establishing an **inventory of actual and potential performance** within the undertaking to provide a basis for manpower planning

- Monitoring the undertaking's **initial selection procedures** against the subsequent performance of recruits, relative to the organisation's expectations

- **Improving communication** about work tasks between different levels in the hierarchy

1.3 **The need for appraisal**

(a) Managers and supervisors may obtain **random impressions** of subordinates' performance (perhaps from their more noticeable successes and failures), but rarely form a coherent, complete and objective picture.

(b) They may have a fair idea of their subordinates' shortcomings - but may not have devoted time and attention to the matter of **improvement and development**.

(c) Judgements are **easy to make**, but **less easy to justify** in detail, in writing, or to the subject's face.

(d) **Different assessors** may be applying a **different set of criteria**, and varying standards of objectivity and judgement. This undermines the value of appraisal for comparison, as well as its credibility in the eyes of the appraisees.

(e) Unless stimulated to do so, managers rarely give their subordinates adequate **feedback** on their performance.

Activity 10.1

List four disadvantages to the individual of not having an appraisal system.

1.4 **Three basic problems for appraisers**

(a) The **formulation and appreciation of desired traits and standards** against which individuals can be consistently and objectively assessed.

(b) **Recording assessments.** Managers should be encouraged to utilise a standard and understood framework, but still allowed to express what they consider important, and without too much form-filling.

(c) **Getting the appraiser and appraisee together,** so that both contribute to the assessment and plans for improvement and/or development.

2 THE PROCESS OF APPRAISAL

2.1 **A typical appraisal system**

Step 1. **Identification of criteria** for assessment, perhaps based on job analysis, performance standards, person specifications and so on.

Step 2. The preparation by the subordinate's manager of an **appraisal report.** In some systems both the appraisee and appraiser prepare a report. These reports are then compared.

Step 3. An **appraisal interview,** for an exchange of views about the appraisal report, targets for improvement, solutions to problems and so on.

Step 4. **Review of the assessment** by the assessor's own superior, so that the appraisee does not feel subject to one person's prejudices. Formal appeals may be allowed, if necessary to establish the fairness of the procedure.

Step 5. The preparation and implementation of **action plans** to achieve improvements and changes agreed.

Step 6. **Follow-up:** monitoring the progress of the action plan.

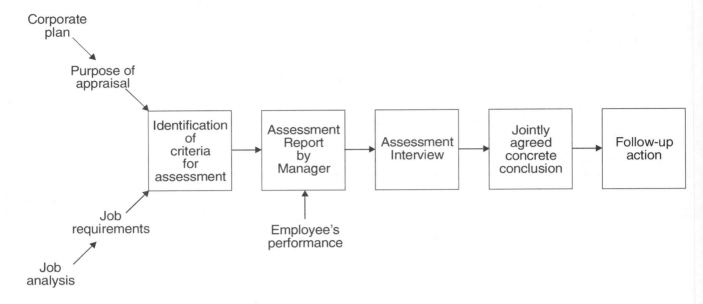

2.2 An **appraisal report** is written before the interview.

(a) Key issues relate to the **job description**.

(b) **Personality** is not relevant unless specifically related to performance.

(c) A **competence** is an observable skill or ability to complete a particular task successfully. It can include the ability to transfer skills and knowledge to new situations. The AAT qualification is based in part on this approach.

Activity 10.2

Identify specific competences which may be relevant to some jobs of your choice.

2.3

Appraisal techniques	
Overall assessment	The manager writes in narrative form his judgements about the appraisee. There will be no guaranteed consistency of the criteria and areas of assessment, however, and managers may not be able to convey clear, effective judgements in writing.
Guided assessment	Assessors are required to comment on a number of specified characteristics and performance elements, with guidelines as to how terms such as 'application', 'integrity' and 'adaptability' are to be interpreted in the work context. This is more precise, but still rather vague.
Grading	Grading adds a comparative frame of reference to the general guidelines, whereby managers are asked to select one of a number of levels or degrees to which the individual in question displays the given characteristic. These are also known as **rating scales**. Numerical values may be added to ratings to give rating scores. Alternatively a less precise **graphic scale** may be used to indicate general position on a plus/minus scale. *Factor: job knowledge* High __√__ Average _____ Low

Appraisal techniques	
Behavioural incident methods.	These concentrate on **employee behaviour**, which is measured against typical behaviour in each job, as defined by common **critical incidents** of successful and unsuccessful job behaviour reported by managers.
Results-orientated schemes	This reviews performance against specific targets and standards of performance **agreed in advance by manager and subordinate together**. The advantages of this are as follows.

> (i) The subordinate is more involved in appraisal because he/she is able to evaluate his/her success or progress in achieving specific, jointly-agreed targets.
>
> (ii) The manager is therefore relieved, to an extent, of a critic's role, and becomes a counsellor.
>
> (iii) Learning and motivation theories suggest that clear and known targets are important in modifying and determining behaviour.
>
> The effectiveness of the scheme will still, however, depend on the **targets set** (are they clearly defined? realistic?) and the **commitment** of both parties to make it work.

Activity 10.3

What sort of appraisal systems are suggested by the following examples?

(a) The Head Teacher of Dotheboys Hall sends a brief report at the end of each term to the parents of the school's pupils. Typical phrases include 'a satisfactory term's work', and 'could do better'.

(b) A firm of auditors assess the performance of their staff in four categories: technical ability, relationships with clients, relationships with other members of the audit team, and professional attitude. On each of these criteria staff are marked from A (= excellent) to E (= poor).

(c) A firm of insurance brokers assesses the performance of its staff by the number of clients they have visited and the number of policies sold.

The appraisal interview

2.4 The process of the interview is given below.

Step 1. **Prepare**

- Plan and place, time and environment
- Review employee's history
- Consult other managers - let employee prepare
- Prepare report. Review employee's self-appraisal

Step 2. **Interview**

- Listen to employee. Discuss, don't argue
- Encourage employee to talk, identify problems and solutions
- Be fair
- Gain employee commitment
- Agree plan of action
- Summarise to check understanding

Step 3. **Complete appraisal report**, if not already prepared

Step 4.   **Follow up**

- Take action as agreed
- Monitor progress
- Keep employee informed

Interview and counselling

2.5   The report may be shown to the appraisee and thus form a basis for discussion. Three types of approach to the appraisal interview are discussed below.

2.6   **The tell and sell method**. The manager tells the subordinate how he/she has been assessed, and then tries to 'sell' (gain acceptance of) the evaluation and the improvement plan. This requires unusual human relations skills in order to convey constructive criticism in an acceptable manner, and to motivate the appraisee to alter his/her behaviour.

2.7   **The tell and listen method**. The manager tells the subordinate how he/she has been assessed, and then invites the appraisee to respond. The manager therefore no longer dominates the interview throughout, and there is greater opportunity for **counselling** as opposed to pure **direction**. The employee is **encouraged to participate** in the assessment and the working out of improvement targets and methods.

2.8   **The problem-solving approach**. The manager abandons the role of critic altogether, and becomes a helper. The discussion is centred not on the assessment, but on the employee's **work problems**. The employee is encouraged to think solutions through, and to commit himself to the recognised need for personal improvement.

Activity 10.4

What approach was taken at your last appraisal interview? Could it have been better?

2.9   Even the most objective and systematic appraisal scheme is subject to problems.

- Appraisal is often **defensive on the part of the subordinate,** who believes that criticism may mean a low bonus or pay rise, or lost promotion opportunity.

- Appraisal is often **defensive on the part of the superior**, who cannot reconcile the role of judge and critic with the human relations aspect of interviewing and management.

- The superior might show **conscious or unconscious bias** in the appraisal or may be influenced by rapport (or lack of it) with the interviewee.

- The manager and subordinate may both be **reluctant to devote time and attention to appraisal.**

- The organisational culture may **simply not take appraisal seriously.**

Activity 10.5

This activity shows some of the problems of operating appraisal schemes in practice.

It is time for Pauline Radway's annual performance appraisal and Steve Taylor, her manager, has sought your advice on two problem areas which he has identified as 'motivation' and 'the organisation's systems'.

The appraisal system has a six point rating scale:

1	Excellent	4	Acceptable
2	Outstanding	5	Room for improvement
3	Competent	6	Unacceptable

The annual pay increase is determined, in part, by the overall rating of the employee.

Pauline was recruited into Steve's section 18 months ago. She took about five months to learn the job and achieve competence. Accordingly, at last year's appraisal she and Steve agreed that an overall rating of '4' was appropriate.

Over the next six months Pauline worked hard and well and in effect developed her job so she was able to accept more responsibility and expand her range of activities into areas which were both interesting and demanding.

During the last six months the section has been 'rationalised' and the workforce has been reduced (although the workload has increased). Steve is under pressure to contain costs - particularly in the area of salary increases.

Steve now has to rely on Pauline performing her enriched job which, taking the past six months as a whole and given the increased pressure, she performs 'satisfactorily' rather than 'outstandingly'; there are aspects of her performance in this enriched job which she could improve.

When Steve met Pauline to agree the time for the appraisal interview she said - only half jokingly - 'I warn you, I'm looking forward to a respectable pay rise this year.'

Task

(a) Outline the problems for Steve that arise from the above scenario:

    (i)   in relation to Pauline's feelings;

    (ii)   in relation to the organisation's systems.

(b) Suggest how Steve should proceed.

3 FOLLOW-UP

3.1 After the appraisal interview, the manager may complete the report, with an overall assessment, assessment of potential and the jointly-reached conclusion of the interview, with **recommendations for follow-up action**. The manager should then discuss the report with the counter-signing manager (usually his or her own superior), resolving any problems that have arisen in making the appraisal or report, and agreeing on action to be taken. The report form may then go to the management development adviser, training officer or other relevant people as appropriate for follow-up.

3.2 Follow-up procedures

- **Informing appraisees of the results** of the appraisal, if this has not been central to the review interview

- **Carrying out agreed actions** on training, promotion and so on

- **Monitoring the appraisee's progress** and checking that he/she has carried out agreed actions or improvements

- Taking necessary steps to **help the appraisee to attain improvement objectives**, by guidance, providing feedback, upgrading equipment, altering work methods or whatever

Activity 10.6

What would happen without follow-up?

DEVOLVED ASSESSMENT ALERT

The operation of an appraisal scheme might be one of the key issues in improving the effectiveness of your section. So you can identify this as an opportunity.

4 DEVELOPMENT AND THE ROLE OF TRAINING

4.1 Training and development are ways by which organisations seek to improve the performance of their staff and, it is hoped, of the organisation.

KEY TERMS

- **Development** is 'the **growth or realisation of a person's ability and potential** through the provision of learning and educational experiences'.

- **Training** is 'the planned and systematic **modification of behaviour** through learning events, programmes and instruction which enable individuals to achieve the level of knowledge, skills and competence to carry out their work effectively'.

    (Armstrong, *Handbook of Personnel Management Practice*)

There is an important distinction to be made between training and development. Perhaps the easiest way to grasp the difference is to see training as immediately practical and connected to job performance. On the other hand, development may have no immediate practical application but tends, over time, to enable a person to deal with wider problems.

Development is more relevant to more senior people. In the rest of this chapter, try to distinguish when we are talking about training, when about development and when about both.

4.2 **The overall purpose of employee and management development** is to **ensure** the firm meets current and future performance objectives by **continuous improvement** of the performance of individuals and teams, and **realising people's** potential for growth (and promotion).

4.3 **Development activities**
- Training, both on and off the job
- Career planning
- Job rotation
- Appraisal
- Other learning opportunities

Activity 10.7

Note down key experiences which have developed your capacity and confidence at work, and the skills you are able to bring to your employer (or indeed a new employer!)

Training and the organisation

4.4 **Benefits for the organisation of training and development programmes**

Benefit	Comment
Planning can minimise the learning costs of obtaining the skills the organisation needs	Ad hoc courses can increase cost and fail to address real training needs.
Lower costs and **increased productivity**, thereby improving performance	Some people suggest that higher levels of training explain the higher productivity of German as opposed to many British manufacturers
Fewer accidents, and better health and safety	EU health and safety directives require a certain level of training. Employees can take employers to court if accidents occur or if unhealthy work practices persist.
Less need for detailed supervision	If people are trained they can get on with the job, and managers can concentrate on other things. Training is an aspect of **empowerment**.
Flexibility	Training ensures that people have the **variety** of skills needed – multi-skilling is only possible if people are properly trained.
Recruitment and succession planning	Training and development attracts new recruits and ensures that the organisation has a supply of suitable managerial and technical staff to take over when people retire.
Change management	Training helps organisations manage change by letting people know why the change is happening and giving them the skills to cope with it.
Corporate culture	(1) Training programmes can be used to build the corporate culture or to direct it in certain ways, by indicating that certain **values** are espoused. (2) Training programmes can **build relationships** between staff and managers in different areas of the business
Motivation	Training programmes can increase commitment to the organisation's goals

Training and the individual

4.5 For the individual employee, the benefits of training and development are more clear-cut, and few refuse it if it is offered.

Benefit	Comment
Enhances portfolio of **skills**	Even if not specifically related to the current job, training can be useful in other contexts, and the employee becomes more attractive to employers and more promotable
Psychological benefits	The trainee might feel reassured that he/she is of continuing value to the organisation
Social benefit	People's social needs can be met by training courses – they can also develop networks of contacts
The job	Training can help people do their job better, thereby increasing job satisfaction

5 IDENTIFYING TRAINING NEEDS

The training process in outline

5.1 In order to ensure that training meets the real needs of the organisation, large firms adopt a planned approach to training. This has the following steps.

Step 1. Identify and define the **organisation's skills requirements**. It may be the case that recruitment might be a better solution to a problem than training

Step 2. **Define the learning required** – in other words, specify the knowledge, skills or competences that have to be acquired. For technical training, this is not difficult: for example all finance department staff would have to become conversant with a new accounting system.

Step 3. **Establish training objectives** – what must be **learnt** and what trainees must be **able to do** after the training exercise

Step 4. **Plan training programmes** – training and development can be planned in a number of ways, employing a number of techniques, as we shall learn about in Section 3. (Also, people have different approaches to learning, which have to be considered.) This covers:
- Who provides the training
- Where the training takes place
- Divisions of responsibilities between trainers, line managers or team leaders and the individual personally.

Step 5. **Implement the training**

Step 6. **Evaluate** the training: has it been successful in achieving learning objectives?

Step 7. Go back to Step 2 if more training is needed.

Activity 10.8

Draw up a training plan for introducing a new employee into your department. Repeat this exercise after you have completed this chapter to see if your chosen approach has changed.

5.2 Training needs analysis covers three issues.

Current state	Desired state
Organisation's current results	Desired results, standards
Existing knowledge and skill	Knowledge and skill needed
Individual performance	Required standards

The difference between the two columns is the **training gap**. Training programmes are designed to improve individual performance, thereby improving the performance of the organisation.

Setting training objectives

5.3 The **training manager** will have to make an initial investigation into the problem of the gap between job or competence **requirements** and current **performance**.

5.4   If training would improve work performance, training **objectives** can then be defined. They should be clear, specific and related to observable, measurable targets, ideally detailing:

(a)   Behaviour - what the trainee should be able to do.

(b)   Standard - to what level of performance.

(c)   Environment - under what conditions (so that the performance level is realistic).

5.5   EXAMPLE

'At the end of the course the trainee should be able to describe ... or identify ... or distinguish x from y ... or calculate ... or assemble ...' and so on. It is insufficient to define the objectives of **training** as 'to give trainees a grounding in ...' or 'to encourage trainees in a better appreciation of ...': this offers no target achievement which can be quantifiably measured. However, the aims of **development** will be less specific.

5.6   Training objectives link the identification of training needs with the content, methods and technology of training. Some examples of translating training needs into learning objectives are given by Torrington and Hall.

Training needs	Learning objectives
To know more about the Data Protection Act	The employee will be able to answer four out of every five queries about the Data Protection Act without having to search for details.
To establish a better rapport with customers	The employee will immediately attend to a customer unless already engaged with another customers.
	The employee will greet each customer using the customer's name where known.
	The employee will apologise to every customer who has had to wait to be attended to.
To assemble clocks more quickly	The employee will be able to assemble each clock correctly within thirty minutes.

Having identified training needs and objectives, the manager will have to decide on the best way to approach training: there are a number of types and techniques of training, which we will discuss below.

6   METHODS OF DEVELOPMENT AND TRAINING

Incorporating training needs into an individual development programme

6.1   Any scheme of training should incorporate these general features:

(a)   **Establish learning targets**. The areas to be learnt should be identified, and specific, realistic goals (eg completion dates, performance standards) stated by agreement with the trainee.

(b)   **Plan a systematic learning and development programme.** This will ensure regular progress, appropriate stages for consolidation and practice.

(c)   **Identify opportunities for broadening the trainee's knowledge and experience:** eg by involvement in new projects, placement on inter-departmental committees, suggesting new contacts, or simply extending the job, adding more tasks, greater responsibility etc.

(d)   **Take into account the strengths and limitations of the trainee** in learning, and take advantage of learning opportunities that suit the trainee's ability, preferred style and goals.

(e)   **Exchange feedback.** The coach will want to know how the trainee sees his or her progress and future. He or she will also need performance information in order to monitor the trainee's progress, adjust the learning programme if necessary, identify further needs which may emerge and plan future development for the trainee.

> ## KEY TERM
>
> A **personal development plan** is a 'clear developmental action plan for an individual which incorporates a wide set of developmental opportunities including formal training.'

6.2   **Purposes of a personal development plan**

- Improving performance in the existing job
- Developing skills for future career moves within and outside the organisation.

> ## KEY TERM
>
> **Skills:** what the individual needs to be able to do if results are to be achieved. Skills are built up progressively by repeated training. They may be manual, intellectual or mental, perceptual or social.

Preparing a personal development plan involves these steps.

Step 1.   **Analysis** of the current position. You could do a personal SWOT (strengths, weaknesses, opportunities, threats) analysis. The supervisor can have an input into this by categorising the skills use of the employee on a grid as follows, in a **skills analysis**.

		Performance	
		High	*Low*
Liking of skills	*High*	Like and do well	Like but don't do well
	Low	Dislike but do well	Dislike and don't do well

The aim is to try to incorporate more of the employees' interests into their actual roles.

Step 2.   **Set goals to cover performance in the existing job,** future changes in the current role, moving elsewhere in the organisations, developing specialist expertise. Naturally, such goals should have the characteristic, as far as possible of SMART objectives (ie specific, measurable, attainable, realistic and time-bounded).

Step 3.   **Draw up action plan** to achieve the goals, covering the developmental activities listed in paragraph 3.1

Activity 10.9

Draw up a personal development plan for yourself over the next month, the next year, and the next five years. You should include your AAT activities.

Formal training

6.3 **Formal training**

(a) **Internal courses** are run by the organisation's training department or may be provided by external suppliers.

(b) **Types of course**

- **Day release**: the employee works in the organisation and on one day per week attends a local college or training centre for theoretical learning.

- **Distance learning, evening classes and correspondence courses**, make demands on the individual's time outside work. This is commonly used, for example, in accountancy training.

- **Revision courses** are often used for examinations of professional bodies.

- **Block release** courses may involve four weeks at a college or training centre followed by a period back at work.

- **Sandwich courses** usually involve six months at college then six months at work, in rotation, for two or three years.

- A **sponsored full-time course** at a university may last for one or two years

(c) **Computer-based training** involves interactive training via PC. The typing program, Mavis Beacon, is a good example.

(d) **Techniques**

- Lectures
- Seminars, in which participation is encouraged
- Simulation. For example, you may have been sent on an audit training course.

6.4 **Disadvantages of formal training**

(a) An individual will not benefit from formal training unless he or she **wants to learn**. The individual's superior may need to provide encouragement in this respect.

(b) If the **subject matter** of the training course does not **relate to an individual's job**, the learning may quickly be forgotten.

(c) Individuals may not be able to carry over what they have learned to their own particular job.

On the job training

6.5 **Successful on the job training**

(a) The assignments should have a **specific purpose** from which the trainee can learn and gain experience.

(b) The organisation must **tolerate any mistakes** which the trainee makes. Mistakes are an inevitable part of on the job learning.

(c) The work should **not be too complex**.

6.6   **Methods of on the job training**

(a) **Demonstration/instruction:** show the trainee how to do the job and let them get on with it. It should combine **telling** a person what to do and **showing** them how, using appropriate media. The trainee imitates the instructor, and asks questions.

(b) **Coaching:** the trainee is put under the guidance of an experienced employee who shows the trainee how to do the job.

(c) **Job rotation:** the trainee is given several jobs in succession, to gain experience of a wide range of activities. (Even experienced managers may rotate their jobs, to gain wider experience; this philosophy of job education is commonly applied in the Civil Service, where an employee may expect to move on to another job after a few years.)

(d) **Temporary promotion:** an individual is promoted into his/her superior's position whilst the superior is absent due to illness. This gives the individual a chance to experience the demands of a more senior position.

(e) **'Assistant to' positions:** a junior manager with good potential may be appointed as assistant to the managing director or another executive director. In this way, the individual gains experience of how the organisation is managed 'at the top'.

(f) **Action learning:** a group of managers are brought together to solve a real problem with the help of an 'advisor' who exposes the management process that actually happens.

(g) **Committees:** trainees might be included in the membership of committees, in order to obtain an understanding of inter-departmental relationships.

(h) **Project work**. work on a project with other people can expose the trainee to other parts of the organisation.

Activity 10.10

Suggest a suitable training method for each of the following situations.

(a)   A worker is transferred onto a new machine and needs to learn its operation.

(b)   An accounts clerk wishes to work towards becoming qualified with the relevant professional body.

(c)   An organisation decides that its supervisors would benefit from ideas on participative management and democratic leadership.

(d)   A new member of staff is about to join the organisation.

Induction training

6.7   On the first day, a manager or personnel officer should welcome the new recruit. He/she should then introduce the new recruit to the person who will be their **immediate supervisor.**

6.8   The immediate supervisor should commence the **process of induction**.

Step 1.   Pinpoint the areas that the recruit will have to learn about in order to **start the job**. Some things (such as detailed technical knowledge) may be identified as areas for later study or training.

Step 2.   Explain first of all the nature of the job, and the goals of each task, both of the recruit's job and of the department as a whole.

Step 3. Explain about hours of work, and stress the importance of time-keeping. If flexitime is operated, the supervisor should explain how it works.

Step 4. Explain the structure of the department: to whom the recruit will report, to whom he/she can go with complaints or queries and so on.

Step 5. Introduce the recruit to the people in the office. One particular colleague may be assigned to the recruit as a **mentor**, to keep an eye on them, answer routine queries, 'show them the ropes'.

Step 6. Plan and implement an appropriate **training programmes** for whatever technical or practical knowledge is required. Again, the programme should have a clear schedule and set of goals so that the recruit has a sense of purpose, and so that the programme can be efficiently organised to fit in with the activities of the department.

Step 7. Coach and/or train the recruit; and check regularly on their progress, as demonstrated by performance, as reported by the recruit's mentor, and as perceived by the recruit him or herself.

6.9 After three months, six months or one year the performance of a new recruit should be formally appraised and discussed with them. Indeed, when the process of induction has been finished, a recruit should continue to receive periodic appraisals, just like every other employee in the organisation.

Activity 10.11

'Joining an organisation with around 8,500 staff, based on two sites over a mile apart and in the throes of major restructuring, can be confusing for any recruit. This is the situation facing the 20 to 30 new employees recruited each month by the Guy's and St Thomas' Hospital Trust, which was formed by the merger of the two hospitals in April.

In a climate of change, new employees joining the NHS can be influenced by the negative attitudes of other staff who may oppose the current changes. So it has become increasingly important for the trust's management executive to get across their view of the future and to understand the feelings of confusion new staff may be experiencing.'

Personnel Management Plus, August 1993

See if you can design a 9-5 induction programme for these new recruits, in the light of the above. The programme is to be available to **all** new recruits, from doctors and radiographers to accountants, catering and cleaning staff and secretaries.

7 LEARNING

7.1 There are different learning theories which explain and describe how people learn.

7.2 Whichever approach it is based on, learning theory offers certain useful propositions for the design of **effective training programmes**.

Proposition	Comment
The individual should be **motivated** to learn	The advantages of training should be made clear, according to the individual's motives - money, opportunity, valued skills or whatever.
There should be clear **objectives and standards** set, so that each task has some meaning	Each stage of learning should present a challenge, without overloading the trainee or making them lose confidence. Specific objectives and performance standards for each stage will help the trainee in the process of learning, and providing targets against which performance will be measured.
There should be timely, relevant **feedback** on performance and progress	This will usually be provided by the trainer, and should be prompt. If progress reports or performance appraisals are given only at the year end, for example, there will be no opportunity for behaviour adjustment or learning in the meantime.
Positive and negative **reinforcement** should be judiciously used	Recognition and encouragement enhance an individuals confidence in their competence and progress: punishment for poor performance - especially without explanation and correction - discourages the learner and creates feelings of guilt, failure and hostility
Active **participation** is more telling than passive reception (because of its effect on the motivation to learn, concentration and recollection).	If a high degree of participation is impossible, practice and repetition can be used to reinforce receptivity. However, participation has the effect of encouraging 'ownership' of the process of learning and changing - committing the individual to it as their **own** goal, not just an imposed process.

Learning styles

7.3 The way in which people learn best will differ according to the type of person. That is, there are **learning styles** which suit different individuals. *Honey and Mumford* have drawn up a popular classification of four learning styles.

(a) **Theorists**

Theorists seek to understand **underlying concepts** and to take an intellectual, 'hands-off' approach based on logical argument. They prefer training to be:

- Programmed and structured.
- Designed to allow time for analysis.
- Provided by teachers who share his/her preference for concepts and analysis.

Theorists find learning difficult if they have a teacher with a different style (particularly an activist style); material which skims over basic principles; and a programme which is hurried and unstructured.

(b) **Reflectors**

- **Observe** phenomena, **think** about them and then **choose** how to act.
- Need to work at their own pace
- Find learning difficult if forced into a hurried programme with little notice or information.
- Produce carefully thought-out conclusions after research and reflection
- Tend to be fairly slow, non-participative (unless to ask questions) and cautious.

(c) **Activists**
- Deal with practical, active problems and who **do not have much patience with theory**.
- Require training based on **hands-on experience**.
- **Excited by participation** and pressure, such as making presentations and new projects.
- Flexible and optimistic, but tend to rush at something without due preparation, take risks and then get bored.

(d) **Pragmatists**
- Only like to study if they can see its direct link to practical problems - they are not interested in theory for its own sake.
- Good at learning new techniques in on-the-job training which they see as useful improvements.
- Aim is to implement action plans and/or do the task better.
- May discard as being impractical good ideas which only require some development.

The implications for management are that people react to problem situations in different ways and that, in particular, training methods should be tailored to the preferred style of trainees where possible. Moreover, training interventions should ideally be designed to accommodate the preferences of all four styles. This can often be overlooked especially as the majority of training staff are activitists.

Activity 10.12

With reference to the four learning styles drawn up by Honey and Mumford, which of these styles do you think most closely resembles your own? What implications has this got for the way you learn?

---

8 THE SUPERVISOR'S ROLE

The trainee

8.1 Many people now believe that the ultimate responsibility for training and development lies, not with the employer, but with the individual. People should seek to develop their own skills, to improve their own careers rather than wait for the organisation to impose training upon them.

(a) **Delayering** means there are fewer automatic promotion pathways; promotion was once a source of development but there might be no further promotions available.

(b) **Technological change** means that new skills are always needed, and people can find new work by learning new skills.

The human resources department should be heavily involved

8.2 The human resources department should be heavily involved with developing people. As far as managers are concerned, many large organisations have extensive management development and career planning programmes. These shape the progression of individuals through the organisation, in accordance with their performance and potential and the needs of the organisation.

8.3 The HR department performs an administrative role by recording what training and development opportunities an individual might be given – in some firms, going on a training programme is an entitlement, which the HR department might have to enforce.

The supervisor and manager

8.4 Line managers and supervisors discharge some of the responsibility for training and development within the organisation by identifying four things.

- The training needs of the department or section
- The current competences of the individuals within the department
- Opportunities for learning and development on the job
- When feedback is necessary.

Mentoring

> **KEY TERM**
>
> **Mentoring** is the use of specially trained individuals to provide guidance and advice which will help develop the careers of those allocate to them. A person's line manager should not be his or her mentor.

8.5 Mentors can assist in several ways.

- Drawing up personal development plans
- Advice with administrative problems people face in their new jobs
- Help in tackling projects, by pointing people in the right direction

---

Key learning points

- Appraisal is part of the system of **performance management.**

- The main difference in emphasis is that **appraisals are backward looking**, whereas performance management as a whole looks to the future.

- Appraisal can be used to reward but also to **identify potential**.

- Three basic problems are defining **what** is to be appraised, **recording** assessments, and **getting the appraiser and appraisee together**.

- Normally a report is written - but both manager and appraisee can contribute to the process, hence the value of self-appraisal.

- Problems with appraisal are its implementation in practice and the fact that it ignores, by and large, the context of performance.

- In order to achieve its goals, an organisation requires a **skilled workforce**. This is partly achieved by training.

- The main purpose of training and development is to **raise competence and therefore performance standards**. It is also concerned with **personal development**, helping and motivating employees to fulfil their potential.

- A thorough analysis of **training needs** should be carried out as part of a systematic approach to training, to ensure that training programmes meet organisational and individual requirements. Once training needs have been identified, they should be translated into **training objectives**.

- Individuals can incorporate training and development objectives into a personal development plan.

- There are different schools of thought as to how people learn. Different people have different learning styles.

- There are a variety of training methods. These include:

  - Formal education and training
  - On-the-job training
  - Awareness-oriented training

Quick quiz

1   What are the purposes of appraisal?

2   What bases or criteria of assessment might an appraisal system use?

3   What is a results-oriented approach to appraisal?

4   What follow-up should there be after an appraisal?

5   What kinds of criticism might be levelled at appraisal schemes by a manager who thought they were a waste of time?

6   What is the difference between performance appraisal and performance management?

7   List examples of development opportunities within organisations.

8   List how training can contribute to:

(a)   Organisational effectiveness.
(b)   Individual effectiveness and motivation.

9   Define the term 'training need'.

10   How should training objectives be expressed?

11   What does learning theory tell us about the design of training programmes?

12   List the four learning styles put forward by Honey and Mumford.

13   List the available methods of on-the-job training.

14   What is the supervisor's role in training?

Answers to quick quiz

1   Identifying performance levels, improvements needed and promotion prospects; deciding on rewards; assessing team work and encouraging communication between manager and employee.

2   Job analysis, job description, plans, targets and standards.

3   Performance is assessed against specific mutually agreed targets and standards.

4   Appraisees should be informed of the results, agreed activity should be taken, progress should be monitored and whatever resources or changes are needed should be provided or implemented.

5   The manager may say that he has better things to do with his time, that appraisals have no relevance to the job and there is no reliable follow-up action, and that they involve too much paperwork.

6   Appraisal *on its own* is a backward-looking performance review. But it is a vital input into performance management, which is forward-looking.

7   Career planning, job rotation, deputising, on-the-job training, counselling, guidance, education and training.

8   (a)   Increased efficiency and productivity; reduced costs, supervisory problems and accidents; improved quality, motivation and morale.

(b)   Demonstrates individual value, enhances security, enhances skills portfolio, motivates, helps develop networks and contacts.

9   The required level of competence minus the present level of competence.

10   Actively - 'after completing this chapter you should understand how to design and evaluate training programmes'.

11   The trainee should be motivated to learn, there should be clear objectives and timely feedback. Positive and negative reinforcement should be used carefully, to encourage active participation where possible.

12   Theorist, reflector, activist and pragmatist.

13   Induction, job rotation, temporary promotion, 'assistant to ' positions, project or committee work

14   Identifying training needs of the department or section, identifying the skills of the individual employee, and deficiencies in performance. Providing or supervising on-the-job training (eg coaching). Providing feedback on an individuals performance.

Answers to activities

Answer 10.1

Disadvantages to the individual of not having an appraisal system include: the individual is not aware of progress or shortcomings, is unable to judge whether s/he would be considered for promotion, is unable to identify or correct weaknesses by training and there is a lack of communication with the manager.

Answer 10.2

You might have identified such things as:

(a) Numerical ability applicable to accounts staff, say, more than to customer contact staff.
(b) Ability to drive safely, essential for transport workers - not for desk-bound ones.
(c) Report-writing (not applicable to manual labour, say).

Answer 10.3

(a) Overall assessment of the blandest kind.
(b) This is a grading system, based on a guided assessment.
(c) Results orientated scheme.

Answer 10.5

(a) *Steve's problems*

    (i) *Pauline's feelings*

        Pauline, makes a connection between performance and reward. She feels she has worked hard and that this should be recognised in financial terms. Steve, on the other hand, is under pressure to keep costs under control.

        Pauline, however, does make a crude assumption that effort equals performance. She is highly motivated at the moment, but her performance is not outstanding. Her performance is only satisfactory in her changed job, and therefore it would not be appropriate to tell her otherwise.

        Steve is thus faced with a dilemma. If she is not rewarded, it is likely that she will make less effort to perform well. Steve will suffer, as the rationalised department depends on her continual hard work.

        Another factor is fairness. Pauline cannot expect special treatment, when compared to other workers, who may have made an equal effort. Over-rewarding average performance, despite the effort, might demotivate other staff who will accuse Steve of favouritism.

    (ii) *The organisation's systems*

        It is clear that Steve is having to negotiate the requirements and failings of 3 different systems here.

        (1) The budgetary control system, restricting pay rises.
        (2) The appraisal system, which contributes to pay rises.
        (3) The remuneration system, by which pay rises are awarded.

        Finally, Pauline's job is very different from what it was when she first started.

        The source of the problem is the failure to recognise that Pauline is now doing a different job. Her job should have been re-evaluated. If this were the case, Steve could assess her reward on the basis of the performance in this re-evaluated job. She would have higher pay, commensurate with her enhanced responsibilities, but not an unfairly favourable grading.

        However, Steve realises that the appraisal system is the one over which he has most direct control. He is in a position to reward her effort, but her performance in the new job is not exceptional. Yet her enhanced responsibilities need to be recognised somehow, although Steve, under pressure from the budgetary control system, may not be able to reward it financially.

        There is little Steve can do about the budgetary factors, apart from stating to Pauline that everybody is in the same boat. There might be non-financial rewards that he can offer her. Pauline might like to have her own separate office space, for example, if it were available, or Steve might be able to offer her increased annual leave or a unique job title.

Pauline might also resent waiting for the outcome of a job re-evaluation exercise, as, from her point of view, that is the organisation's problem, not hers.

(b)   *What Steve should do*

Steve has a choice either to overrate Pauline, according to the appraisal system, in recognition of her efforts rather than her performance in the changed job, or, alternatively, to try and negotiate a job re-evaluation first, with the risk that Pauline will become demotivated.

Steve needs to consider the effects of an unfairly favourable appraisal grading on the other staff. There are good reasons to believe that, while it might let him off the hook immediately, it would have bad long term repercussions, as it would send the wrong signals to Pauline about her current performance. Next year, for example, if her performance had not improved, he would have to downgrade her.

He will have to try and persuade Pauline of the complexities of the situation.

Steve can promise Pauline that the job will be re-evaluated. This might be a long term objective. He can promise Pauline that he will be supportive in the re-evaluation exercise, and involve her in any input to it.

Steve can also suggest new targets for Pauline to achieve in her changed job, to give her something to aim for. This might still motivate her, providing Steve can explain to her the slightly difficult situation he is in.

He might give her formal recognition of her status, and allow her more autonomy in planning her work, if she is sufficiently competent.

Obviously he cannot guarantee the result of the job evaluation system, but he can make some effort to solve the problem.

Answer 10.6

Nothing. There would be no momentum.

Answer 10.7

Few employers throw you in at the deep end – it is far too risky for them! Instead, you might have been given induction training to get acclimatised to the organisation, and you might have been introduced slowly to the job. Ideally, your employer would have planned a programme of tasks of steadily greater complexity and responsibility to allow you to grow into your role(s).

Answer 10.10

Training methods for the various workers indicated are as follows.

(a)   Worker on a new machine: on-the-job training, coaching.

(b)   Accounts clerk working for professional qualification: external course - evening class or day-release.

(c)   Supervisors wishing to benefit from participative management and democratic leadership: internal or external course. However, it is important that monitoring and evaluation takes place to ensure that the results of the course are subsequently applied in practice.

(d)   New staff: induction training.

Answer 10.11

Here is the actual programme for new recruits (of all types) at Guy's and St Thomas' Hospital Trust, as published in *Personnel Management Plus*.

9.00	Welcome	
9.05	Introduction	*Ground rules and objectives for the day*
9.25	Presentation	*The history of Guy's and St Thomas' hospitals*
10.25	Presentation	*Talk on structure of the management team, trust board and executive*
10.45	Group exercise	*With chief executive Tim Matthews on patient care, funding, hospital processes and measuring the care provided*
12.20	Lunch	
1.15	Tour of Guy's	
2.30	Presentation	*Looking at trust with new eyes - suggestions for change*
2.20	Presentation	*Information on staff organisations*
3.10	Presentation	*Security issues, fire drills, health and safety (including handouts)*
3.30	Presentation	*Session on occupational health*
3.40	Presentation	*Local areas and staff benefits*
3.45	Tour of St Thomas'	
4.30	Presentation	*Facilities management and patient care*
4.45	Closing session	*Evaluation and finish*

Particularly important is the focus on patient care and the group exercises. 'Feedback from the participants shows that they enjoy the discussions and learn a lot more about their colleagues and the trust by participating rather than being talked at.'

Answer 10.12

Depending on your answer you will learn most effectively in particular given situations. For example, the theorist will learn best from lectures and books, whereas the activist will get most from practical activities.

Part C
Preventing fraud

Chapter 11 Fraud and its implications

Chapter topics

1 Recent frauds

2 What is fraud?

3 Implications of fraud

4 Types of fraud

5 Computer fraud

6 Conclusion

Learning objectives

On completion of this chapter you will be able to:

	Performance criteria	Range Statement
• Evaluate existing systems for preventing fraud	10.3.1	1, 2, 3
• Identify potential areas of fraud	10.3.1	1, 2, 3
• Report areas of concern and weakness to management	10.3.4	1, 2, 3
• Give examples of control avoidance	10.3.2	1, 2, 3

BPP PUBLISHING

1   RECENT FRAUDS

1.1   In recent years the UK has witnessed a number of high profile frauds, most notably the BCCI, Maxwell and Barings Bank cases. These incidents clearly illustrate how far-reaching the implications of fraud can be. The real incidence of fraud is difficult to gauge, however, particularly because companies are often loath to publicise such experiences. Nonetheless, there is little doubt that fraudulent activities are widespread.

2   WHAT IS FRAUD?

KEY TERM

No precise legal definition of fraud exists. However, **fraud** may be generally defined as 'deprivation by deceit'.

2.1   In a corporate context, fraud can fall into one of two main categories.

- **Removal of funds** or assets from a business
- **Intentional misrepresentation** of the financial position of the business

2.2   The most obvious example of (a) above is outright **theft**, either of cash or of other assets. However, this form of fraud also encompasses more subtle measures, such as overstatement of claims, 'creation' of liabilities, undisclosed creation of credit and the manipulation of the company's relationships with suppliers or customers.

2.3   Intentional misrepresentation ((b) above) includes the **omission or misrecording of the company's accounting records.**

2.4   We will look at examples of these in greater detail later.

3   IMPLICATIONS OF FRAUD

3.1   Whilst it is clear that fraud is bad for business, the precise ways in which the firm is affected depends on the type of fraud being carried on.

(a)   **Removal of funds or assets from a business**

    (i)   **Immediate financial implications**

        Profits are lower than they should be. The business has less cash or fewer assets, and therefore the net asset position is weakened. Returns to shareholders are likely to fall as a result.

    (ii)   **Long term effects on company performance**

        The reduction in working capital makes it more difficult for the company to operate effectively. In the most serious cases, fraud can ultimately result in the collapse of an otherwise successful business, such as Barings.

(b)   **Intentional misrepresentation of the financial position of the business**

    (i)   Financial statements do not give a true and fair view of the financial situation of the business. Results may be either artificially enhanced or, less frequently, under-reported.

    (ii)   It is also possible that managers in charge of a particular **division** can artificially enhance their division's results, thereby deceiving senior management.

Activity 11.1

Try to think of reasons why someone might want to:

(a) artificially enhance the results
(b) under-report the results

3.2 **If results are overstated**:

- A company may **distribute too much** of its profits to shareholders.

- **Retained profits will be lower than believed**, leading to potential shortfalls in working capital. This makes the day-to-day activities more difficult to perform effectively.

- **Incorrect decisions will be made**, based on inaccurate knowledge of available resources.

3.3 This type of fraud can sometimes explain why a firm may be experiencing going concern difficulties whilst apparently reporting healthy profits.

3.4 The effects of fraudulent activities can also affect **stakeholders** if the financial statements upon which they rely are misrepresentations of the truth.

- **Investors** making decisions based on inaccurate information will find their expected returns deviating substantially from actual returns.

- **Suppliers** will extend credit without knowing the financial position of the company.

3.5 If results are **understated**:

- Returns to investors may be reduced unnecessarily.

- If the company is quoted on the stock exchange, the share price might fall and market strength may be eroded.

- Access to loan finance may be restricted if assets are understated.

3.6 Even if the fraud is discovered and addressed, the **negative publicity** can contribute to the demise of the business by affecting the public's perceptions. Consumer confidence, once lost, can be difficult to regain.

3.7 **Legal consequences**. Finally, fraudsters open themselves up to the possibility of arrest. Depending on the scale and seriousness of the offence some, such as Nick Leeson, may even find themselves in facing a prison sentence.

3.8 All businesses, without exception, face the risk of **fraud** and the directors' responsibility is to manage that risk. It is naïve to ignore the possibility.

4 TYPES OF FRAUD

4.1 To recap, fraud in business organisations tends to fall into one of two categories - removal of funds or assets or intentional misrepresentation of the financial position of the business.

Let us consider some practical examples within each category.

Removal of funds or assets from a business

4.2 **Theft of cash.** Employees with access to cash may be tempted to steal it. A prime example is theft from petty cash. Small amounts taken at intervals may easily go unnoticed.

Retail businesses offer another common example. Cashiers may not ring up all the sales on the cash register and merely pocket the amount not recorded.

4.3 **Theft of stock.** Similarly, employees may pilfer items of stock. The most trivial example of this is employees taking office stationery, although of course larger items may be taken also.

These examples are of unsophisticated types of fraud, which generally go undetected because of their immateriality. On the whole, such fraud will tend to be too insignificant to have any serious impact on results or long-term performance.

4.4 **Payroll fraud.** Employees within or outside the payroll department can perpetrate payroll fraud.

(a) Employees external to the department can falsify their timesheets, for example by claiming overtime for hours which they did not really work.

(b) Members of the payroll department may have the opportunity deliberately to miscalculate selected payslips, either by applying an inflated rate of pay or by altering the hours to which the rate is applied.

(c) Alternatively, a fictitious member of staff can be added to the payroll list. The fraudster sets up a bank account in the bogus name and collects the extra cash himself. This is most feasible in a large organisation with high numbers of personnel, where management is not personally acquainted with every employee.

4.5 **Teeming and lading.** This is one of the best known methods of fraud in the sales ledger area. Basically, **teeming and lading** is the theft of cash or cheque receipts. Setting subsequent receipts, not necessarily from the same debtor, against the outstanding debt conceals the theft. This process can continue until the fraudster repays the amount or, more likely, leaves the firm or is discovered.

4.6 **Fictitious customers.** This is a more elaborate method of stealing stock. Bogus orders are set up, and goods are despatched on credit. The 'customer' then fails to pay for the goods and the cost is eventually written off as a bad debt. For this type of fraud to work, the employee must have responsibility for taking goods orders as well as the authority to approve a new customer for credit.

4.7 **Collusion with customers.** Employees may collude with customers to defraud the business by manipulating prices or the quality or quantity of goods despatched.

(a) For example, a sales manager or director could **reduce the price** charged to a customer in return for a cut of the saving. Alternatively, the employee could write off a debt or issue a credit note in return for a financial reward.

(b) Another act of collusion might be for the employee to **suppress invoices** or under-record quantities of despatched goods on delivery notes. Again, the customer would probably provide the employee with a financial incentive for doing this.

In all these situations, both the employee and the customer benefit at the firm's expense.

4.8 **Bogus supply of goods or services**. This typically involves senior staff who falsely invoice the firm for goods or services that were never supplied. One example would be the supply of consultancy services. To enhance authenticity, in many cases the individual involved will set up a personal company that invoices the business for its services. This type of fraud can be quite difficult to prove.

4.9 **Paying for goods not received**. Staff may collude with suppliers, who issue invoices for larger quantities of goods than were actually delivered. The additional payments made by the company are split between the two parties.

4.10 **Meeting budgets/target performance measures**. Management teams will readily agree that setting budgets and goals is an essential part of planning and an important ingredient for success. However, such targets can disguise frauds. In some cases, knowing that results are unlikely to be questioned once targets have been met, employees and/or management siphon off and pocket any profits in excess of the target.

4.11 **Manipulation of bank reconciliations and cash books**. Often the simplest techniques can hide the biggest frauds. We saw earlier how simple a technique teeming and lading is for concealing a theft. Similarly, other simple measures such as incorrect descriptions of items and use of compensating debits and credits to make a reconciliation work frequently ensure that fraudulent activities go undetected. For example, an entry in the cash book with the narrative 'missing cheques' may be all that is needed to ensure that stolen cheques do not appear in the bank reconciliation as a reconciling item.

4.12 **Misuse of pension funds or other assets**. This type of fraud has received a high profile in recent years, not least in the Maxwell case. Ailing companies may raid the pension fund and steal assets to use as collateral in obtaining loan finance. Alternatively, company assets may be transferred to the fund at significant over-valuations.

4.13 **Disposal of assets to employees**. It may be possible for an employee to arrange to buy a company asset (eg a car) for personal use. In this situation, there may be scope to manipulate the book value of the asset so that the employee pays below market value for it. For example, this could be achieved by over-depreciating the relevant asset.

DEVOLVED ASSESSMENT ALERT

When trying to identify areas of potential fraud, it is often easiest to consider the company on a department by department basis, eg sales, purchases, credit control, payroll etc. Think about the functions of each department and the ways in which staff could abuse the systems.

Intentional misrepresentation of the financial position of the business

4.14 Here we consider examples in which the intention is to overstate profits. Note, however, that by reversing the logic we can also use them as examples of methods by which staff may deliberately understate profits. You should perform this exercise yourself.

4.15 **Over-valuation of stock.** Stock is a particularly attractive area for management wishing to inflate net assets artificially. There is a whole range of ways in which stock may be incorrectly valued for accounts purposes.

    (a) Stock records may be manipulated, particularly by deliberate miscounting at stock counts.

    (b) Deliveries to customers may be omitted from the books.

    (c) Returns to suppliers may not be recorded.

    (d) Obsolete stock may not be written off but rather held at cost on the balance sheet.

4.16 **Bad debt policy may not be enforced.** Aged debtors who are obviously not going to pay should be written off. However, by not enforcing this policy management can avoid the negative effects it would have on profits and net assets.

4.17 **Fictitious sales.** These can be channelled through the accounts in a number of ways.

- Generation of false invoices
- Overcharging customers for goods or services
- Selling goods to friends with the promise of buying them back at a later date

4.18 **Manipulation of year end events.** Cut off dates provide management with opportunities for window dressing the financial statements. Sales made just before year end can be deliberately over-invoiced and credit notes issued with an apology at the start of the new year. This will enhance turnover and profit during the year just ended. Conversely, delaying the recording of pre-year-end purchases of goods not yet delivered can achieve the same objective.

4.19 **Understating expenses.** Clearly, failure to record all expenses accurately will inflate the reported profit figure.

4.20 **Manipulation of depreciation figures.** As an expense that does not have any cash flow effect, depreciation figures may be easily tampered with. Applying incorrect rates or inconsistent policies in order to understate depreciation will result in a higher profit and a higher net book value, giving a more favourable impression of financial health.

5 COMPUTER FRAUD

5.1 Organisations are becoming increasingly dependent on computers for operational systems as well as accounting and management information. With this dependency comes an increased **exposure** to fraud. The computer is frequently the vehicle through which fraudulent activities are carried out.

5.2 Problems particularly associated with computers.

    (a) **Computer hackers.** The possibility of unknown persons trying to hack into the systems increases the potential for fraud against which the firm must protect itself.

    (b) **Lack of training within the management team.** Many people have an inherent lack of understanding of how computer systems work. Senior management can often be the least computer literate. They may also be the most reluctant to receive training, preferring to delegate tasks to assistants. Without management realising it, junior staff can secure access to vast amounts of financial information and find ways to alter it.

(c) **Identifying the risks.** Most firms do not have the resources to keep up to date with the pace of development of computer technology. This makes it ever more difficult to check that all major loopholes in controls are closed, even if management are computer literate.

(d) **Need for ease of access and flexible systems.** In most cases, a firm uses computers in order to simplify and speed up operations. To meet these objectives, there is frequently a need for ease of access and flexible systems. However, implementing strict controls can sometimes suppress these features.

Types of computer fraud

5.3 Three main types of computer fraud exist. They relate directly to the key stages in computer processing.

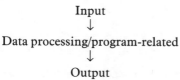

Input
↓
Data processing/program-related
↓
Output

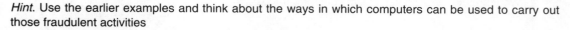

Activity 11.2

Try and come up with examples of input-related fraud, program-related fraud and output-related fraud.

Hint. Use the earlier examples and think about the ways in which computers can be used to carry out those fraudulent activities

6 CONCLUSION

6.1 We have considered the implications of fraud for a business and looked at some examples of how fraud may be carried on. Variations of all of the frauds discussed in this chapter are very common in practice. While some, such as outright theft, are easily visible, others are difficult to detect. The implementation of internal controls to detect fraud therefore is an essential element of any business. It is crucial to be alert to signs that something may not be quite right. In the next chapter, we turn our attention to methods by which firms can try to prevent and detect fraud.

Activity 11.3

Report: exposure to fraud

Smiths Ltd is a small, family-run manufacturing firm that makes office furniture. The directors, Stuart and his sister Michelle, share responsibility for running the business, although Stuart concentrates on trying to bring in new business while Michelle takes a more active role in day-to-day management.

John runs the purchasing department. Martha, who has just recently been recruited to the firm, looks after the cash book and is responsible for performing monthly bank reconciliations.

John keeps records of all purchases and related expenses as well as looking after creditor accounts. When an invoice comes in, he checks the details against the purchase ledger details. If he is satisfied that the invoice is correct, he draws up a cheque for Michelle to sign. He also supervises Martha's work.

All accounting systems are computerised. The firm employs one staff member, Craig, in an IT capacity. Craig has full control of the computer network, with access to all programs and reporting systems.

You are required to produce a report to the directors in which you advise them on ways in which the firm is exposed to the risk of fraud.

BPP PUBLISHING

Key learning points

- The purpose of this chapter has been to outline in broad terms different types of fraud and their implications for businesses.

- Fraud may be generally defined as 'deprivation by deceit'.

- In a corporate context, fraud can fall into one of two main categories:

  o Removal of funds or assets from a business; and/or
  o Intentional misrepresentation of the financial position of the business

- **Computers** are frequently used as a means of carrying out fraudulent activities.

- The three main types of computer fraud are **input-related, program-related and output-related** fraud

Quick quiz

1 What is fraud?

2 What are the two main types of fraud from a corporate perspective?

3 Give two consequences of each type.

4 Give three examples of each type.

5 Why do computers increase the risk of fraud?

6 What are the three main types of computer fraud?

Answers to quick quiz

1 Fraud may generally be defined as 'deprivation by deceit'.

2 The two types of corporate fraud are removal of funds or assets from a business and intentional misrepresentation of the financial position of the business.

3 Consequences of the former include lower profits and a reduction in working capital. Consequences of the latter include incorrect decision-making by management or by investors and fluctuations in share price.

4 Examples of the former include theft of cash or other assets, payroll fraud and teeming and lading. Examples of the latter include overvaluation of stock, failure to adhere to bad debt or depreciation policy and manipulation of year-end events.

5 Computers tend to increase exposure to fraud because they are frequently the vehicles through which fraudulent activities are carries out.

6 The three main types of computer fraud are input-related, program-related and output-related fraud.

Answers to activities

Answer 11.1

(a) Reasons for overstating profits and/or net assets:

- To ensure achievement on paper, may have to meet targets in order to secure a promotion, bonuses or remuneration may be linked to performance

- Trying to conceal another form of fraud, such as theft

- Need a healthy balance sheet to convince bank to give loan finance

- Ailing company may be trying to entice equity investors

(b) Reasons for understating profits and/or net assets

- To facilitate a private purchase of an asset from the business at less than market value

- To defraud the Inland Revenue by reducing taxable profits or gains

- Trying to force the share price down so that shares can be bought below market value by friends or relatives

Answer 11.2

Input-related fraud

- Creation of input
- Amendment of input
- Deletion of input
- Duplication of input
- Abuse of access privileges

Program-related fraud

- Unauthorised program changes
- Abuse of access privileges
- Unauthorised access to data manipulation utilities

Output-related fraud

- Suppression or destruction of output
- Creation of fictitious output
- Improper amendment of computer output prior to transmission
- Theft of output

Answer 11.3

Report: exposure to fraud

Date: 30 June 19X7
To: Stuart and Michelle Smith, Directors, Smiths Ltd
From: Accounting Technician
Subject: Risk of fraud

You have asked me to advise on ways in which Smiths Ltd is exposed to the risk of fraud. My report has been based on discussions with you both about the established work practices and on a review of the company's books.

Findings

Due to the small number of staff employed by the firm, there is little segregation of duties. This automatically enhances exposure to risk of fraud.

(a)   Martha is responsible for both the cash book and bank reconciliations. This makes it easy for her to conceal theft or to manipulate accounting records. Simple measures such as the use of compensating debits and credits to make the reconciliation work or incorrect narratives facilitate such frauds.

(b)   John keeps the records of all purchases and expenses but yet he is also responsible for confirming that invoice details agree to purchase ledger details and for maintaining creditor accounts. He therefore has ample opportunity to manipulate accounting records, such as turnover figures. He is also responsible for drawing up the cheques for Michelle to sign. This means he could easily steal from the firm by drawing up cheques for fictitious creditors.

(c)   Craig has sole control of all computer systems. He has unlimited access to files and is in a unique position to carry numerous types of fraud. The firm essentially relies on nothing more than trust to ensure that he does not engage in any fraudulent activities.

(d)   As Stuart focuses almost entirely on bringing in new business, he has little time to spend on the supervision of day-to-day activities. The bulk of this work falls on Michelle. The sheer weight of her responsibilities means that in many cases there is little independent review or supervision of her work.

Overall, the firm suffers from a high level of exposure to risk. In order to manage that risk effectively, a system of internal controls should be introduced to prevent and detect incidences of fraud.

Chapter 12   Detecting fraud

Chapter topics

1 Relying on hindsight

2 Prevention and detection

3 Assessing the risk

4 Common indicators of fraud

5 Internal controls

6 Controls against computer fraud

7 Conclusion

Learning objectives

On completion of this chapter you will be able to:

	Performance criteria	Range Statement
• Identify areas of potential fraud and assess the risk.	10.3.3	1, 2, 3
• Identify methods of avoiding the risk	10.3.5	1, 2, 3
• Make recommendation to the appropriate people	10.3.6	1, 2, 3

BPP PUBLISHING

1 RELYING ON HINDSIGHT

1.1 Hindsight is a wonderful thing. Journalists reporting high profile frauds frequently raise the question of why nobody noticed earlier that something was wrong. They ask why the warning signs that should have signalled that all was not well were missed somehow. The answer is usually that there were **insufficient internal** controls in place.

1.2 In this chapter we focus on indicators of fraud and the internal controls that firms can use as tools to prevent and detect fraud.

2 PREVENTION AND DETECTION

2.1 A primary aim of any system of internal controls should be to prevent fraud. However, the very nature of fraud means that people will find ways to get around existing systems.

DEVOLVED ASSESSMENT ALERT

Controls should exist to try to prevent fraud from ever occurring at all. However, to manage the risk of fraud effectively, it is equally important to recognise that controls must also be devised to ensure that if fraud is happening, it will be detected.

2.2 In a **limited company** or **plc**, it is the **responsibility of the directors** to prevent and detect fraud. They should do three things.

- Ensure that the activities of the entity are conducted honestly and that its assets are safeguarded.

- Establish **arrangements to deter fraudulent or other dishonest conduct** and to detect any that occurs.

- Ensure that, to the best of their knowledge and belief, financial information, whether used internally or for financial reporting, is reliable.

3 ASSESSING THE RISK

3.1 The starting point for any management team wanting to set up internal controls to prevent and detect fraud must be an assessment of the extent to which the firm is exposed to the risk of fraud.

3.2 What follows is a guideline of how such a task might be approached.

DEVOLVED ASSESSMENT ALERT

The key to devising successful internal controls is to identify the risks clearly first. If the risks are not known, they cannot be managed effectively.

3.3 The best approach is to consider separately the extent to which **external** and **internal** factors may present a risk of fraud.

3.4 **External factors**

Step 1. First, consider the market place as a whole. The general environment in which the business operates may exhibit factors that increase the risk of fraud. For instance, the trend to 'de-layer' may reduce the degree of supervision exercised in many organisations, perhaps without putting anything in its place.

Step 2. Next, narrow the focus a little and consider whether the industry in which the firm operates is particularly exposed to certain types of fraud. For example, the building industry may be particularly prone to the risk of theft of raw materials, the travel industry may face risks due to the extensive use of agents and intermediaries, the retail industry must be vigilant to the abuse of credit cards and so on.

Activity 12.1

Think of some examples of such general external factors that might influence the degree of risk that a company is exposed to.

3.5 Internal factors

Having considered the big picture, the next step is to apply the same logic at a company level. Focus on the general and specific risks in the firm itself.

Be alert to circumstances that might increase the risk profile of a company.

- Changed operating environment
- New personnel
- New or upgraded management information systems
- Rapid growth

- New technology
- New products
- Corporate restructuring
- New overseas operations

4 COMMON INDICATORS OF FRAUD

4.1 A number of factors tend to crop up time and time again as issues that might indicate potential fraud. Attention should be drawn to them if any of these factors come to light when assessing external and internal risks.

4.2 Business risks

An alert management team will always be aware of the industry or business environment in which the organisation operates.

(a) **Profit levels/margins deviating significantly from the industry norm**

As a rule of thumb, if things seem too good to be true, then they generally are. If any of the following happen, alarm bells should start ringing.

- The company suddenly starts to exhibit profits far above those achieved by other firms in the same industry.

- Turnover rises rapidly but costs do not rise in line.

- Demand for a particular product increases significantly.

- Investors seem to find the firm unusually attractive.

Such patterns can indicate problems such as the manipulation of accounting records, collusion with existing customers or the creation of fictitious customers.

Similarly, results showing that the organisation is under-performing relative to competitors may be an indication of theft, collusion with suppliers or deliberate errors in the accounting records.

(b) **Market opinion**

If the market has a low opinion of the firm, this might indicate something about the company's products, its people or its way of doing business.

(c) **Complex structures**

- Organisations with complex group structures, including numerous domestic and overseas subsidiaries and branches, may be more susceptible to fraud.

- The sheer size of the group can offer plenty of opportunities to 'lose' transactions or to hide things in intercompany accounts.

- Furthermore, vast staff numbers contribute to a certain degree of employee anonymity, making it easier to conceal fraudulent activities.

4.3 **Personnel risks**

Fraud is not usually an easy thing to hide. A person's behaviour often gives clues to the fact that they are engaging in fraud. Some of the most common indicators are listed below.

(a) **Secretive behaviour**

A High Court judge once described secrecy as 'the badge of fraud'. If an individual starts behaving in a more secretive way than is generally considered normal, then there may be cause for concern.

(b) **Expensive lifestyles**

A well-known indicator of fraud is a life-style beyond an individual's earnings. A recent case involved an Inspector of Taxes who started driving expensive sport cars, taking lavish holidays and so forth. It was later discovered that he was being paid by a wealthy businessman in return for assisting him to evade tax. Life-styles of work colleagues may not always be apparent but fraudsters often cannot resist the temptation to flaunt their new-found wealth. You should not necessarily take at face value the standard stories about wealthy spouses or sudden inheritances.

(c) **Long hours or untaken holidays**

Workaholics and staff who do not take their full holiday entitlement may be trying to prevent a temporary replacement from uncovering a fraud. Also, staff who insist that certain tasks be left for them to complete upon their return from holiday might do so because they have something to hide.

(d) **Dominant personality**

Some fraudsters were able to get away with it for so long because they were dominant personalities in very senior positions. The prime example is Robert Maxwell. Junior staff members are often loath to question the decisions or actions of an aggressive manager or director. A forceful personality may be sufficient, therefore, to ensure that a fraud remains undetected, at least for a considerable period of time.

(e) **Autocratic management style**

In some organisations a sole manager or director has exclusive control over a significant part of the business. This can provide ample scope for fraud, particularly when the situation is compounded by little, if any, independent review of those activities by anyone else at a senior level.

(f) **Lack of segregation of duties**

Employees occasionally have more than one area of responsibility, particularly in small businesses where staff numbers are low. This can make it easy for the employee to conduct and conceal fraudulent actions. For example, if the employee who prepares the payslips were also the person who authorises the payments, payroll fraud would be relatively simple to put into practice.

(g) **Low staff morale**

One motive for fraud is resentment towards the firm. Staff may start defrauding the firm because they feel that they are not rewarded sufficiently for their work or because they were passed over for a promotion that they believed they deserved. Alternatively, low staff morale may lead indirectly to fraud, insofar as employees fail to take pride in their work and start to cut corners. This can lead to the breakdown of internal controls, yielding opportunities for fraud.

DEVOLVED ASSESSMENT ALERT

Just because these factors are evident does not mean that a fraud *is* taking place – so don't start libelling your colleagues!

5 INTERNAL CONTROLS

5.1 Controls must be developed in a structured manner, taking account of the whole spectrum of risk and focusing on the key risks identified in each area of the business.

5.2 We looked at internal controls generally in chapter 7. Let us think about appropriate controls that could be introduced to combat fraud. The paragraph below gives you a flavour of the means by which management can fight fraud.

5.3 **Physical controls**. Basic as it seems, physical security is an important tool in preventing fraud. Keeping tangible assets under lock and key makes it difficult for staff to access them and can go a long way towards discouraging theft.

5.4 **Segregation of duties.**

(a) Staff who have responsibility for a range of tasks have more scope for committing and concealing fraud. Therefore the obvious way to control the risk is to segregate duties.

(b) If an employee's duties do not extend beyond one domain, it will be more difficult for an employee to conceal a fraud. It is more likely that it will be picked up at the next stage in the process.

(c) So, for example, the employee responsible for recording sales orders should not be the same person responsible for maintaining stock records. This would make it more difficult to falsify sales records, as a discrepancy between sales figures and stock balances would show up. For the same reason, it makes it more difficult to amend stock records.

(d) Segregating responsibility for packaging goods for delivery from either of the recording tasks **would also help** to minimise the risk of theft and increase the likelihood of detection.

5.5 **Authorisation policies**

Requiring written authorisation by a senior is a good preventative tool. It increases accountability and also makes it harder to conceal a fraudulent transaction.

BPP PUBLISHING

5.6 **Customer signatures**

Requiring customers to inspect and sign for receipt of goods or services ensures that they cannot claim that the delivery did not match their order.

It also provides confirmation that the delivery staff actually did their job and that what was delivered corresponded to what was recorded.

5.7 **Using words rather than numbers**

Insist that all quantities be written out in full. It is much more difficult to change text than to alter a figure. This is particularly useful in the payroll department. For example it is very easy to change, say, '1.5' to look like '15' but it is very difficult to change 'one and a half' to look like 'fifteen'.

5.8 **Documentation**

Separate documents should be used to record sales order, despatch, delivery and invoice details. A simple matching exercise will then pick up any discrepancies between them and lead to detection of any alterations.

5.9 **Sequential numbering**

Numbering order forms, delivery dockets or invoices makes it extremely simple to spot if something is missing.

5.10 **Dates**

Writing the date on to forms and invoices assists in cut-off testing. For example, if a delivery docket is dated pre-year end but the sale is recorded post-year end it is possible that results are being manipulated.

5.11 **Standard procedures**

Standard procedures should be defined clearly for normal business operations and should be known to all staff. For example:

- Independent checks should be made on the existence of new customers.

- Credit should not be given to a new customer until his/her credit history has been investigated.

- All payments should be authorised by a senior member of staff.

- Wages/payslips must be collected in person.

Any deviations from these norms should become quite visible.

5.12 **Holidays**

As we have said, fraud is difficult to conceal. Enforcing holiday policy by insisting that all staff take their full holiday entitlement is therefore a crucial internal control. A two-week absence is frequently sufficient time for a fraud to come to light.

However, it is equally important to ensure that adequate cover is arranged in good time.

5.13 **Recruitment policies**

Personnel policies play a vital part in developing the corporate culture and deterring fraud. Something as obvious as checking the information and references provided by applicants may reduce the risk of appointing dishonest staff.

6 CONTROLS AGAINST COMPUTER FRAUD

6.1 Any situation involving the use of computers opens up a whole new set of risks. Controls must be specifically tailored to deal with these additional risks.

Activity 12.2

Try to come up with ideas of possible controls which management could use to combat the specific computer risks identified in the previous chapter.

(a)   Input-related fraud
(b)   Program-related fraud
(c)   Output-related fraud

---

7 CONCLUSION

7.1 The overriding message of this chapter is that identifying the risks and deciding what controls to use are complex challenges. It is clear that a structured approach is vital to managing risk successfully.

7.2 We have learnt about some of the most common indicators of fraud and considered practical examples of internal controls used to tackle the problem. You should now understand how to evaluate systems and identify potential risk areas. You should also be able to suggest possible ways of avoiding the risks and detecting incidences of fraud.

Activity 12.3

[This case study is a continuation of the scenario set out in the case study in chapter 11.]

Due to the small number of staff employed by Smiths Ltd, there is little segregation of duties. This automatically enhances exposure to risk of fraud.

Martha is responsible for both the cash book and bank reconciliations. This makes it easy for her to conceal theft or to manipulate accounting records.

John keeps the records of all purchases and expenses but he is also responsible for confirming that invoice details agree to purchase ledger details and for maintaining creditor accounts. He therefore has ample opportunity to manipulate accounting records, such as turnover figures. He is also responsible for drawing up the cheques for Michelle to sign. This means he could easily steal from the firm by drawing up cheques for fictitious creditors.

Craig has sole control of all computer systems. He has unlimited access to files and is in a unique position to carry numerous types of fraud. The firm essentially relies on nothing more than trust to ensure that he does not engage in any fraudulent activities.

As Stuart (one of the two directors) focuses almost entirely on bringing in new business, he has little time to spend on the supervision of day-to-day activities. The bulk of this work falls on Michelle (the second director). The sheer weight of her responsibilities means that in many cases there is little independent review or supervision of work.

Overall, the firm suffers from a high level of exposure to risk. You are asked to write a report to the directors suggesting a system of internal controls that could be introduced to prevent and detect incidences of fraud.

Key learning points

- It is the responsibility of the directors to take such steps as are reasonably open to them to **prevent and detect fraud**.

- The key to devising successful internal controls is to **identify the risks** clearly first. If the risks are not known, they cannot be managed effectively.

- A number of factors tend to crop up time and time again as issues that might indicate potential fraud situations. These can be categorised under **business and personnel risks.**

- **Controls must be developed in a structured manner**, taking account of the whole spectrum of risk and focusing on the key risks identified in each area of the business.

Quick quiz

1   What is the key to devising successful internal controls?

2   What is the first step in assessing the risks faced by an organisation?

3   List five common indicators of fraud

4   In what manner should controls be developed?

5   List five examples of internal controls (not computer-related).

Answers to quick quiz

1   The key to devising successful internal controls is to identify the risks clearly first.

2   The first step is to consider separately the extent to which external and internal factors may present a risk.

3   Common indicators of fraud include trends that start to deviate from the industry norms, complex changes to business structures, secretive behaviour, evidence of an expensive lifestyle not commensurate with earnings and an autocratic management style.

4   Controls must be developed in a structured manner, taking account of the whole spectrum of risk and focusing on the key risks identified in each area of business.

5   Examples include physical controls, segregation of duties, authorisation policies, using words rather than numbers and enforcing holiday policy.

Answers to activities

Answer 12.1

You might have thought of some of the following.

(a)   Technological developments.
(b)   New legislation or regulations.
(c)   Economic or political changes.
(d)   Increased competition.
(e)   Changing customer needs.

Answer 12.2

Possible controls include the following.

(a)   **Input-related fraud**

   (i)   Segregation of duties in user areas and between users and IT staff.
   (ii)   Independent reconciliations.
   (iii)   Authorisation of changes to standing data.
   (iv)   Access controls over data files, e.g. password protection.

(v)   Period listing and review of standing data.

(b)   **Program-related fraud**

(i)   Authorisation and testing of program changes

(ii)   Restricting access to system libraries containing live programs

(iii)   Using special utility programs to compare changed versions of programs to original versions to make sure that only authorised amendments have been made

(iv)   Reducing dependence on key systems staff

(c)   **Output-related fraud**

(i)   Segregation of duties in user areas
(ii)   Independent reconciliations
(iii)   Good custodial controls over sensitive print-outs
(iv)   Strong access controls

Answer 12.3

Report: Internal controls to prevent and detect fraud

Date: 30 June 19X7
To: Stuart and Michelle Smith, Directors, Smiths Ltd
From: Accounting Technician
Subject: Internal controls

You have asked me to suggest some internal controls that could be introduced to reduce the extent to which the firm is exposed to the risk of fraud. My recommendations include the following measures.

Potential internal controls

(a)   *Reallocation of work*

It may be worth training Martha so that she could take over control of the creditor accounts from John. Martha should check invoice details against the purchase ledgers maintained by John. Responsibility for drawing up cheques could also be passed to her. John could take over the running of the cashbook instead. This would separate out responsibility for related accounting functions somewhat.

(b)   *Independent review and supervision*

As staff numbers are limited and it is not possible to segregate duties as much as you would wish, I would suggest that you recruit one more employee to act as an assistant director. This would take some of the pressure off Michelle and would ensure facilitate better supervision and review of work. As director, Michelle should ensure that cheques are matched to invoices before she signs them.

(c)   *Reduction of dependence on Craig*

Computer fraud is very prevalent and steps should be taken to reduce dependence on just one person. Apart from the risk of fraud, other problems could arise, eg if Craig fell ill and was off work for any length of time.

It may be worth considering subscribing to a software helpdesk. Most software suppliers offer this type of service. Staff could also be trained to bring their skills up to a particular level of competence so that they can deal with more things themselves.

(d)   *Authorisation policies*

Policies should be introduced requiring your authorisation before any program changes or changes to standing data can be made. Reports could be generated on a regular basis summarising changes that have been made over the relevant time period.

There are numerous controls that could be implemented to assist in the prevention and detection of fraud. The cost of introducing such controls must be weighed up against the perceived risk from fraud arising out of not having them in place.

List of key terms and index

BPP PUBLISHING

Index

ORDER FORM

Any books from our AAT range can be ordered by telephoning 020-8740-2211. Alternatively, send this page to our address below, fax it to us on 020-8740-1184, or email us at **publishing@bpp.com.** Or look us up on our website: www.bpp.com

We aim to deliver to all UK addresses inside 5 working days; a signature will be required. Order to all EU addresses should be delivered within 6 working days. All other orders to overseas addresses should be delivered within 8 working days.

To: BPP Publishing Ltd, Aldine House, Aldine Place, London W12 8AW

Tel: 020-8740 2211 **Fax: 020-8740 1184** **Email: publishing@bpp.com**

Mr / Ms (full name): _____

Daytime delivery address: _____

_____

Postcode: _____ Daytime Tel: _____

Please send me the following quantities of books.

	5/00 Interactive Text	8/00 DA Kit	8/00 CA Kit
FOUNDATION			
Unit 1 Recording Income and Receipts	☐	☐	
Unit 2 Making and Recording Payments	☐	☐	
Unit 3 Ledger Balances and Initial Trial Balance	☐	☐	
Unit 4 Supplying information for Management Control	☐	☐	
Unit 20 Working with Information Technology (8/00 Text)	☐		
Unit 22/23 Achieving Personal Effectiveness	☐		
INTERMEDIATE			
Unit 5 Financial Records and Accounts	☐	☐	
Unit 6 Cost Information	☐		
Unit 7 Reports and Returns	☐	☐	
Unit 21 Using Information Technology	☐		
Unit 22: see below			
TECHNICIAN			
Unit 8/9 Core Managing Costs and Allocating Resources	☐		☐
Unit 10 Core Managing Accounting Systems	☐	☐	
Unit 11 Option Financial Statements (Accounting Practice)	☐		☐
Unit 12 Option Financial Statements (Central Government)	☐		
Unit 15 Option Cash Management and Credit Control	☐	☐	
Unit 16 Option Evaluating Activities	☐	☐	
Unit 17 Option Implementing Auditing Procedures	☐	☐	
Unit 18 Option Business Tax FA00(8/00 Text)	☐	☐	
Unit 19 Option Personal Tax FA00(8/00 Text)	☐	☐	
TECHNICIAN 1999			
Unit 17 Option Business Tax Computations FA99 (8/99 Text & Kit)	☐	☐	
Unit 18 Option Personal Tax Computations FA99 (8/99 Text & Kit)	☐	☐	
TOTAL BOOKS	☐ +	☐ +	☐ = ☐

Postage and packaging:

UK: £2.00 for each book to maximum of £10

Europe (inc ROI and Channel Islands): £4.00 for first book, £2.00 for each extra

Rest of the World: £20.00 for first book, £10 for each extra

@ £9.95 each = £ ☐

P & P £ ☐

► Unit 22 Maintaining a Healthy Workplace Interactive Text (postage free) ☐ @ £3.95 £ ☐

GRAND TOTAL £ ☐

I enclose a cheque for £ _____ (cheques to BPP Publishing Ltd) or charge to **Mastercard/Visa/Switch**

Card number ☐☐☐☐☐☐☐☐☐☐☐☐☐☐☐☐☐☐☐

Start date _____ Expiry date _____ Issue no. (Switch only)___

Signature _____

REVIEW FORM & FREE PRIZE DRAW

All original review forms from the entire BPP range, completed with genuine comments, will be entered into one of two draws on 31 January 2001 and 31 July 2001. The names on the first four forms picked out on each occasion will be sent a cheque for £50.

Name: _____   Address: _____

_____

_____

How have you used this Interactive Text?
(Tick one box only)

☐ Home study (book only)

☐ On a course: college _____

☐ With 'correspondence' package

☐ Other _____

Why did you decide to purchase this Interactive Text? *(Tick one box only)*

☐ Have used BPP Texts in the past

☐ Recommendation by friend/colleague

☐ Recommendation by a lecturer at college

☐ Saw advertising .

☐ Other _____

During the past six months do you recall seeing/receiving any of the following?
(Tick as many boxes as are relevant)

☐ Our advertisement in *Accounting Technician* magazine

☐ Our advertisement in *Pass*

☐ Our brochure with a letter through the post

Which (if any) aspects of our advertising do you find useful?
(Tick as many boxes as are relevant)

☐ Prices and publication dates of new editions

☐ Information on Interactive Text content

☐ Facility to order books off-the-page

☐ None of the above

Have you used the companion Assessment Kit for this subject?   ☐ Yes   ☐ No

Your ratings, comments and suggestions would be appreciated on the following areas

	Very useful	Useful	Not useful
Introductory section (How to use this Interactive Text etc)	☐	☐	☐
Chapter topic lists	☐	☐	☐
Chapter learning objectives	☐	☐	☐
Key terms	☐	☐	☐
Assessment alerts	☐	☐	☐
Examples	☐	☐	☐
Activities and answers	☐	☐	☐
Key learning points	☐	☐	☐
Quick quizzes and answers	☐	☐	☐
List of key terms and index	☐	☐	☐
Icons	☐	☐	☐

	Excellent	Good	Adequate	Poor
Overall opinion of this Text	☐	☐	☐	☐

Do you intend to continue using BPP Interactive Texts/Assessment Kits? ☐ Yes   ☐ No

Please note any further comments and suggestions/errors on the reverse of this page.

Please return to: Nick Weller, BPP Publishing Ltd, FREEPOST, London, W12 8BR

REVIEW FORM & FREE PRIZE DRAW (continued)

Please note any further comments and suggestions/errors below

FREE PRIZE DRAW RULES

1   Closing date for 31 January 2001 draw is 31 December 2000. Closing date for 31 July 2001 draw is 30 June 2001.

2   Restricted to entries with UK and Eire addresses only. BPP employees, their families and business associates are excluded.

3   No purchase necessary. Entry forms are available upon request from BPP Publishing. No more than one entry per title, per person. Draw restricted to persons aged 16 and over.

4   Winners will be notified by post and receive their cheques not later than 6 weeks after the relevant draw date.

5   The decision of the promoter in all matters is final and binding. No correspondence will be entered into.